D0040774

“I’ll never forget the first time I met Bill McCartney. There was something about the strength in his handshake and the look in his eyes that told me this is a man who is very serious about who he is. That brief moment was in itself a challenge to me. As an athlete I respected his contribution to his sport. However, it is his life after football which has demonstrated to me just how truly *sold out* a man can be.”

—Dave Dravecky, former all-star pitcher for the San Francisco Giants, author, and founder of Outreach of Hope Ministries

“In *Sold Out*, Bill McCartney shows us that godly change to our nation, to our governments, to our churches, and to our families begins with us through the development of personal intimacy with Almighty God. Bill’s humility and openness will help every reader see that it is Christ in us, the hope of glory, who is the source of true, godly change.”

—Tony Evans, senior pastor of Oak Cliff Bible Fellowship, Dallas, Texas, and author of *What a Way to Live!*

“Bill McCartney’s desire to make a difference in the lives of others and his love for his wife and family permeates everything he does. I truly know of no man who loves God more.”

—John Maxwell, founder of INJOY

“The words ‘sold out’ can be construed as a case of human compromise, or as a commitment to a holy mission. Bill McCartney’s life and words are both crystal clear—total commitment to Christ is *his* definition. Here’s a handbook on power-filled, practical, and penetrating faith.”

—Jack W. Hayford, author and senior pastor of The Church on the Way

“If you’re a man who has grown comfortable in your complacency and has become mellowed by mediocrity, God can use Bill and Lyndi’s message to turn your life upside down for Christ.”

—Gary J. Oliver, professor, Denver Seminary, and author of *Made Perfect in Weakness*

"Bill, a coach, is a modern Nehemiah, chosen to 'rebuild the walls of the souls of men.' Through his own rebuilding process, he became an instrument for the healing and restoration of others."

—Danny de Leon, senior pastor of Templo Calvario,
Santa Ana, California

"Bill McCartney strikes a chord in the heart of every man who has 'sold out' to something. Bill and Lyndi's life experiences teach us to give our all to the One who sold out for us—Jesus Christ."

—Grant Teaff, former head coach, Baylor University Football

"*Sold Out* is far more than an entertaining biography. Truth will confront you with no forewarning. You will be faced with the unshakable conviction that you can no longer remain neutral. Open its first pages and buckle your seatbelt tight. Turn its final page and be man enough to make a difference—sold out!"

—James Ryle, pastor of Boulder Valley Vineyard

"*Sold Out* reaches into the hearts of not only men, but women as well. Thanks, Bill, for letting women see a man's inside battles, and thanks, Lyndi, for an example of Godly womanhood."

—Rachael Crabb, author of *The Personal Touch*

"There's a love story here—but not a spiritualized cover-up crafted to keep up a public image, the kind we read but never quite believe. Rather, one that reveals common mistakes that can threaten any marriage. Bill and Lyndi's story is just getting good! Those who learn from it can change the direction of their own love story to make it all that God intends."

—Connie Neal, author of *Dancing in the Arms of God*

Sold Out:

Becoming Man Enough to Make a Difference

By Bill McCartney
with
David Halbrook

WORD PUBLISHING
Nashville•London•Vancouver•Melbourne

SOLD OUT

Published in association with Sealy M. Yates, Literary Agent, Orange, California.

Library of Congress Cataloging-in-Publication Data

McCartney, Bill.

Sold out : becoming man enough to make a difference / Bill McCartney

p. cm.

ISBN 0-8499-1515-5

1. Christian life. 2. McCartney, Bill. 3. Men—Religious life.
4. Promise Keepers (Organization) I. Title.

BV4501.2.M187 1997

267'.23'092—dc21 97-36710

[B] CIP

Printed in the United States of America

7 8 9 0 1 2 3 4 BVG 9 8 7 6 5 4 3 2 1

Lyndi and I would like to dedicate this book to our mothers:

Ruth McCartney, 87

and

Milli Taussig, 86

the two women who have been necessary and integral to all we are, and everything we do. We thank God for your long lives and lasting support.

Contents

Sold Out: Becoming Man Enough to Make a Difference

Contents

Sold Out: Becoming Man Enough to Make a Difference

Foreword

THE FIRST TIME I EVER SPOKE with Bill McCartney, he told me that he believed there was a message which was heavy on God's heart; and Bill wondered out loud with me if that might mean he should write another book. He had already written his autobiography *Ashes to Glory* in 1989. He was uncertain whether there was anything more for him to put into a book. But, he shared with me, there was a different message that the Holy Spirit seemed to be burdening him with. It was a message he felt God wanted him to address now: a message to believers, especially Christian men, born out of Bill's continuing personal spiritual journey, calling all of us to live for Christ so radically that our world will be turned upside down by the example of our love for Almighty God and by our faith in action. The message would include how living such a radical life for Christ is a lifetime process that allows Jesus to make us His intimate friends, little by little, day by day.

What you hold in your hands is the book we believe to be the direct result of Bill's obedience to God's leading. It is a result of much prayer and hard work by Bill and the team that God recruited to work with him. God has been at work in all our lives throughout this project, and we have been wonderfully blessed by

His work. I sincerely believe that, by reading this book, you will also be the beneficiary of His work.

For twenty-six years, I have been working with Christian authors and Christian publishing houses, and I have been privileged to have worked with many of the best and most talented people in Christian publishing. God has blessed me incredibly to be able to use my professional education, gifts, and experience in ministry as He called me to work as a lawyer as a part of the Body of Christ. I am honored to have had the opportunity to work with Bill and Lyndi McCartney and to have been given a small part in this very unique project.

In March 1996, Pete Richardson, vice president of creative services for Promise Keepers, asked me if I would be willing to speak with Bill about assisting him with the publication of a book. I agreed, and for the next several months Bill, David Halbrook, and I prayed together about this project. We met several times to discuss among ourselves what we thought it was that God wanted Bill to say in this book. Bill told David Halbrook and me that it was imperative for us to diligently seek God's will regarding whether we should join with Bill to write and publish this book. He cautioned us that, if we were to join him as part of the team the Holy Spirit was recruiting, he believed our health, our personal well-being, and that of our family members and of any who would join our team would be at severe risk from attacks by the enemy.

On December 7, 1996, Bill and Lyndi McCartney, David Halbrook, and I met, got on our knees before Almighty God, and committed ourselves to be a part of the team that God was to assemble to write and publish this book. We determined that God wanted us to publish a book about living for God in a world hostile to those who were truly committed in their Christian faith, a book which would encourage others to live as though they really believed what they read in God's Word. That Saturday morning the four of us made a covenant with each other and with our Lord that we would hold each other, and all of our family members, up in prayer daily until the book was written and published. We also agreed that day that we would only work with a publishing house to publish the book if its management team was prepared to join in our covenant.

On January 15, 1997, the management team at Word Publishing joined our covenant team as we all determined to move forward in humility, fear, and obedience. In an unprecedented step, we all agreed to put our covenant in writing and to make it a part of the publishing agreement between us. In that covenant, we each agreed that, from the date of the agreement until the book was published, we would pray daily for the spiritual and physical covering protection of God over each other, our spouses, our children, and our grandchildren and for protection for the publishing house and for Promise Keepers.

Spiritual attacks can come in many forms. Our enemy is extremely clever, and he will use anything he can to discourage or distract us from being obedient to what God would have us do. Without intending to suggest that Satan is behind everything bad that happens in our lives, but acknowledging that we are in a spiritual battle that requires all the prayer and mutual support we can give for each other, there were some very serious and distracting things that occurred after we made our mutual covenant, which felt to us like attacks from the enemy:

Kip Jordon, publisher at Word Publishing, had to have surgery to remove a malignant tumor from his colon;

My son, Curtis, a senior at Westmont College, was involved in an accident during a practice for a theatrical performance at the college during which Curtis's roommate, Patrick Steele, was flipped over Curtis's back as a part of the choreography for the performance. Patrick fell to the ground and broke his neck, and he remains paralyzed today;

David Halbrook and his wife, Francie, became pregnant then lost the baby to a miscarriage;

Lyndi McCartney's brother, Chase, was suddenly stricken with leukemia and died within weeks after being diagnosed; and

Joey Paul, associate publisher for Word Publishing, and his wife, Sharon, have faced some very serious threats to Sharon's health.

There have been many others behind the scenes who have also felt the attack of the enemy but who have kept on praying daily for the McCartneys and the Halbrooks as they have worked. What I have shared (and this is, of course, only a small view of all that has happened in the past year) is not intended to draw attention to ourselves or to look for Satan under every rock. However, we are reminded that, as believers, we face a spiritual battle every day, we must be prepared, and we really need one another. As Chuck Swindoll says, "The enemy will not go away, but we are perfectly equipped to handle him. The letter to the Ephesians reminds us that we have available God's 'full armor' and all we have to do is put it on and stand firm against the enemy. We can do that—and we *must* do that if we hope to walk in victory" (see Ephesians 6:10–17).

We believe that what God has done is to deliver to you a book that neither Bill nor any of us could have written on our own. Through Bill, who has opened himself up to reveal his spiritual journey, both the good and the bad, and through Lyndi, who has been gracious enough to respond with her wonderful, revealing, and helpful insights into what she has seen God doing in Bill and in their home, we believe that God has put together an example that will help us all as we move, little by little, toward becoming promise keepers and people of God who are truly sold out; people who want to love God with all their hearts, with all their souls, and with all their minds; people who want to love *all* their neighbors as themselves.

Here is the spiritual covenant which we made part of our publishing agreement. We believe God has blessed each of us as we have worked together to bring this book to you, and we trust that He will bless you as you read and consider with us what it means to be *SOLD OUT*.

Foreword

God, in His infinite wisdom, has made it very clear to the parties to this Agreement that He requires more from them in this relationship of author, writer, agent, and publisher than their mutual promises to each other concerning writing, publishing, and financial details. The parties believe that this Agreement concerns the publication of a book that will reflect the heart of God for this time. It concerns the responsibilities that the parties believe the Father of the Lord Jesus Christ desires that each of them shall accept with regard to the development, delivery, and distribution to His people of a book that the parties believe the Holy Spirit desires to use to change them for His glory, and that He wants to use to help people who are standing outside the gates of faith so that they can see God at work. The parties also understand that, because God has such a purpose for them with respect to the delivery and distribution of that book, Satan and his armies intend to do all they can to attack and defeat them and all God has for them to do in that regard.

Therefore, the parties believe that they must establish a covenant relationship that involves the deepest spiritual bond between each of them and the God who has called them to this publishing task. With that being fully understood, and praying that Jehovah Jireh ("The Lord Who Provides") will give to each of them all that is needed to keep their covenants, Bill McCartney, Lyndi McCartney, David Halbrook, Sealy Yates, Tom Thompson, Byron Williamson, Kip Jordon, Joey Paul, and David Moberg hereby covenant with each other and with the Father, Son, and Holy Spirit that, from the date of this Agreement until the book reflecting the heart of God is published, they will each:

1. Pray daily for the covering and protection of the blood of Christ over each of the others, their spouses, children, and grandchildren, and over the Nelson/Word Publishing venture and Promise Keepers so that Satan will not have any opportunity to attack those and cause a spiritual weakness in the covenant relationship of the team that God wants to use to deliver and distribute the book that is on His heart to the people He has determined to bless;

> *2. Live a life of purity, free from intentional sin that would cause a separation and a breach of fellowship between themselves and their heavenly Father so as to allow Satan or his angels the opportunity to destroy what God wants to do through this covenant relationship; and*
>
> *3. Pray that the Holy Spirit will give all the wisdom that is needed by Bill McCartney, Lyndi McCartney, and David Halbrook as writers and Joey Paul and Sealy Yates as editor and consultant to write a manuscript that will deliver the message that does in fact reflect the heart of God for this hour.*

It is our sincere prayer that you will read this book with a heart and mind set toward God, and then with grace and courage move forward, day by day, little by little, toward intimacy with Jesus that can result in a lifetime of *Sold Out* obedience to Him.

—SEALY M. YATES
Orange, California
October 1997

Acknowledgments

THE AUTHORS WOULD LIKE TO THANK the following individuals for their steadfast encouragement, prayer, and assistance in helping us bring this book to completion.

Connie Neal, a skilled writer and author who lent us her talents at a late stage in the manuscript's development, assisting Lyndi with the vision, coordination, and writing of her key observations and impressions throughout this book.

Bobb Biehl, President of Masterplanning Group International, who provided much-needed wisdom and strategic counsel at a critical stage in the writing process.

Francie Halbrook, beloved wife of the co-author, who offered endless encouragement and patience as this book unfolded, who served as a valuable sounding board, and who proved to be a talented proofreader and manager of countless behind-the-scenes details without which this book would not have been possible.

Tom Thompson, associate literary agent with Yates and Greer—a diligent trouble shooter who lent much encouragement and hands-on assistance in helping clear away a host of potential roadblocks to the project's completion.

Dave Plati, sports information director at the University of Colorado, a speedy, invaluable source of information throughout.

Pete Richardson, Vice President of Creative Services for Promise Keepers, who put us in contact with our literary agent, Sealy Yates (a God-send), at the outset of the project and who offered vital input from beginning to end.

Carolyn Bearse and *Sidney Rainwater*, Mac's administrative and special assistants at Promise Keepers, who served as valuable facilitators throughout.

We would also like to personally thank everyone, known and unknown, who prayed for this project from beginning to end; each of the members of our spiritual covenant teams, those from Word Publishing and Yates and Greer, who prayed daily and faithfully for the protection and safety of our families—that Jesus' will would be done and His name glorified by the end result; and the dear brothers and sisters who daily prayed for the author's and co-author's families, for our protection, and for God's inspiration and anointing over the writing process.

—*David Halbrook*
Longmont, Colorado
October 1997

Introduction

SOME MONTHS BACK, my wife Lyndi and I began something new: We began to recite our wedding vows to one another. We now try to do it every morning before I go to work. It helps me to have the words fresh on my mind as the busy day gets underway. For most of our thirty years of marriage, I not only never *thought* of our vows, I doubt if I could have told you what they *meant*. They were just words from a long-forgotten ceremony.

Over these past months, however, they've become part of me. They're conventional vows. My part reads: "I, Bill, take thee, Lynne, for my lawful wife, to have and to hold from this day forward, for better, for worse, for richer, for poorer, in sickness and in health; and, forsaking all others I solemnly vow before God in the power of the Holy Spirit to love, honor, cherish, and obey and be faithful to you all the days of my life."

I can't tell you who wrote them, or where they originated. But having taken the opportunity to recite them, meditate on them, and simply allow them to sink in, I have become very convicted by the single phrase: "forsaking all others."

In all honesty, when Lyndi and I first started this, I assumed "forsaking all others" merely implied that I was to forsake other *women*. That's certainly true, but as I've had the chance to chew on it, I realize it means exactly what it says: *forsake all others*. On my wedding day, December 29, 1962, I vowed to Lyndi that I would forsake all others. I promised I would put all others—men, women, friends, co-workers, even our children—second to her. I solemnly vowed to God that, second only to Him, I would always put Lyndi *first*.

Sadly, I spent the better part of our adult lives forsaking my vow. Rarely did I forsake all others, much less *things* or goals, in favor of Lyndi. The truth is, until the day I resigned as head football coach at the University of Colorado in November 1994, I usually forsook Lyndi in favor of *all others*. I can tell you their names: success, competition, career, *football*.

We titled this book *Sold Out* because, for most of my life, I *have* been undeniably sold out—feverishly committed to and wholeheartedly invested in whatever goals and challenges I chose to pursue. Sold out is generally viewed as the opposite of lukewarm, the word which likely describes much of mankind. The lukewarm seldom realize they're lukewarm; in fact, they're among the most self-satisfied folks around, thinking everything's just fine. Yet for any who fall into this category, the Lord Jesus Christ has harsh words: "So, because you are lukewarm—neither hot nor cold—I am about to spit you out of my mouth" (Revelations 3:16).

The lukewarm are not hard to find. They're everywhere. We live in a society that *promotes* passive indifference. Regardless of cultural background or creed, it's the rare individual in today's culture who is genuinely excited about *anything*. And all too often, when we do manage to get ourselves pumped up or excited, it's a fleeting feeling. That's because the objects of our passion are either vain or superficial.

In and of itself, the state of being completely sold out is not necessarily cause for celebration either. What are we sold out to? In all my years as an athlete and a coach—and later in my role with Promise Keepers—I can safely say I have *never* lacked for zeal. It's just part of my genetic make-up, I'm afraid. From the time I took my first communion as a child, in fact, I've been almost belligerently sold out to God, to church, to sports. Growing up, this trait served me well in realms where dogged determination and the will to succeed meant everything. But increasingly, this zealous bent led me into headier realms where it's also an advantage to be superficial and self-serving.

Football is a passionate game. For a hyper-competitive man like me, it was the easiest thing to be sold out, heart and soul, to football. It fed into my strengths; it was intoxicating. It's now been almost three years since I stepped away from what many might consider a major college "dream job." I do still, however, watch an occasional game on TV. I recall a recent Monday Night Football game at Texas Stadium featuring the Dallas Cowboys and the Philadelphia Eagles. It was a hard-fought, fiercely-executed game that ended in Dallas's favor when the Eagles botched a last-second, point-blank field goal. Those who saw the game can attest to the fact that both teams played themselves to exhaustion on a dripping hot September night. A handful of players battled until they literally dropped.

I admire their effort. I support them. It's even scriptural. It says in Colossians 3:23, "Whatever you do, work at it with all your heart. . . ." It pleases God when we put all of our hearts into significant endeavors. For more than thirty years, I poured my heart and soul into competing and coaching on the gridiron. I left nothing on the field. I put *all* of my heart and every ounce of energy into it. It paid handsome dividends. Yet as admirable as this type of behavior seems, God looks first at our motive. The second half of the verse says, "work at it with all your heart, *as working for the Lord*, not for men, since you know that you will receive an inheritance from the Lord as a reward. *It is the Lord Christ you are serving*" (Colossians 3:23–24, emphasis added).

The athletes who poured it all out on Monday Night Football went home and rested the next day. Some took it easy in practice the following week to heal up, or simply to save themselves for the next game. A small handful, I suspect, crawled out of bed the next morning, ignoring their pain and stiffness, and headed to the weight room; a few probably rose early to start watching film. These are the players who flat out love to win, who play the game for the love of it, who simply want to be the best. They're not in it just for the money, the nice car, or the big home.

In my opinion, that's what God's looking for—a people who will rise early, or carve out a special time in each day, to be with Him just because they love Him. The great psalmist, King David, said this of a man who loves God with all his heart: "His delight is in the law of the LORD, and on his law he meditates day and night. He is like a tree planted by streams of water, which yields its fruit in season and whose leaf does not wither. Whatever he does prospers" (Psalm 1:3). This is not the portrait of a lukewarm man. It's the portrait of a man who's *hot* after God. Delighting in the Word of God is not lukewarm. A tree planted by streams of water is not just surviving—it's a flourishing, thriving, towering tree. A man who prospers in all he does can't possibly be lukewarm. He's energized, focused, dedicated to the task at hand.

God is looking for those who go after Him seven days a week with the same feverish intensity in which a professional football player dives for the end zone on a Sunday afternoon. God knows that if a man's motive is *anything* else—whether it be pleasing the boss, impressing one's friends, gaining financial security, winning the big promotion, or wearing the Super Bowl ring—that man will lose gusto. His strength will fade and his zeal will wither. But the man who yearns after the Lord with all of his heart, day and night delighting in and meditating on His Word, *that* man will prosper in everything he does. He will be like a well-watered tree growing strong and vibrant, able to withstand long droughts and formidable adversity.

In many respects, my story is a testament to the striking contrast between being sold out and lukewarm. It's equally the story of misdirected passion set aright by God's Spirit. In this spiritual journey I take pains to revisit the turbulent, sometimes disastrous turns a man can make when he charges out to the front of the pack, navigating his own course without God's Spirit dwelling within. Thankfully, it's also the account of a profound, providential moment when Christ came in and began to rebuild and rehabilitate—of becoming, one piece at a time, sold out to the right things, to things that last. It meant coming to terms with God and reconciling the anguished gap between my public persona and my private *person*. It meant salvaging a bankrupt marriage and reclaiming the priceless treasure of my family.

In these pages you will see my life examined from the perspective of one who also lived through it—my beautiful wife. After all these years, that Lyndi is still in my corner and willing to participate in this, at times, excruciating exercise, is the most compelling proof of God's willingness to heal and redeem us. Lyndi's pointed counterpoints to my reflections complete the story.

In the end, *Sold Out* is about the process of deciding where we stand on the important issues of our day; it is about the costs incurred and the blessings realized by *taking* that stand, and then becoming highly intentional about making the right choices. It's not just about *finding* truth, or examining it—it's about learning to carve our bedrock convictions from the ways in which we spend our time and lavish our affections. Some who read this book may walk away feeling disoriented, even threatened, sensing an entire world view has been dismantled. Others may, in much the same way as I have, sense that they have stumbled upon the "pearl of great value" Jesus cites in Matthew 13:45–46. They may find themselves uncharacteristically bold and undaunted, having discovered that they, too, are willing to sell all to know the One who sold all to know us.

Prologue

My Father's Team and the Game of Life

You have made known to me the path of life;
you will fill me with joy in your presence, with eternal
pleasures at your right hand.

—Psalm 16:11

The Team

Let me tell you about an uncommon team I joined in 1974. Though it's never won a national championship, it's the most successful team of all time. Its consistency and longevity are unmatched—two thousand years and counting. This team's overall wealth and membership are beyond calculation. Every player is a stockholder, and the team never changes management. Though it has suffered setbacks and occasionally stumbles, the team never has been, and never will be, beaten.

It is not like any other team you've ever known. The power and authority at its disposal can shake the nations, yet it never intimidates or overpowers its foes. Rather, its strength is in its meekness, its brilliance in its humility. Players are required to be totally committed to a rigorous policy of moral purity, obedience, loyalty, and sacrificial love.

Our Coach

Let me tell you about Coach. He's a proven leader. In His playing days, He was the all-time champ. He knows what it takes to win.

He's a brilliant, patient teacher. He's never in a hurry but is always on time. He makes sure His players know their individual roles and takes great pains to see that they all have opportunities to meet their potential. The team delights in Coach's presence, and it is inspired by His unselfish nature and spotless character. Many players on the team are so devoted to Coach that they give their lives defending His honor.

Our Coach handcrafted the team with single-minded vision, handpicking each player, expending every resource, and sparing no expense in the recruiting process. He's intimately aware of each player's strengths, weaknesses, and flaws. He wrote their names on His roster and assigned each a spot on the squad before there was even a team.

Coach is both our guiding mentor and loving dad. Think of the finest father figure you've ever known or *imagined*, magnify his qualities as far as your mind allows, gift him with supernatural power and *willingness* to satisfy your deepest needs and longings, and he would still fall embarrassingly short of Coach. Intimately aware of our greatest failures and grandest dreams, Coach works tirelessly to train, cheer, and whip us into shape so we can serve the team effectively.

Like no other team I know, my spot on the roster doesn't depend on my performance. Because He loves me for who I am, Coach wants to keep on working with me until I get it right. He bought my rights for the highest price—*much* more than I was worth—then signed me to the richest contract in history. The duration of my contract goes way beyond "lifetime." It keeps earning interest into eternity. No matter how badly I blow it, no matter how undeserving I am, He never shops me around, discards, or trades me for a higher draft pick. Why? Because He drafted me not just to support the team but to become part of His extended family. One day He will invite me to come live in His mansion.

Our Play Book

Let me tell you about our Play Book. It's unlike any other play book. It's flawless; it holds the keys to wisdom and illustrates the perfect play for any situation. More than that, it's a personal strategy for a life of significance, which Coach knows is every player's dream. Coach penned each word as a blueprint for what He calls "abundant life": what it means to be a real player, how to treat the other team members, the importance of trusting in the wisdom and play-calling of our Coach, and, most importantly, how to be in a tight, healthy relationship with Him. Our Play Book lays out the plan for the game of life, not just for easy victories. When the game's on the line, the team trusts in the Play Book. Each player is taught that if they execute its game plan, victory is guaranteed.

The Game Plan

Coach doesn't give us His game plan, then turn us loose. He doesn't just bark orders from the sideline. He leads us on to the field, helps us call the play, and throws the first block. He knows what to do in every situation. His game plan is simple—it never deviates from the Play Book. No one rides the bench in His game plan; every player is an active participant. We all get to carry the ball. We're always excited, on the alert, knowing at any moment He might call our number. By simply playing the game, all players discover gifts and talents they've never known.

The Opposition

The opposing team has a fast offense. It's free-spirited, reckless, over-confident. Its style of play forces each player to compete feverishly for a spot on the line-up. Performance is everything; built-in incentives force each player to vie for individual glory rather than for the team's success. There was a time when we all played on this team.

The opposing coach is clever, ingenious, deceptive. He, too, is a skilled motivator. He has coaxed some of our best friends and loved ones into lifetime contracts. They can't see that he's not committed to their well-being but is secretly motivated by deep hatred. He doesn't love his players, could care less about their dreams, and, most of all, doesn't want them to even hear about the love of our Coach. A pathological liar, he twists the truth, pointing his team down a dead-end path of pleasure-seeking and self-gratification, knowing they will ultimately lose the game. In the end, players for the opposing team will know they poured out their peak performances on a counterfeit promise. The worst part is they will realize that they have forfeited the staggering joy and privilege of playing for our Coach.

Rules and Tools of the Game

Coach demands obedience to a fair set of rules and, as such, invests heavily in our education. Faith, repentance, confession, and obedience are our disciplines; they are the mighty engine behind our Coach's powerful offense. Our uniform is truth, righteousness, peace, joy, and purity. When worn properly, and when exercised with radical faith according to our Coach's matchless counsel, our tools and uniform serve as impenetrable armor on the battlefield.

Coach firmly advises us to communicate with Him every hour of every day. For this He has installed an audible system called "prayer" that permits us to call the right play every time. When we use this audible system properly—fixing our eyes on Him, focusing on His voice alone, trusting in His perfect plan—our precision is exact, our execution flawless.

It's no surprise that our best players are the ones who spend the most time with our Coach and who play the game completely sold out to Him. They love the sound of His voice; they delight in asking Him questions; they find strength in His example. When the game is on the line, those who trust Him most strike fear in the hearts of the opposition.

His Love for Me

The most incredible thing about Coach is that He loved each of us before we loved Him. He proved His love by paying history's highest price to include each of us on the team. Knowing we could never understand or earn His gift on our own—and even while we were still fiercely loyal to the opposition—He removed His coach's hat and took the field on our behalf, as a *player*. He knew that by offering Himself as our substitute at a key point in the game, He would gain the victory, win back our rights, and release us from our one-sided contracts. In return, Coach asks for nothing but our total love and trust in His hard-won stewardship over our lives.

I love my Coach. He keeps encouraging me. He expects perfection but is easy to please. I've dropped the ball, thrown interceptions, been offsides, committed personal fouls, and even helped the other team score, but He never changes. He keeps sending me back in the game and enlisting me to do my best. He keeps telling me that, no matter what, He still loves me. I believe Him. He is my best Friend.

Victory Is Assured

We have only one team but many squads competing around the globe. Our sole mission is to share the good news about playing for our Coach. We taste our sweetest victories when members of the other team rip up their contracts and join us. One day we'll all be on the same field, celebrating a triumphant reunion with our conquering Coach. It excites me to think of carrying Him off the field after all the years He has carried us.

Chapter 1
Legacy of Pain

MY DATE WAS IN TEARS. She and her girlfriend were terrified that I was going to kill us all on the icy road. I wasn't too concerned. I was drunk. Angry. I was out of control, playing the daredevil, gunning the gas and swerving my borrowed car through the snowbound lanes of Columbia. We'd slid off the road once already, high-centering the car in someone's front lawn. It didn't phase me, barely slowed me down. A good friend of mine and teammate, who was along for this outlandish double-date, helped me push the car out. Then I immediately swerved back out into the frozen suburbs bordering the University of Missouri. My buddy was in no better condition than I; we were behaving like idiots—laughing, joking, merrily dismissing our dates' frantic pleas to stop the car. Their squeals only egged me on. I punched the gas and fishtailed around another hairpin turn.

Crunch!

I'm certain it was the loud crashing sound that finally got my attention. Or maybe it was the violent, whiplashing jolt of metal crushing metal on a quiet winter's night. Either way, it snapped me to attention. While I knew it was a car I'd struck at thirty miles per hour, I now discerned that it had an official-looking emblem on the side, and what appeared to be a red light on top. Not good. By now it had become preposterously clear that my long-awaited date with the woman of my dreams was a complete catastrophe.

It was the dead of winter, 1961. Our little group had spent the evening at a fraternity party near the University of Missouri campus. It was attended by some Tiger football teammates of mine and billed as a sort of post-season celebration—a fancy term for "kegger." The football season had ended on a high note a few weeks back. We beat Kansas in a tough road game in Lawrence to end the year 7-2-1. By rights we should have been preparing for a bowl game. The past two years our team had appeared in consecutive Orange Bowls, the last an historic 1961 win over Navy and its Heismann Trophy tailback Joe Bellino. But this season the coaching staff seemed to suspect that, perhaps, we weren't as good as our record suggested. They were probably right. We'd consistently struggled against some average teams, and in those days the financial incentives for a school to accept a bowl bid weren't nearly as lucrative as today. It wasn't unheard of for some schools to decline their bowl invitation, which is what Mizzou did in 1961. Though disappointed, most of the players bought into the prevailing consensus: "Why spoil a decent record with a possible bowl loss," especially the year after the school's Orange Bowl jubilation. The season was over. I was a senior, and my football-playing days were over. Other pursuits beckoned.

The night of the fraternity party was one of my first dates with a young lady named Lyndi Taussig. She attended Stephens College across town—the infamous rich girls' school. In some respects, I feared I was in over my head. I certainly wasn't what you'd call suave or debonair when it came to courting matters. I was a *lineman*. My gift was cracking heads at the line of scrimmage, not making fashionable small talk with a classy debutante. Some of my teammates chided me, "Mac, give it up; she's too good for you. You're gonna blow it."

No matter. I set aside my doubts and pressed stubbornly on.

Lyndi was sweet, extremely witty and fun-loving, and also quite attractive. Something about her really appealed to me. She made me laugh, and from what I knew, she was everything I'd ever wanted in a partner. We seemed comfortable together. I was curious to see where a little perseverance might lead. When she said she'd accompany me to my so-called "jock" party, I was really excited. I couldn't wait to introduce her to the guys as "my date."

Unfortunately, it wasn't the dream date I'd hoped for. It was more like the date from hell. Things deteriorated almost the minute we showed up at the kegger. Once at the party, I began jawing and clowning with my comrades-in-arms. Soon, all pretense at good manners and polite introductions flew out the window. My brief stabs at charm and sophistication yielded to more pressing business: draining the keg as fast as possible. It wasn't long before Lyndi was justifiably ticked off. Oh, how I'd wanted to impress her, but I still couldn't resist knocking down a few quick beers with the fellas. And those were days when a few beers always led to a few more, until. . . .

To this day I am mystified at how some guys can drink and get all lighthearted and cheerful, or become charming romantics or armchair philosophers. Not me. Pour me a few rounds and it could be a harrowing scene. From shy and painstakingly courteous, I'd change into an ill-tempered, belligerent jerk looking for trouble and inevitably finding it. It was a failing well-documented through many sordid exploits in college, yet it was something over which I seemingly had little control.

Lyndi hadn't seen this side of me yet, at least not the full extent of it. She'd had little tip-offs, though, like the first time we met at a campus watering hole. A friend of mine was trying to set us up, but, having had a few beers, I was reportedly rude and tactless. It was nothing compared to what she was now about to witness. With her proud escort occupied over at the keg, Lyndi was trying hard to mix with the rough-edged crowd of half-lit frat boys and jocks. From across the room, I heard her cracking jokes with some of the guys. Then—I couldn't believe my ears—she casually used the Lord's name in vain. It was very off-handed and probably just slipped out, but I almost dropped my beer cup. I swung around and glared at her. She glanced over with a look that said, "Uh-oh!"

It's important to understand here that, to this died-in-the-wool Catholic with a spiked blood alcohol level, Lyndi—*my* date, the woman with whom I'd already pictured myself walking down the aisle—had burst my bubble. Using God's name in vain at all, much less around my teammates, for heaven's sake, was like committing the unpardonable sin. Never mind that I was obnoxiously ignoring my own drunken stupor. I clamped down on her innocent slip with all the irrational fury of a pit bull. I *exploded.* To her shock, I turned mean and berated her for her careless blasphemy. She was speechless, horrified, embarrassed. She said she was sorry, but I rejected her frantic apologies. Instead, I barked, "C'mon, we're leaving!" Ordering her outside into the car was like pouring gasoline over our big date and striking a match to it. This was how alcohol affected me. My friend and his date tagged warily along behind us. I put Lyndi in the car, slammed the door, and sped off into the freezing night.

The guy who loaned me his car for the night, a truly generous, kindhearted friend, would have never consented to hand me the keys if he had foreseen how it would end. Like a kamikaze bobsled pilot, I lost control on the ice and skidded smack into a parked Columbia police car directly in front of Lyndi's dorm at Stephens. The officer was sitting in the front seat, quietly minding his own business, when I creamed him. Thankfully, from what I recall, damage to both cars was minimal, and no one was injured.

My eyes regained focus in time to see most of the all-girl student body at Stephens, including the Dean of Students, crowding on the front lawn. Drawn by the sound of the crash, Lyndi's classmates were standing wide-eyed, hands over their mouths. The dazed policeman emerged from his car looking disheveled and disbelieving. Flashlight in hand, he approached my driver's side window.

Under similar circumstances, I suppose wiser men would have seen the potential for real ugliness brewing and done their best to quickly sober up. They would have become really polite, deferential—*obedient*. But, as I've noted, after a few pitchers I was always ready with the crude retort or cutting insult. When the officer leaned in and asked me to get out of the car, I quite casually replied, "I don't think you're *big* enough to get me out of this car!"

Everyone was silent—dumbfounded! The officer stared at me as if I were insane. On the lawn, dozens of jaws fell open. My friend and his date held their breath in the back seat. Lyndi's face turned ghost white. Me? I had a stupid grin on my face. I thought it was a witty quip. No one laughed, least of all the police officer. Mortified, Lyndi leaned back, planted both feet on my back, and literally kicked me out of the car into the policeman's waiting handcuffs. I staggered to my feet, but the show wasn't over.

As the officer began to wrestle me past the crowd of gawkers, something strange and spontaneous came over me. I suddenly became that incurable romantic I'd always admired. Spinning around with swashbuckling bravado, I grabbed Lyndi in both arms, gave her a big bear hug, and bellowed, "Oh Lyndi, I love you!" The officer went flying; Lyndi looked as if she were about to die; her classmates all looked as if they'd seen a UFO land and ask directions. Satisfied, I resumed my march to jail. I'm told that this spectacle by a Mizzou football player stirred Columbia's gossip mill for weeks running.

The aftermath of this debacle was truly wretched. Not only was I barred by Stephens from seeing Lyndi again, but less than a week after my arrest I received the biggest blow of my life. The University of Missouri Athletic Department very matter-of-factly notified me that my football scholarship had been revoked. Stripped. Canceled. Voided. It was very cut and dried. My first thought was, *Oh no, God, this has to be a mistake*. But it was no mistake. Nothing could have hurt worse. I was disgraced; I was devastated.

The humiliation of being kicked off scholarship over a drunk-

and-disorderly incident was beyond catastrophic (ironically, I would in years to come be faced with similar decisions regarding my own players). But it was even worse than that. I genuinely, desperately, needed the scholarship money to complete my education degree. I had played out my four years of eligibility, but I still had a semester or so of classes to finish up. Losing the scholarship guaranteed I would finish my college career financially destitute.

In fairness to the university, they had little choice in the matter. They were simply making a firm, categorical statement: University of Missouri student athletes would *not* drink and drive, smash into parked police cars, and resist arrest. It was impossible to argue. At the same time, I felt deeply persecuted and betrayed. That scholarship represented years of hard work, years of punishing my body and training my mind to compete at a major college level. If the truth were known, it represented most of what I considered worthwhile about myself. I'd completed my athletic obligation and given the university the best four years of my life. To my thinking, it didn't seem like too much to ask for the school to extend some grace, even over an admittedly reckless blunder. Cutting me loose now that my playing days were over seemed the height of disloyalty. For a long time I found it simply impossible to swallow; I was hurt and disillusioned. The pain and abandonment of that decision haunted me a long time.

The Birth of a Paradox

Here would be a great place to say this foul episode marked the end of the foolishness, that with the loss of my scholarship and estrangement from my girlfriend I hit rock bottom. I wish I could say that, as a well-intentioned college senior, I woke up, smelled the coffee, and righted the listing ship that was my life—or that I learned my lesson, quit drinking cold turkey, got my priorities in order, and lived happily ever after. It would make a great made-for-TV movie. It would be wonderful to be able to say all that, but the fact is, the story was only beginning.

Those who know, or *think* they know, Bill McCartney, are probably shaking their heads at this story. They probably see me in much simpler terms: a devoted, sold-out Christian—maybe a bit overboard—but clearly on fire for and passionately committed to Jesus Christ. For those, this bewildering episode of youth might not add up. Others who have heard me speak somewhere in a stadium full of men as the founder of Promise Keepers—a Christian men's organization committed to raising up a new generation of godly men in our country—would think the incident crude and incongruous. Who would expect such behavior, even far back in his impetuous youth, from a man who now calls men to uncompromising, *radical* purity, holiness, integrity, and commitment?

There will always be those who retain images of me as the former coach of the University of Colorado Buffaloes. In that high-profile role, I was a strict disciplinarian who held his own players to a fair, if inflexible, code of conduct. "How could 'Preacher Bill' have squandered his own football scholarship during an irresponsible night of drunk driving?" they might indignantly ask.

It's reasonable to ask, "Who is this guy I thought I had a handle on?" Or, "How does such a loose cannon get from *there* to *here?*" The truth is, if this story demonstrates anything, it's that the person many think they know has been, and continues to be, a paradox. The fabric and flow of my life has, in most respects, been an ebbing, flowing, baffling contradiction.

Tucked away in the folds of my life are countless episodes that coldly strip away the mystique and pretense of what some think of me. A.W. Tozer once described how an admirer of the godly Macarius of Optino wrote that his spiritual counsel had been helpful. "This cannot be," Macarius wrote in reply. "Only the mistakes are mine. All good advice is the advice of the Spirit of God, His advice that I happen to have heard rightly and to have passed on without distorting it."[1] In like fashion, now more than ever, mine is the story of a highly flawed, ordinary man who has made it through only with the help of an extraordinary God.

In this respect it is an instructive, even inspiring, commentary. But to leave it at that would deny a cornerstone piece of the puzzle needed to bring the picture of Bill McCartney into tighter focus. For within the shifting frontiers of all this confounding contradiction, there has been one enduring constant: the unsettling quality of being doggedly, unconventionally *sold out* and *radically* committed to my goals, whatever they happen to be. We're talking full throttle, all or nothing, pedal to the metal, go for broke, *sold out*, every day of my life.

Don't think this eases the paradox. It compounds it. For on the one hand I've been sold out to highly significant challenges and pursuits—meaty ventures and substantial goals that brought great satisfaction and lasting spiritual and material returns. For this I have been undeservedly blessed. Yet, by the same token, there have been serious missteps; I've also been misguided and sold out to false dreams and enticements, ideals that became idols, risks that turned sour, blind allies that brought pain and devastation to those I love. This almost unconscious, compulsive drive to give myself over (often to the exclusion of everything else) to whatever challenge I bit into, for too long took the form of selfish ambition. This knack of turning the simplest idea into a highly-public personal crusade and, like a 350-pound tackle, rolling over any obstacle was frequently insensitively imposed upon my marriage and family, bringing both to the brink of ruin. In other ways it cluttered my thinking, stalled my spiritual growth, and exposed me in stages as a fraud to the beliefs I held dear.

Thankfully, the story doesn't end here. In the final analysis, there is something wonderful, integral, about being hopelessly and incurably sold out to one's causes. It's a gift, a strength, a blessing bestowed from above. I still thank God endlessly for depositing this nature within me, because I've learned to ask Him: What are the causes worth being sold out to? I'm being taught. I'm learning that this bent, softened and refocused, is the path to otherwise unapproachable depth in our lives, loves, and relationships. It's the sold-out heart that breaks chains of bondage and releases power. It's the zealous, no-holds-barred heart that grants us intimate access into the sweet presence of the Almighty. It's the red hot, unfearing determination to surrender all that brings cleansing redemption to our souls. Radical, breathless, sold-out commitment to the *right* causes generates boundless power to give and receive. How do I know? Because only my stubborn tenacity to lay hold of God's best has enabled me to crawl back through the burnt rubble of my neglect and failure to start over.

Yes! Being sold out is a *good* thing—the *best* thing. But there is a battle to be waged. It's a drama that continues to play itself out in my life; it begins to explain how an angry, inebriated young man rampaging through the streets of Columbia gets *here* from *there*. It's worth taking a look back at the root of, or in my case the *seeds* that gave rise to, a sold-out heart.

It doesn't take a genius to see that the young man who clobbered a parked Columbia police car in 1961 didn't have a clue. What winding route landed him in handcuffs that night? Where did his dreams take him from there? How did a stubborn, willful athlete, radically sold out to football, career, and his own whims, become a fifty-seven-year-old man sold out, more and more, to God and his family—to the *right* things? It's a journey of years, tears, crippling setbacks, and agonizingly slow progress. It's a path of unexpected twists and unlikely turns, speaking poignantly, often disturbingly, yet, perhaps best of all, *triumphantly*, to God's mercy. Most of all, it speaks to the relentless, fiery pulse of God's sold-out heart toward me.

Lyndi: Young Love and Hope for the Future

The first time I ever laid eyes on Bill McCartney I prayed for him. I prayed God would make him all right again. It was a cold October afternoon in 1960, and I was with my school friends watching the Missouri Tigers beat up on another team. I attended an all-girls school, so I had a tendency to gravitate to where the men were, and they were typically at the football game.

I was on my way to the first aid station when Bill's name came echoing over the public address system. He had been injured and was being wheeled to an awaiting ambulance. That's where we first came face to face. The nurse was treating my toes for frostbite as Bill lay motionless on a stretcher nearby. He looked dead to me; he was so gray and pale. It really frightened me; so I prayed for him. He was hoisted into the ambulance, and it sped away. I wouldn't see him again until the following Spring or be introduced to him for another year.

Bill and I finally met in December 1961. We only had one date before I left for Christmas break. I didn't often date football players; they seemed to be too much into themselves. But Bill was different. He was such a well-mannered gentleman. When he was willing to attend a Christmas musical with me—something I loved that was worlds apart from his interests—I thought, *Here is a guy who is open to experiencing things I enjoy!* That impressed me! He had a tender way about him and a love for family and God that drew me in.

We had no time to establish any real connection. I figured I'd never see him again because I had to leave immediately for Christmas break. During those three weeks at home, I cherished a wistful longing to have a real and safe connection with someone with whom I could share my life and dreams of family. In the midst of these idealized longings stood the memory of a young man named Bill McCartney. He held promise.

The bus ride back to school evoked in me a loneliness for an indefinable something I could not seem to grasp. I was staring out the window of the bus feeling very sad inside as we pulled into the small station in Columbia, Missouri. There was a familiar figure in the distance. I couldn't believe my eyes—it was Bill. I gathered my things quickly and raced off the bus. I called out to him, in a most unladylike fashion, even though he was halfway down the street. He turned and ran to me. I had no idea he would be there. Bill had no idea what bus I would be on. He had been meeting buses all day. He was waiting for me. I was amazed! No one had ever made me feel so valuable, so special.

Bill and I saw each other nearly every day for the next six months, getting to know all about each other and falling in love. We talked incessantly, studied, played, and began to sketch a future together. The ugly drinking incident Bill referred to marred the pretty picture I had developed about us. It stood in stark contrast to the image I held of the man I was beginning to see as the one who would love me and help me find my way to the kind of life, family, and future I longed for. In the glow of young love, the negative image of that drunken man faded as I chose to focus on the bright image I had seen of Bill.

It's funny, though, how the real man has a way of confusing a woman's fantasies of him. I had dreamed of the day Bill would confess his love for me. In the midst of the bizarre events Bill recounted for you, a single memory would stand out for me. Bill first told me he loved me while he was handcuffed to a police officer. It still makes me laugh! How absurd! The next time he told me he loved me, he got my name wrong. He used his old girlfriend's name. That was perhaps my first clue that Bill was a paradox.

I was not blind; I saw the man at his worst. I also saw the promise of the man he longed to be; that was the man I fell in love with. He seemed to have everything I hoped for in a man. Bill and I attended his church together every week. That told me he was a man who could be trusted. In my mind, if God didn't play a big role in our life together, nothing would ever work out right. Bill had been devoted to God and his church from childhood. I longed for a man who would make his wife and children a high priority. That's what Bill wanted too. I felt assured that he would have enough love for me and our future children to last a lifetime. His certainty and clarity of his career gave me a feeling of security. I felt safe in his arms and safe in his presence, and above all else, I needed to feel safe. At that time, nothing took precedence over it. All dreams, all important matters, all duties seemed to flow through our relationship. I felt loved, valued, and perfectly connected to Bill.

This romantic notion of my husband was not just girlish fantasy. It was inscribed in more than thirty romantic and beautiful love letters Bill wrote to me during our separation in the summer of 1962. On top of each page were the letters JMJ, which stood for Jesus, Mary, and Joseph—a habit Bill developed in Catholic grade school. To me, JMJ represented the sacredness of family, designed by God. Each letter Bill wrote me ended with a decree to pray for me and a promise of unending love. This was the man who drew my heart into his, and I wanted to stay there for the rest of my life.

In this chapter, Bill raised two questions. He asked how that stubborn, willful, drunken man became who he is today—a man who is calling a new generation of men to holiness and integrity. He also set forth the goal of being wholeheartedly invested in love of God and family and asked how we get from wherever we are to that goal. The answers to both questions are one and the same. The way Bill McCartney got from there to here is the way God will get you from wherever you are to where He wants you to be. He will get you there little by little.

When the children of Israel were going into the Promised Land, Moses told them, "The LORD your God will drive out those nations before you, *little by little*. You will not be allowed to eliminate them all at once, or the wild animals will multiply around you" (Deuteronomy 7:22, emphasis added). While they may have wanted to take the land all at once (which surely is how my husband would have wanted to take it if he had been there), God knew that there were wild beasts to be driven out little by little. God also knew that what He had promised, and put in their hearts to desire, would be fulfilled. But for the men and women leading their families through the wilderness, gazing intently toward the Promised Land, the journey was often harrowing. It was the same way for Bill and me as we journeyed through life. No doubt, it's the same for all God's children. We see it. We long for it. We know God wants us to have it. And we want it now. But reality seems to hold us back. We want the promise, and yet we live with the paradox.

Be encouraged, wives of men who are seeking to be sold out to God—wives who see the paradox of the man who says he wants to love God with all his heart but comes home drunk; the man who says he wants to put his family before his career but can't make the time. I've lived with that paradox, and I have come to make peace with it. You can too.

When a man says he wants what God wants for him and his family, to me that shows that he is setting out for the Promised Land. But wanting it doesn't make it so, no matter how sold out he may be, no matter how zealous. My husband is as zealous as they come, and he, too, could only possess the promises of God for himself and his family little by little. That's how we can learn to live with the paradox—not only the paradox we see in our husbands' lives, but in our own. Before any of us can possess the promises of God, we must set our hearts to journey in that direction. We must state our intentions. We must also recognize that we all have our own wild beasts that must be driven out before we can possess the life God intends in its fullness. But while we live with the paradox, we rely on the fact that God has called us to the life we long for and has promised to bring us in and help us fight off the wild beasts, little by little. God is the great Promise Keeper.

Chapter 2
The Privilege of Prayer

"In every thing let your request be made known unto God." You may pray about the smallest and the greatest thing. You not only may pray for the Holy Spirit, but you may pray for a new pair of boots. You may go to God about the bread you eat, the water you drink, the clothing you wear, and pray to Him about everything. Never say that daily necessities are too little for Him to notice; everything is little in comparison with Him.[1]

—CHARLES SPURGEON

Journal Entry 1/25/97—*As I prayed this morning, I was realizing what Jesus has saved us from and what He has saved us into. If we could comprehend the true contrast of life without Christ and life with Him, we would be overwhelmed and would praise and thank God nonstop. If we realized who God is—how extraordinary, how glorious, how loving and kind—if we could clearly distinguish who we are and who He is, all of us would repent that we had not prayed and prayed and prayed.*

—BILL McCARTNEY

The memory is still as fresh as yesterday, though it happened more than fifty years ago. I was seven years old, sitting by myself during a Christmas party at the Catholic grade school I attended in Trenton, Michigan. It was the type of party where, at the end of the cake, ice cream, and games, every kid would pick a present from a big box in the center of the room. It was a random drawing. We'd been told to spend no more than a dollar on our gifts. So even back in 1947 the best we could expect were little gag toys or trinkets. But I had a secret.

As the games ended, the whole class started milling about waiting for the grand finale. I was off in a corner praying under my breath. I had one simple request, and I wanted God to answer it. A close friend had pulled me aside before the party started. Whispering, he told me he'd splurged on his gift—he'd spent *five* dollars on a brand new leather wallet. He and I were the only ones who knew. I began thinking that somewhere in the communal gift box was a neatly gift-wrapped wallet, with *my* name on it!

The teachers called us up by rows, telling us to close our eyes, reach in, and grab a gift.

My prayers turned urgent. "Oh, please, God. If You knew how much I want that wallet. Could I have it, please? I do need a wallet, after all, and I'll do anything You say. But God, *pleeese* help me to pick that wallet."

Our row stood and walked single file past the box. At my turn, I whispered one last prayer, took a deep breath, closed my eyes, and reached in. I picked a package and walked back to my chair. My heart was pounding. Slowly, I removed the gift wrapping and lifted out a small brown box, taped shut. Tenderly, I peeled away the tape and opened the box. Pushing aside the tissue packing and removing the contents, I sat there looking at my gift. There it was. My *wallet!*

There it was! I couldn't believe it. I wanted to cheer. Of dozens of gifts in that box, I got my wallet, exactly as I'd prayed. It took every ounce of will power not to sprint to the front of the room and scream to the whole class how God answered my prayer. I thought better of it, realizing it might raise more questions than it would answer. So I sat there grinning from ear to ear, marveling in my wonderful secret. As it says in the Bible, my joy was complete. It had nothing to do with the wallet anymore. All I kept thinking was, "Wow! *God answered my prayer!* He *heard* me." It boggled my young mind, stretched my imagination to its limits. I mean, if I could call on God for something like a five dollar wallet, what else could I pray for? The implications were staggering. It meant that I could call on God for . . . *anything!*

It was a landmark moment that probably changed my life irrevocably. I was set on a new course. This startling development stirred everything up. It confirmed everything I'd been hearing in catechism and already strongly suspected: There really *is* a God. He really *does* love me. I could actually talk to the God of the universe and expect Him to hear. I could possibly even, maybe someday, get to *know* Him. Maybe He really did know each and every hair on my head. It was a tremendous revelation to a thoughtful seven-year-old who'd already taken a deadly serious interest in religion.

Faith, or something like it, was already brewing within me, or I never would have prayed for the wallet in the first place. My teachers had shown us scripturally that the full purpose of man is to know, love, and serve God. I had no doubt there *was* a God; I might have even thought I knew what He was like. But how to approach God or *relate* to Him remained fuzzy. Wouldn't you know it, God took care of it for me. He took the occasion to lean down, answer a silly prayer, and make Himself real to a curious child. It was simple, miraculous, and cost God less than the blink of an eye. But in doing so, He taught me infinitely more than a lifetime of catechism classes about His tender love for His children.

Drawn by Tradition

In our family photo album is a telling photo of me at age six. In it, I'm taking my first communion. Kneeling, elbows propped on a table and hands folded at my chin, I'm looking heavenward with eyes as big as half dollars. Draped around my fingers are rosary beads. But it's the expression on my face that says it all. It registers such sincerity that a person would have to be blind not to see how desperately important it was to me. The eyes, the stiff posture, certainly reflected deep, abiding respect and reverence. But a pure childhood innocence also comes through. It's the face of a child who, perhaps, wasn't grasping it all, but nonetheless embraced each moment with unreserved indulgence. That's how I related to God: He sent chills down my spine.

I still remember my first communion. I thought that day would never arrive. As all Catholics know, it's the first time a child is fully admitted into the breadth of church life. It's something like the *bar mitzvah* for a young Jewish boy, a time when family and friends gather to celebrate his arrival at a stage of religious responsibility. It's a coming-of-age ceremony that provided me a delicious first taste of privilege and entitlement. For one, I was finally allowed to go forward with the rest of the church when the congregation took communion. It may not seem like a big deal to non-Catholics, but imagine yourself as a youngster sitting in church month after month. Every time the congregation stands to take communion, your father says, "Not this time. You wait here." It's something a child begins to look forward to and desire, and, in my case, *yearn* for.

I grew up in a family where church and its activities were held in highest regard and attended with due homage. The day of my first communion families drove in from great distances. There was a lavish party. For one day, at least, I was the center of attention. Reexamining that photo, I see the pensive face of one who is already sold out, mind and body, to the notion that, perhaps, God was gazing down for the first time and taking note of a little boy who was on fire to know Him.

It's difficult to understand if you didn't grow up in my home. But nothing could be clearer to me. Without hesitation, I trace my religious affinity to three sources, three spiritual mentors, if you will, who modeled it: my older brother, Tom; my grandmother, Mary; and my dad, William Patrick. They were the catalysts for my enthusiasm. Take note, adults: Sold-out role models produce sold-out devotees. (My mother, Ruth, who was always a gentle, steadying influence in our family, gave her life to the Lord in 1989. And my younger brother, John Richard McCartney, also received Christ and is an active member of his church in Lansing, Michigan.)

My brother Tom is two years, eleven days older than me. As with most things he did, Tom set the example for me at church. He did everything before me, and he did it well. His example was a strong early impression. I looked up to him. What I saw was an older brother who *always* took a very serious and devout approach to life. Before I even had a clue about it, I watched Tom prepare for his first communion. Tom was never half-hearted or indifferent about anything, but he approached his first communion with a maturity and a sense of honor and duty that belied his age. When that day arrived, he conducted himself with military precision and attention to detail. Do you wonder why it made such an impression on me? I mean to tell you, he whet my appetite.

It was always a distinct privilege to follow in Tom's footsteps. Tom went on to be an altar boy and took part in the major events at church. Even at those young ages, I was simply awestruck by his sincere, wholehearted demeanor. His example followed me into adulthood, where I took great pains to be equally wholehearted in everything I did.

My dad's mother, Mary, died when I was fifteen. My recollection of her is that she was the most godly woman I have ever known. My youth was richly embroidered with tales about grandmother—stories my father told about her noble character and passion for God. Rarely a day passed without us hearing something new about her. Dad liked to say, "If my mother doesn't go to heaven, none of us have a chance." To him, she was the most wonderful person on the face of the earth, and he made sure we all knew that what set her apart was her all-out pursuit of the Lord. She was such a hero to my dad that she became a hero to me. I absorbed those stories and found myself embracing her values.

Grandma Mary raised eight kids of her own. When she wasn't at home tending to everyone's needs, she was at church or in prayer. Knowing that made *me* want to pray. (Interestingly, Lyndi's grandmother had very similar spiritual qualities, and I can't help but believe the prayers of these two godly women helped sustain us and our family over the years).

Grandma made no secret that her favorite day of the year was the Catholic feast day in August known as the Feast of the Assumption of Mary. Every year as the day approached, Grandma got excited and started preparations, making sure we all knew too. After a long, fruitful life, Grandmother passed away in 1955, on August 8, the very day the Feast of the Assumption fell on that year. We were stunned. It left me with the lasting impression that she was very special in the eyes of God, that she must have known God so personally and loved Him so dearly that He brought her home to be with Him on the day she treasured. Her life, and now her death, demonstrated, even to a preoccupied teenager, that God takes special interest in those who are impassioned toward Him. Neither catechism nor Sunday Mass had brought this to life like my grandmother's legacy. She showed me that, if I chose, I too could have a fiery hot relationship with God.

Dad

Within an hour of meeting my dad, most people would agree he was four things: Irish, Catholic, Democrat, and Marine. These things not only defined my dad's primary convictions, they were his heart, soul, and constitution, the pillars of his personality. And he wasn't shy about telling you so. Dad was the walking definition of "sold out." First, he was sold out to his Irish heritage—fiercely, passionately loyal to his roots. On St. Patrick's Day, our family didn't just *recognize* St. Patrick, we *celebrated* the day as if it were a major national holiday. Dad didn't go in for this wishy-washy "put on some green socks" or "pin a piece of green ribbon to your T-shirt." No, when St. Patrick's Day arrived, our entire family was *decked out* in full green regalia. If you had seen our entire family walking down the street together on St. Patrick's Day, you might have thought a giant lime tree had sprouted arms and legs.

Dad was just as radically loyal to the Democratic Party and to FDR. Growing up, we thought Franklin Roosevelt was the greatest American in history. *And* he was loyal to the Marines with whom he served in World War II. To hear Dad tell it, the Marines were single-handedly responsible for saving civilization while, perhaps, the military's other branches sat back sipping coffee and nibbling doughnuts. The first song I ever learned, Dad taught me: "From the Halls of Montezuma." We'd sing that song as a family from time to time, my dad leading the chorus like Tony Bennett. Tom joined the Marines when he turned seventeen, and while I never entered the service, I, too, was a Marine at heart. Dad was Irish, I was Irish; Dad was Democrat, I was Democrat; Dad was a Marine, I was a Marine. And the only reason I identified with any of these is because Dad so completely, energetically, aggressively identified himself with each of them. Sold-out dads produce sold-out sons.

More than anything, Dad was Catholic. The prominent ideal he imparted to me as a child was his love and allegiance to the Catholic church. Growing up, for example, we lived just across the street from the public school. I could hear the school bell ring every morning. But Dad bussed us across town to the Catholic school. On Sunday mornings he didn't *send* us to church; he *took* us to church. Rain or shine, blizzard or drought, hail or high water, we were there without fail. When your father is as devoutly, faithfully Catholic as mine, it meant, of course, that we were huge Notre Dame fans (and so, we naturally assumed, was God). Well past my college years, if you'd have ever asked me, I would have insisted that Catholics alone were heaven-bound.

In any event, you can see that from an early age I was surrounded by wholehearted, sold-out people, literally immersed in the lives of mentors and role models who didn't just share their religious beliefs and leave it at that. These were not shrinking violets. They poured themselves into their convictions with gusto. They weren't indifferent but were bona fide leaders who taught me that total, all-out commitment was the only way to live life. It was certainly the only way to approach God. I watched and emulated them, and through their diligence and forthrightness I saw the physical evidence of God's undergirding presence about them. There is no doubt—*they* were the seeds and I am their legacy. God joined my heart to His through theirs, meeting me in the crosscurrents of their passion, calling out to me, wooing me, and drawing me in. To whatever extent God set His sights on me, it is to the honor of those who boldly represented Him to a trusting child.

Chapter 3
Seeds of a Lifelong Obsession

HOW DOES IT HAPPEN? How does a stirring pastime become a suffocating obsession? How does something that starts out enlivening one's heart turn into a brass idol? I've come to understand that there are two basic forms of idolatry: worshiping something other than God, and worshiping God other than He is. Attaching worth to something in excess of what we give to God makes it an idol. It offends the heart of God, who created us to worship Him alone. For thoughts of God, heaven, and church to occupy such an exalted position in my adolescent hierarchy of interests speaks clearly to something good and pure at work in me. It speaks to God's hand on me, and it carried over and sustained me through many difficult years to come. Yet God was not without rival in my impressionable young heart. Seeds of another sort had already sent down deep shoots, and would grow to crowd and challenge my First Love. By age seven, the year of my "miracle wallet," serious competition from another quarter had begun to monopolize my affections.

Were these the seeds of idolatry? If I were to tell you that by age seven I already suspected that I would be a coach, you probably wouldn't believe me. But it's the honest truth. It wasn't just a case of being inordinately enthusiastic about coaching, or thinking I might make a good coach, or even seeing coaching as one of several viable career choices. No, even if it meant instructing tee-ball at the local YMCA, given the opportunity, I would have gladly done it full-time. From roughly the same time that I took my first communion, I was becoming consumed by the idea of sports and coaching.

Allow me to explain: Career options where I grew up in Riverview, Michigan, weren't exactly jumping out at kids. My neighborhood, just off Lake Erie in a southern suburb of Detroit, was a classic blue-collar community. My friends' dads worked in factories or at the automobile plants. My dad worked for Chrysler, where he helped make the old De Soto. Kids in Riverview didn't grow up pining to be doctors or lawyers or accountants. In this pinched economic climate, my folks never rubbed shoulders with people who had lots of money. We never had a physician over for dinner, for instance, and I didn't know any kids whose fathers were corporate CEOs. We didn't begrudge these people—we just never mixed with them. The notable folks in our community, those whom kids looked up to, were public servants: firemen, policemen, teachers, priests, *coaches*. In the late 1940s, these were the jobs kids in Riverview grew up revering. With such a narrow range of options, wanting to be a coach when I grew up wasn't so odd. Make no mistake, I knew I wanted to be a coach.

Still, an instinctive love for coaching comes from somewhere. In my case it grew out of a childhood obsession with sports: competing in sports, reading about sports, dreaming about sports, idolizing great athletes. We're all born with natural fascinations and abilities. With me it was sports. It was my gift. Take my grandson, Timothy Chase. T.C. just turned eight years old. Already he's showing signs of being a great athlete. He loves football, basketball, and baseball. He won a ball-throwing competition in first grade, so he's already showing potential as a pitcher or quarterback. I helped introduce him to these sports, and I've been there to encourage him. But T.C. also loves to fish, play roller-blade hockey, and swim, and he's taken a real liking to golf—he has a natural swing. The point is, he didn't learn any of these sports from me or any other adult. He's just a natural athlete drawn to sports, period.

My natural inclinations were nourished by a daily regimen of sports, sports, sports. In my neighborhood, we played ball morning, noon, and night from the time we were old enough to run, chew gum, and swing a bat. Riverview was a relaxed, fairly innocent, family-oriented town—a safe place to raise kids. Most kids didn't have a ton of chores, and there simply weren't a lot of other diversions. On a sunny day, you wouldn't find me hanging out in the library. I was out on the sand lot.

Don't forget, my older brother Tom excelled in sports. Much like my first communion, he paved the way in sports as well. He was an avid influence, guiding me early into organized sports: football, basketball, baseball, and track. That's how we spent our time. Every day after school we'd be out in the grass playing football or shooting hoops on the asphalt. Practically every memory I have as a kid has something to do with a ball.

I enjoyed some benefits of proximity. Our home sat right across the street from the high school ball fields. Most afternoons I watched the older kids practice from behind the fence. I loved to listen to the coaches barking orders, demonstrating techniques, calling plays, exhorting the team. Over time I made friends with both players and coaches. Later, I used these contacts to hitch rides on the team bus as they traveled to away games. I'd be the only kid on board, soaking up the excitement and energy of it all, joking with the players, absorbing the sights, sounds, and smells. It was like a dream. On the way home from games, I'd chime in with the players singing "Ninety-nine Bottles of Beer on the Wall."

It was the culture I was raised in. My neighborhood was literally an athletic training ground. And from the beginning I had a natural curiosity about the finer points of each sport. Watching from the sideline, dozens of questions raced endlessly through my mind: What made this team better than that? Why does that guy's jumpshot swish while the other guy clangs it off the iron? Why does that play go for a touchdown while this one goes for a ten-yard loss? What makes one athlete superior to another? I had a hunger to learn, and I'd go to great lengths to find an answer. Many things I just instinctively understood, and I had the ability to explain them to others.

My obsession with sports would have been a serious letdown if I had turned out to be a lousy, or mediocre, athlete. The fact is, passing through grade school, junior high, and into high school, I was competitive. Because of my knowledge of most sports, I could lead on the court, in the huddle, or on the diamond. I was a guy who'd draw the play in the dirt and say, "You run a down-and-out, and I'll throw it to you," or "Let's trap that guy at half-court and steal the pass." By the time I was in the fourth grade, if I wasn't chosen in the first three picks on the playground, I was the one doing the choosing. The fact is, I took immense pride in always being one of the better athletes in my age group. It made for easy acceptance. The other kids liked and befriended me. It only encouraged a childhood longing to succeed.

Basketball was always my favorite sport. Yet, by the time I was in the eighth grade, I was the leading scorer on the football team as a halfback and the leading scorer on the basketball team as a guard, and I batted third in the line-up in baseball. I was awarded an individual trophy at our eighth-grade sports banquet that year for "Outstanding Ability." Let me tell you, that trophy told me everything I needed to know about myself. It affirmed me and told me exactly where my strengths lay. I was a young athlete on the rise.

Looking back at it, something else was happening through all this affirmation. Subtly, unmistakably, I began to equate my self-worth, indeed, my very identity, with my athletic performance. And why wouldn't I? It's where all my positive feedback came from. Being recognized in the community as "above the norm" athletically is heady stuff to a kid. It makes you feel good about yourself. It's where the seeds begin to germinate, where the system of performance that defines our culture begins wrapping itself around young minds. Performance-based approval in childhood comes in all forms, such as music, grades, allowance. With me, wildly positive strokes from coaches, parents, and peers only led me into a deeper commitment, a more eager embrace, a more strident work ethic. From a young age, I was hooked, sold out.

The Sixth Sense

At Riverview High School, I went on to become a three-year varsity starter in football, basketball, and baseball. I was a rough, rawboned kid, but I was never the kind of natural, dominating athlete who could singlehandedly take over a game. I knew I never would be. So I plugged away, overcompensating with hard work, thorough preparation, and, of course, my biggest asset—my head. I had a sixth sense about what to do in a game. I was also extremely intense and aggressive. As a linebacker, I was very active. Whenever I'd make good contact, stick a solid tackle, or sack the quarterback, the coaches would get excited, run up to affirm me, heap on the praise, and say, "Get in there and do it again." With such positive strokes, it doesn't take long to start believing your clippings. And to someone like me, who still harbors a thousand secret insecurities about himself, the underlying message was, "I'm more acceptable as an athlete than as just plain old Bill McCartney." I sensed I would never get that kind of attention outside of athletics, so I pursued sports with a vengeance.

Scholastically, I was a slightly above-average student. But my sights were set on sports, on coaching. I lost interest if I suspected a particular class wasn't preparing me for my chosen profession. Some teachers used sports as a carrot. When assigned a book report, I'd write a paper on the week's top sports headline. My research papers invariably profiled top professional athletes. It's not something I boast of today, though I am indebted to some of my teachers for their forbearance, but that's who I was. Sports is what held my attention.

Through it all, my childhood vision to coach kept getting stronger. I knew I'd never play professional sports, but I also knew I'd never *not* be involved in sports, somehow. Coaching simply made sense. Almost every coach I ever had made a huge impact on me. They were my *heroes*, the picture of success. I could see they really enjoyed their jobs. During summers as I got older, I worked some tough construction jobs, everything from manual labor to lugging concrete-reinforced steel. Some of it paid pretty well, but it was grueling, gut-wrenching, sweaty, hard work. It taught me I didn't want to do that the rest of my life. For a kid from Riverview who had only so many options, coaching versus construction? You've got to be kidding. I never saw one of my high school coaches walking around with a pick or a shovel. They always had a *ball* in their hands and a smile on their faces. *What a way to live*, I thought. *I'm cut out for this. When I'm finished playing, I'll stay involved through coaching.*

One last thing: None of my mentors ever so much as snickered at my coaching dream or even *hinted* that coaching wasn't a worthwhile endeavor. That would have crushed me. It was just the opposite. Any adult I ever shared my dream with offered nothing but encouragement. I was *always* affirmed in my dream.

Because of family, heritage, community, the men and women I admired, a portrait has emerged: It's not so different from that photo of a child at his first communion. It portrays a young man at once bristling with passion, fueled by high ideas, and driven by concrete goals. Lukewarm? Indifferent? They were foreign concepts. They weren't options. Rather, the seeds that spawned a hot-blooded, two-track appetite for God and coaching were "breathless conviction" and "feverish aspiration." As I entered college, my path seemed set. I was thoroughly invested. My jaws were clinched, and my motives clear. But an unforeseen bend in the road was coming up fast—faster and larger than I would have expected—and threatened to knock me off course.

Chapter 4
Season of Compromise

THE DAY I LEARNED I'D BEEN offered a football scholarship to the University of Missouri as part of Dan Devine's first recruiting class is the day I thought, *I've finally arrived—the hard work has paid off*. Being pursued by the former coach of Arizona State (and future coach of the Green Bay Packers and Notre Dame) was the overwhelming realization of a lifelong dream.

In the days after signing the letter of intent, I remember strolling around Riverview, imagining that people were eying me and saying things like, "Nobody can deny *now* that that Bill McCartney kid has got something to offer. He's gonna make a name for himself someday." I assumed others who might have begrudged me my tunnel-vision approach to sports would now admit it was all well worth the effort. I had a free ride to play college football at a major university, something I'd dreamed of, worked toward, and prayed about for more than a decade. Proverbs 13:19 says that "a longing fulfilled is sweet to the soul." For me, nothing could have been sweeter than playing center and linebacker for the Missouri Tigers.

My elation stemmed from the fact that a scholarship was never a sure bet. I wasn't exactly a "lock" to play major college football. Coaches didn't use the word "blue chipper" to appraise my ability.

Riverview hadn't had a powerhouse program the years I was there, so our players didn't attract a lot of attention. We were a smaller school with decent, determined athletes, who often played over their heads against much larger schools. Though few expected us to beat some of these teams, it was still a good showcase for a Riverview athlete. If one of us happened to pull out a great performance against top-notch competition, he could attract some attention from scouts stalking the opposing team.

It's how I landed at Missouri. I had the game of my life against one of these imposing opponents. Trenton High School, from the same neighboring town where my parents bussed me to Catholic grade school for six years as a child, provided my moment of glory. Even as a child, I knew about Trenton High. They were a big deal in that town; they always seemed to win. Many successful college careers began on their practice fields. Growing up, I thought of them as the Green Bay Packers of high school. Later, when I entered high school myself, I couldn't wait to test myself against Trenton. I'd worked it up in my mind as a fierce natural rivalry: Trenton's great tradition pitted against Riverview's status as a scrappy underdog was the perfect stage on which to prove one's manhood.

By the time our game rolled around my senior year, Trenton was, as usual, a daunting opponent. Their entire squad had superior talent and depth. They rightly expected to overpower everyone they played. As a linebacker at Riverview, I prospered in a system designed to get me a lot of tackles. For the Trenton game, our coaches tailored the game plan to complement my knack of sniffing out a play and making the quick hit. It put me in the center of the action, and I responded by making more than twenty tackles—a *huge* day by any standard. Our team played great, but Trenton's sheer size and power ultimately wore us down. They narrowly beat us, but my "career performance" stirred up a little buzz about "that hard-hitting linebacker from Riverview." My high school coach, Bud McCourt, sent film of the performance to the few colleges that had expressed an interest.

By rights, Missouri in the late 1950s would never have pursued a player from Michigan, no matter how good he was. But they were in a down cycle at the time, and even with Dan Devine coming in to spearhead a rebuilding program, Missouri was likely having trouble landing top players in their own backyard. It opened the door for a guy like me. When they saw my twenty-plus tackles against Trenton, they apparently figured I'd fallen through the cracks and snapped me up. If I ever doubted that God was orchestrating my life and my football fortunes, uniquely gifting me and helping me make the most of my ability, the Trenton game soundly erased them. It was a divinely inspired performance—a stunning answer to years of prayers. It was my ticket to Columbia.

The Door Cracks Open

I graduated from Riverview in 1958 after four wonderful, whirlwind years. Shortly before graduation, our senior class took a trip to New York City. Sixty-five kids saved for four years to pay for a week in the Big Apple. For this raw recruit from Riverview, it was a sensory explosion. My memories are vivid: riding to the top of the Empire State Building, catching a musical at Radio City Music Hall, surveying the Statue of Liberty. Most fascinating were the mobs of people swarming the sidewalks at all hours—a multiethnic horde racing around, buying, selling, and sampling anything imaginable: fresh fruit and vegetables, fish, pizza, hot dogs, clothes, jewelry, watches. In my wildest dreams, I never would have envisioned so many people in one place, at one time, utterly embracing such brazen chaos. (If I'd known that, forty years later, I'd be back at Shea Stadium helping to host approximately thirty thousand men at a Christian Promise Keepers conference, my brain would have blown a fuse. God's merciful that way.)

The trip was equally memorable for an unflattering controversy that unfolded in our midst. As our excursion neared its end, some of the guys had a bright idea to celebrate by buying some beer. So one night we pitched in and clandestinely bought a six-pack or two, shut ourselves in a hotel room, and let the good times roll. It was my first experience with drinking. It seemed fairly innocent, if a bit chancy. We each drank a couple of beers and got silly. Being rank amateurs in the art of deception, we also got busted.

It was a clear breach of trust on our part and cast an unfortunate pall over the trip. We were embarrassed, and endured some justified ribbing from the kids who'd managed to behave themselves. Our parents received testy letters from the school administration. But beyond that it honestly didn't leave me with much of an impression. I'd already earned my scholarship. I was riding high. School was almost out. I guess it rolled off my back.

In hindsight, my flippancy should have concerned me. Today I see that incident as a tiny seed that may have opened the door, just a crack, to a dark, uncharted facet of my personality. Perhaps my easy tolerance toward some underage drinking was a warning sign. History would prove that, when it came to alcohol, I had blinders on. But back then, who was I to worry? I was young and indestructible. I'd be off to college soon, and once I was on my own, look out! Still, I sometimes wonder how my life might have been different if I'd never taken that first drink.

Rude Awakening

The summer before my freshman year, I traveled to the Columbia campus to get acclimated. It was an exciting time. The university set me up with a summer construction job paying $2.05 an hour, good money in those days. I'd never earned that much back home, and the thought of squirreling away an extra $500 for the school year was irresistible. The athletic department housed us, a handful of incoming freshman signees, in a cheap boarding house. Within a couple of days of my arrival, I was settled in and fully absorbed in the next chapter of my life.

My roommate that summer was an offensive lineman from

Chicago. A decent, fun-loving bruiser, he had done his share of drinking. I was a curious novice. One night after a blistering day at work, he took me out; we bought some liquor and went back to our room. There, behind closed doors, he taught me the ropes of drinking hundred-proof "hard stuff." I'd never sampled hard liquor; it was nothing like those beers I'd sipped in downtown Manhattan. It hit me hard, and at the same time tapped into something unforseen in my character. Never before had I experienced that seductive, total loss of inhibition. To my surprise, I delighted in feeling woozy and being somewhat out of control. One swig led to another, then another, until within the hour I was flat-out bombed. I lapsed into a kind of irrational fog. Another person would have simply realized he'd had too much to drink and stopped. Not me. What I needed was a bucket of hot coffee, a cold shower, and a bed to sleep it off. I'd crossed an unseen line. An untamed spirit had been aroused, and I wasn't about to let the party end.

"We're out of booze," my drinking partner slurred. The words stopped me cold.

"What's that?" I shot back.

"We're all out," he replied. "We drank it all."

It wasn't good news. Indeed, to my addled thinking, it was the worst news since Pearl Harbor. An insatiable craving had welled up in me that was screaming "More!" I could barely stand, but no matter. My belligerent streak exploded like a Roman candle. I didn't *want* to quit drinking. We're on a roll. *Let's keep going!*

Amused by my stupor, my roommate jokingly commented that aftershave cologne contained alcohol.

Really? I thought. *Hmmm. If cologne contains alcohol, that means. . . .* Like a bumbling wino, I lurched to the bathroom, rifling through the medicine cabinet, through the bottles, tooth brushes, razors, till I turned up a bottle of Old Spice. Snatching it from the shelf, I pulled the cap and guzzled a wicked mouthful of aftershave. *Whoooooaa!* It tasted like battery acid. I spewed it out, retching. *Now* the party was over. I stumbled off to bed and collapsed in a ball. As

I drifted off to oblivion, I faintly recall hearing my roommate still roaring in the kitchen.

If there had been a question in my mind about the wisdom of avoiding alcohol, this sordid scene should have stripped away any doubt. It demonstrated that I had a *total* intolerance to liquor. If the New York field trip was a warning whisper of trouble to come, this debacle was a stick of dynamite exploding in my face. In no uncertain terms, while in the grip of alcohol, especially hard booze, I was a walking disaster area. Short of someone calling 911 or strapping me down, I didn't have the wherewithal to stop myself once alcohol's lubricating effects set their hooks. The episode with my roommate didn't teach me much. I continued drinking, occasionally enjoying a cold one or two after work, to no apparent harm. Infrequently, I'd indulge in something harder and suffer for it. But for anyone to suggest in 1958 that someone like me might be an alcoholic wasn't even a consideration. No one knew the dangers; no red flags shot up. And I was too busy chasing my dreams anyway to take much notice.

Trying Not to Disappear

This alarming trait *never* manifested itself during football season. Competing on the college level was far too difficult and all-consuming. The transition from high school to college is drastic enough for the best players, but my youthful bravado was shattered the moment I reported to camp as a freshman and saw the other guys on Missouri's squad. Every insecurity I had flared to the surface: *What am I doing here? Everybody's bigger . . . stronger . . . faster . . . than I am. I'm in* way *over my head.* I was, in addition, totally unprepared and psychologically ill-equipped for the ruthless hazing most freshmen endure. My big nose, skinny legs, and crossed eyes made me an easy target. The locker room can be a brutal environment, and I took my lumps. But in a desperate, do-or-die bid for survival, I quickly learned to give back as good as I took.

Those first weeks were a very insecure, lonely time. I was away from home, I felt physically inferior to the other players, and a helpless fear began to simmer in my gut that I might simply *disappear*. After my high school success, getting my bell rung repeatedly on the field and having my pride cut to ribbons in the locker room was a rude awakening. If I'm not mistaken, there were times when I was tempted to pack my bags and, well, disappear.

But that wasn't me. Never had been. It wasn't who my father, my brother, and all my heroes growing up had raised me to be. I had for years been exclusively *sold out* to the prospect of playing college ball. I was far too stubborn to simply fade away. I came to Missouri to make a significant contribution, to help rebuild a fallen program, to *excel*. This initial shock told me I would have to drastically raise my commitment level. I would have to tap new reservoirs of endurance and perseverance, and adopt a more thoroughly sold-out attitude—one that defiantly declared, "I refuse to quit." With ironclad resolve, I began to channel my fear and zero in on the task at hand. I convinced myself I could accomplish this. I was sold out to leaving everything I had on the field every day.

Before long, I had taken and given enough crisp hits to get the locker room hyenas off my back. If I wasn't as talented as some, they at least knew I was unrelenting. Steadily, I earned a measure of respect. Slowly, methodically, I learned how to compete at this new level. In the process, I rediscovered that sense of belonging and acceptance I had come to crave. Through the fickle measuring rod of performance, I began, once again, to feel good about myself.

In my four years at Missouri, the Tigers went from conference also-rans to a national power. Dan Devine brought in a great group of coaches, revitalized recruiting, and masterfully orchestrated an incredible turnaround. By the time I graduated, some of the biggest, strongest, most dominating players in the country had migrated to Columbia. Not so in the beginning. Coach Devine had to make do with guys of marginal size and skill or, in other words, *me*. Though I never overpowered or outran anybody, I was an aggressive, hard hitter. But my limitations forced me to focus in on other qualities, such as diehard dedication, discipline, sincerity, punctuality, natural instincts, and a quick football mind.

I paid close attention to the technical points of execution and strategy. My knowledge of the game was growing as well. While other players obediently followed instructions, or just instinctively reacted to a situation in the heat of battle, I was assignment conscious to a fault. I was heavily invested in the learning process, painstakingly aware of each opponent's tendencies, strengths, and weaknesses. I listened closely to my coaches and, in a game, was often able to anticipate a play before the snap.

Through it all, my coaching dream loomed large in the back of my mind. I was captivated by football theory, always wondering, always questioning: *Why* did we use certain plays in specific situations. *Why* did we install one formation over another? I played center-linebacker but always tested even with, or right below, the quarterbacks in overall aptitude. OK, I'm the first to admit it wasn't thermonuclear physics or brain surgery. But it repeatedly reconfirmed to me that I *instinctively* had what it took to be a coach.

I started on Missouri's freshman team that first year, then went to being a back-up inside lineman/linebacker as a sophomore and junior, contributing major minutes every game but never cracking the starting line-up. A sophomore highlight was intercepting a Fran Tarkenton pass in the 1960 Orange Bowl, which we lost to the Georgia Bulldogs. I finally broke into the starting line-up as a senior but was always pressed from behind by younger players. Through my entire career at MU, I was in the thick of things, contributing, battling it out every day, but my job was never secure. I never felt my position in the pecking order was settled.

Fateful Celebration

In four years at Mizzou, I never had a drink during football season. It was in the off-season that my drinking resumed with increasing frequency and consequence. Once, at the end of my junior season, following MU's climatic, historic victory over Navy in the 1961 Orange Bowl, I stretched my no-drinking-in-season rule to the breaking point. Missouri had never won a bowl game, and our whole team played extraordinarily well. Our defense did the impossible, holding Heisman trophy winner Joe Bellino to minus eight yards in twelve carries. Navy had never seen a scheme like we threw at them, and they couldn't figure out how to attack us. Our linebackers found themselves largely unblocked the entire game and we recorded several solo tackles. (Many MU alums believe that if voting for the number one team had taken place *after* the bowls back then instead of at the end of the regular season, MU would have been crowned the national champion.)

Either way, when that game ended, no one cared where we were ranked. Everyone was sky high. The team's post-game celebration was at Miami's elegant Indian Hills Creek Country Club. It was a lavish affair. The food was exquisite; several open bars catered to coaches and players from both teams. It was a festive, tempting environment unlike any I'd experienced. The alcohol was flowing, and I was in the mood to celebrate. I spent the evening camped out at the wet bar laughing, carrying on. When all was said and done, I'd become quite inebriated. Rather, I was smashed—so badly that on the bus ride back to the hotel I was doubled over with dry heaves. Some players had to hold my head out a window. Perhaps it was out of respect, or sympathy, but *nobody*, not even the coaches who saw the whole thing, ever mentioned it to me. But I knew I was exposed. I'd debased myself in front of the whole team. It was another tasteless display that should have jolted me awake.

I was in classic denial. The nature and severity of these incidents (not to mention the public humiliation they caused) were infrequently recurring, but nonetheless spectacular proof of a sizeable problem. For a time it was easy to ignore. Folks in Columbia tended to look the other way, especially if an MU athlete was involved. In all fairness, if anybody had ever pulled me aside, or ordered me to see an alcoholic specialist or counselor, it might have made a difference. No one ever did. In those days there were no Betty Ford Centers or alcohol awareness programs for Missouri football players. In my insulated world, there was literally no recognition of alcoholism as a legitimate concern.

However, even in my worst moments, I remained emphatically sold out to my ideals. These minor setbacks hadn't dulled the burning zeal with which I attacked life. I still pursued football and coaching with every fiber of my being; I still prayed regularly and counted myself a pious, model Catholic. I was no less hot-blooded, wholehearted, or fervent. I was a young man tracking his dreams with feverish intensity. And, for what it's worth, when I wasn't drinking (which was the majority of the time), I was seen as a polite, pleasant, low-maintenance, high-achieving individual.

But there was no escaping it—an alarming pattern had emerged. During the off-season I would drink progressively more, act the fool, feel remorse, and grieve with a sense of heavy self-condemnation, bemoaning my inappropriate behavior. I was fully in touch with my poor conduct in key situations. No matter, alcohol was exerting greater and greater influence over me. By the time I started to question myself (around the time I got blitzed, plowed into a Columbia police car, and resisted arrest), I had no leg to stand on. I had a track record.

Chapter 5
The Road Well Traveled

FEW THINGS IN MY LIFE have been as difficult as dredging up these memories forty years after the fact. There remains within me a tendency, an almost irrepressible urge, to simply deny it all happened. It would be tempting to ask God to supernaturally wipe the slate clean and re-write the chapters of my early years before I knew His Son. Each incident, each decision, each consequence, left a permanent stamp in some remote corner of my character. There are times when my heart shrinks back and wants to cry out, "That's not me. I am not that person anymore. Look what God has done!"

But these things *did* happen. Through the passage of years, a thoughtful child grew into a driven young man. At key intersections along the way were defining moments when decisions were made, and he yielded subtly to notions about himself he would one day loathe. He began to passively neglect passions and ideals that once set his spirit soaring. *Sold out?* Always. Naturally. But to what? A thin line separates "sold out" from "*sell out.*" Both are slippery concepts in young, impulsive hands. For while being feverishly sold out is a straight and narrow course, it is entered properly only through the narrow gate of a pure heart. The pure heart has no motives for self and is content to trust God. Choosing the right paths calls for a trustworthy compass. As I progressed through college and started thinking more concretely of career, possible marriage, and new challenges, my field of vision—once wide with childlike awe and hallowed impressions—narrowed to a pinpoint. I needed a competent Pilot, or at least a dependable compass, to help me navigate the twisting byways. Left to myself, I merged comfortably with a wide, well-traveled path, lined with large dreams, sly seductions, and gold-plated trophies that bore little relation to that gloriously pure and narrow starting point.

The Morning After

My, how times have changed. Unbelievably. The extent of my punishment for a drunken tussle with a Columbia police officer after creaming his squad car was a single night in jail. The next day, a visiting judge let me off with a stern warning, mysteriously averting what today would surely be a drawn-out legal ordeal probably resulting in a revoked license, a beefy fine, and perhaps even more jail time. Not that I deserved a speck of mercy, but the traveling magistrate's uncommon leniency put a swift end to the legal woes I might have faced for such an outlandish medley of offenses. But my troubles were just beginning.

It should have come as no surprise when Stephens College, spurred by the dean's eye-witness account of my curbside meltdown, black-balled me from campus and forbade me from seeing Lyndi. I was public enemy number one around there for a while. This is not to imply that Lyndi, for her part, was breathlessly waiting to see me, the guy who'd maligned her character and then scared her witless on a high-speed rampage through Columbia's frozen neighborhoods. Although I'm sure my profession of love while being led away in handcuffs touched her deeply, I'm guessing she doubted wanting any part of this overbearing, moody football player with a taste for large quantities of brewed beverages. Taking all this thoughtfully into account, I was still crushed.

Having already lost my football scholarship, and along with it every shred of dignity and self-worth I'd ever known, being barred from calling on Lyndi or from even trying to repair the breach was like a disabling hit to the midriff.

It's a cruel irony—when people are as soused as I was that night, they rarely think of the consequences of their actions. But the morning after is always dreadful. It's impossible, even forty years later, to describe how bad I felt over my behavior. I kept asking myself, *How can a person with such good intentions and high hopes for a night out with the woman of his dreams instead sabotage—no, incinerate—the rendezvous in a drunken tirade?* I certainly know *how*, but it took me a few more years and countless lurid episodes to fully come to grips with the *why*. The plain truth is, it was the work of an alcoholic. It wasn't just rare bad form or absently losing track of how many trips I'd made to the keg. It was a very real, dark compulsion that overcame me, against which my will power was useless. Back then such thinking was absurd, bogus nonsense. Within a day or two of the incident, I'd already gently reasoned: *OK, so the date was a disaster. I blew it. But life goes on. It's time to move forward and make amends.*

Looking back, it's amazing that Lyndi, a sweet, sophisticated girl, didn't simply turn and run as far away from me as possible. Who could have blamed her? By some miracle she didn't. She stuck it out. Apparently, our time prior to the frat house nightmare helped her understand that my bullheaded persona was probably just an aberration of some kind. It was a reasonable conclusion. Most of our time together had been very sweet and tender. I was by nature scrupulously sincere, polite, a gentleman with impeccable manners, and, some even said, charming.

There were other qualities she liked that temporarily calmed her fears, the first being how wholehearted I was toward my dreams and career plans. She enjoyed listening to me spin my visions and talk about bringing it all to pass. She respected my career choice and appreciated my desire to work with young people. Somewhere in this mix, my devout faith touched a deep chord within her. She regarded my focus on God and my faithful church attendance as a rare trait. It warmed her heart. Growing up, Lyndi found peace and refuge in her hometown church. It helped her through some tough childhood times. She cherished those memories and arrived in adulthood braced with an idyllic view of marriage: It would be very beautiful, filled with lots of children, joy, and laughter, and it depended heavily on a husband who emphasized church and God. Actually meeting someone who held similar beliefs, and who *never* missed a Sunday at church, probably seemed to Lyndi like a direct answer to a childhood prayer.

On balance, all this somehow compensated for my poor showing the night of our date. Lyndi still liked me and wanted to see me. I'd managed to convey my sense of sincerity and principle, and, overall, I guess she concluded I wasn't such a bad guy. I knew already how I felt about her and considered it an act of God that she hadn't simply written me off as an ill-mannered jerk. If I wasn't exactly a knight in shining armor galloping into her dreams on a stallion, she at least saw I had potential; she suspected that I was smitten and granted me another chance.

It took three weeks of phone calls, relentless apologies, even parental intercessions, but finally, with many stipulations and restrictions attached, I was once again allowed to call upon my future wife at Stephens. We were both greatly relieved. We resumed dating under much improved conditions and started spending most of our time together. Our relationship quickly blossomed. Shortly thereafter, I gave Lyndi a commitment pin as a token of my intentions. I was broke, barely scraping by without a scholarship, so I couldn't actually afford to *buy* her a pin. I borrowed one from a friend and presented it to Lyndi, giving her a night to show it off to her friends before I had to return it the next day.

Our affections deepened. By God's grace we were engaged May 8, 1962. We were sitting on a little stone wall in the chapel courtyard at Stephens when I proposed. After momentarily excusing herself to take a phone call, Lyndi ran back outside, lunged into my arms, and shouted, "Yes!" knocking us both off the wall. Those were fun, tender times. It seemed we couldn't spend enough time together, do enough kind deeds for one another, or say enough nice things about each other. We had a sweet, gentle way together. But storm clouds were forming on the horizon. In days to come, our relationship would begin to suffer from stress faults lurking beneath the surface.

After losing my scholarship, a hastily arranged student loan allowed me to stay in school the rest of that winter. But it was a meager stipend. I wasn't sure how I was going to complete my degree the following fall. Lyndi paid for all of our dates, so I never took us anywhere that cost a lot of money. It was embarrassing, completely humiliating, but I was in no condition financially to do anything about it.

The Forgotten Teammate

Within weeks of our engagement, Lyndi and I parted ways for the summer. She went back to her parents' home in Oklahoma. I went back to Michigan. Upon returning to Mizzou the following fall to complete my degree, my mood had turned foul. What might have been a joyful, nostalgic final year at my alma mater—all expenses paid, still on full scholarship, coasting to the finish line—instead took on a somber, impoverished tone. My money problems worsened. I didn't have even enough to take Lyndi to a cheap movie. And the thought of counting pennies at this stage of the game only inflamed my bitterness and frustration.

Most of all, I desperately missed playing football. It was the game I loved. I'd committed the past decade of my life to it. For the first time since junior high, I wasn't spending August in the hot sun gutting it out with the team, or punishing my body through two-a-days and lung-scalding forty-yard sprints. (Boy, those were good times!) For the first time in memory, my mind wasn't completely focused on the season opener. Gone was the adrenaline rush of competing against top-notch talent, gone were the attention and excitement that accompanied the start of football season. It wasn't totally unexpected. Most athletes, from high school through the pros, experience a painful withdrawal when their playing days are over. I've never met anyone, however, who was totally prepared when that day arrived. It's an agonizing transition. As the school year got underway, I still supported the Tigers. I'd sit in the stands, cheering them on. But when all of Columbia is abuzz about football, it hurts to realize you're no longer part of it. The program goes on and prospers without you, never seeming to miss a beat.

There's something about being part of a *team*. For some it's impossible to replace. It stems from the high-spirited camaraderie, the locker room jocularity, and an unparalleled sense of togetherness that can only be forged in the trenches of combat. Occasionally a team just gels—everyone's on the same page, everyone's looking out for his brother—and that's what we had at Mizzou. It's a rare opportunity in life to contribute significantly to something much larger than yourself. It provides a riveting sense of purpose that, for me, had always come from being part of a team. Where else does a young athlete, barely twenty-two years old, find that kind of affirmation? It's what prompts ex-athletes to enter coaching or become weekend softball addicts.

Thank God, not every tie with Mizzou had been cut. The athletic department helped me earn some pocket change by scouting the area high schools, and there were occasional odd jobs to perform here and there for the team. But I was out of the loop—a veritable stranger even to some former teammates. None of the incoming freshmen knew who I was. The emotional cord was cut. I was adrift. Without the sense of *team*, I felt lost and useless. Worse, I didn't know how to channel my lifelong, some would say *overabundant*, surplus of energy.

With no football to fill my days, I lapsed back into some destructive patterns. My drinking picked up pretty much where it left off. But now there was no football, no structure, no discipline, no *team* to hold me in check. The acute sense of loss coincided disastrously with our marriage countdown. Lyndi wasn't faring very well on the other end of my internal tug-of-war. She was bewildered by the change that came over me. I began to withdraw physically and emotionally. Our dates became more infrequent, and when we were together, more often than I care to remember our nights ended up with me passed out drunk on the front seat. She had no choice but to sit there, waiting for me to sober up so I could drive her home. Finally, I just stopped calling.

I was spending more and more of my time with the guys, out drinking, playing cards, and carrying on in truly schizophrenic behavior. I loved Lyndi. I was thrilled with the prospect of marrying this beautiful girl and spending the rest of my life with her. But as the days counted down to our wedding, I listened a little too closely to my poker pals' sarcastic barbs about hen-pecked husbands and the old ball-and-chain. With my thinking becoming increasingly fuzzy, I reasoned that my behavior was merely a harmless attempt to enjoy my remaining days of bachelorhood. Without realizing it, my self-absorption caused Lyndi intense, senseless pain and confusion. My behavior was completely out of line. Lyndi had witnessed the effects of drinking in her life and knew the heartache of abandonment. What was she to make of her fiancé going days on end without calling her, seeming to place a higher priority on partying and playing cards than on planning our lives together? Years later, Lyndi confided that she feared I thought proposing was a colossal mistake; she thought I desperately wanted out. Nothing was further from the truth, but it was impossible to tell from my actions.

The Unseen Foundation

Such sad beginnings; what missed opportunities. A man and woman have but one chance for a strong, healthy beginning. At a stage in our courtship when I should have been laying a firm, nurturing foundation, I was wallowing in nostalgia for my old team and pining for the "good ol' days." What this cost us down the line was enormous: the priceless privilege of launching our lives as a cohesive, impassioned partnership. The truth I failed to see was that Lyndi and I were about to join together as a team of our own. My football playing days were over. I was entering the most important season of my life with the woman I loved. As the man, it was my responsibility to set the moral and spiritual tone of our marriage and, boy, did I. Lyndi had already proven herself faithful and steadfast through some extraordinary trials. Now she was preparing to make a vow of lifetime commitment to our relationship. She has since proven over and over to be the most faithful, giving, selfless teammate I've ever had. No contest! But at the strategic outset of our lifelong adventure, I was aloof, wrapped up in myself, lost in my own fears and insecurities. I can't recall ever asking Lyndi about her dreams or hopes, and she never complained. But because I didn't, we both lost out. In my nearsighted neglect, I committed an infraction I would have considered unthinkable on the gridiron. I was abandoning my teammate in the heat of battle.

Lyndi and I were married December 29, 1962. The months leading up to our wedding were strained. I was floundering. The only foundation I was building was a string of embarrassing incidents that should have stung, jolted, or shamed me into some rigorous self-examination.

A couple of months before our wedding, I attended my brother Tom's wedding in Ohio. Tom had served a tour of duty in the Marines and accepted a scholarship to play football for the University of Toledo. He went on to captain that team and star as an offensive guard and linebacker. Though he was older than I, his military commitment delayed his eligibility. We ended up playing our college careers at the same time. My respect and admiration for him had only grown. Tom was then, as now, the definition of "class act."

From what I remember, it was a beautiful wedding from start

to finish, everything tastefully and carefully rendered. Our family was there, brimming with excitement for Tom on his big day, eager to celebrate his new bride, Bonnie. The reception afterwards was lighthearted and fun, with lots of food, music, and dancing. But in this atmosphere, where others were drinking and having a good time, I proved again I simply couldn't control myself. I got drunk and, once more, made a fool of myself. I was stumbling around on the dance floor, bumping into people, making a scene. When Tom tossed the garter belt, I made a flying leap through the crowd and landed on the floor, face first, with everyone looking on. I'm glad I can't remember Tom's expression as this melodrama unfolded. To an otherwise sweet, dignified affair, I was an ugly footnote.

Today, I still appreciate Tom and Bonnie for the tremendous grace and restraint they showed me following the wedding. They simply loved and consoled me and basically chose to forget the whole mess. That's how it usually worked. I was an earnest, engaging guy, and people tended to look the other way when I drank to excess. They didn't know what to make of my inebriated antics. Most laughed them off and weathered my nonsense with a bemused shrug. With few exceptions, there were no consequences to my actions. Yet, as it sank in the next day, my lack of respect for my brother in his sacred moment almost proved too much for my heart to bear. The whole affair rocked me, forcing me to confront my gross insensitivity. I had always intended to show Tom nothing but my honor and admiration. But in a few moments of monumental carelessness, I had violated a sacred trust between brothers. Now it was out there for even my family to see: When drinking, I was capable of almost anything. Tom and Bonnie attended our wedding a few months later in New York City, deeply honoring Lyndi and me. But their grace and forgiveness were like burning coals on my head.

I came away from that incident knowing I had a bona fide problem. Exactly how severe, I wasn't sure. But this much was clear:

My inability to control myself on the biggest day of my brother's life—the person, mentor, and role model I loved, revered, and credited for much of my success—betrayed my futility in trying to keep my drinking under control, and under wraps. Moreover, I was becoming keenly aware that, beyond the damage I was wreaking on my dearest loved ones, this conduct was dishonoring God. I prayed and searched for power to stop, but try as I might, I wasn't able to begin to address, much less resolve, this distressing pattern. It bled over, unchecked, into my own marriage.

Lyndi began married life isolated and alone. After graduating from college, we stayed for a time in Columbia, where I continued to work a little here and there, sorting through career options, hanging out with the guys. Lyndi was also working, helping us pay for a dingy basement apartment in a rundown boarding house for men. At a time I'm certain she thought our marriage was an unmitigated disaster, she became pregnant. Soon after, while she was at work, she began to miscarry. She didn't know where to find me. I was gone. So she went through the pain and blood and horror of that unfamiliar ordeal alone in our dank apartment. Later, after driving herself and our stillborn child to the hospital, she didn't have enough money to pay the bill. Her heartbreak and humiliation were complete.

Hours afterward, exhausted and still crying, Lyndi tracked me down at a pub on the outskirts of town. I was tending bar, a part-time job I guess I'd forgotten to tell her about. I could see she was devastated, and the news broke my heart. I wished I'd known, but I was, after all, busy working. In her time of need, this stark incident showed just how inaccessible I was. She felt cut off from the flow of my life, like an outsider looking in. Oh, Lord, there were so many lessons I hadn't learned. I loved my wife deeply, was proud and blessed to be with her. She was my prize. She humbled me. If the truth were known, I believed I'd married *way* over my head. So why didn't I show it? Such as I understood it, I treasured my marriage and knew that we'd always be together. But I didn't have a clue how to express any of it. My mind was elsewhere. I was selfish and distracted. I was immature and looking out for myself. My *actions* betrayed me. Lyndi learned quickly what it was to be married to a man sold out and obsessed, but not to her. She started our lives together feeling like a stranger in her own home.

Chapter 6
The Beginning of a Career

AFTER COLLEGE LYNDI AND I zig-zagged from Michigan to Missouri for a couple of years, launching the fast-forward style that would, for the next thirty years, characterize our lives. It was a life spilled out in radical, dogged pursuit of a coaching dream—a dream I hunted with predatory zeal and fury, and which one day would threaten to consume us. I was, at long last, poised at the threshold of an obsession anchored in my earliest childhood daydreams. I was a greyhound flexed at the starting gate, waiting for the starter's pistol. Nothing would stand between me and my prize.

I'd often expressed my dreams to Lyndi, but I doubt she actually ever understood how emphatic I was. If she had, she might have panicked, or simply retreated. As we settled into my first coaching jobs, she may have gathered a sinking, uneasy sense that something about me, and about who we were together, brandished her needs and hopes in a lackluster light, rendering them borderline *insignificant*, disposable. If she didn't already suspect it, she quickly learned that I was privately prepared to pay most any price to harness this burning ambition—this instinctive predisposition of mine to coach—and ride it out as far as I could.

Shortly after I graduated from MU, we traveled back to Michigan to spend the summer at my parents' home. I worked construction, hung out with my old friends, and sent out feelers about coaching openings. Lyndi spent her time competing with my family and friends for a little of my attention.

Inexperienced as I was in the art of self-promotion, I wasn't sure how to begin to pursue a coaching career. I decided I couldn't go wrong by seeking out the best coach around, someone I could learn from, and find a way onto his staff. By late August of 1963, I'd been hired as an assistant football coach in St. Charles, Missouri, where I joined the highly capable staff of Jim Rash, Pat Leahy, and Rich Greer. It seemed to both Lyndi and me that we were finally going to get our lives underway.

The night before we left for St. Charles, some friends gathered at my parents' house to bid us farewell. As usual, a poker game broke out. That night we played for money. At the end of the evening, Lyndi was still alive in the bidding. She wanted to fold and walk away, but she had a good hand, and I was coaching her on. By this time in the game, all of our money—every dollar of savings, and our travel money—sat in the pile in the middle of the table. Lyndi lost the hand. We left the next day for St. Charles with twenty dollars. If I recall, Lyndi didn't have much to say to me on that trip.

In the early '60s, coaching salaries were small, but our lifestyle in St. Charles turned out quite pleasant and peaceful. As we sat destitute in a local cafe on our first day in town, sipping glasses of water, some very kind people helped us settle into an apartment without money up front. The coaching staff was an unexpected blessing as well. They were older, upright, more mature men who'd worked hard and tasted their share of success. They all shared values I badly needed. It was obvious that they placed a much higher priority on marriage and family than on work. They were husbands and fathers first, *then* coaches. They made no secret of the fact that they treasured the rural lifestyle. Their lives reflected harmony and balance.

It was a good year for Lyndi and me. St. Charles was a community straight out of a Norman Rockwell painting. We led an extremely modest lifestyle, renting an old military Quonset someone had converted into stuffy duplexes. Even more than for Lyndi, the change of pace was good for me. The wisdom and sturdy temperaments of my associates rubbed off on me. They were solid mentors who taught me more about life than about coaching. Proverbs 13:20 says, "He who walks with the wise grows wise, but a companion of fools suffers harm." That verse describes my early coaching days to a tee. Walking with these fine men, I began to embrace their values and covet their companionship. That year, I rarely drank; I never once got drunk. A big night out on the town consisted of taking our wives out for a salad and soft drink at the diner. Lyndi thought she was in heaven. We spent quality, satisfying time together. Our marriage settled into a pleasant pattern, and we enjoyed some long-overdue healing.

Settling down long in St. Charles, however, wasn't an option. For me the thought of putting down roots in a small town, perhaps one day working my way up to head coach, held little appeal. It wasn't in the plan. Early on I approached each job strictly as a stepping stone to bigger things, a small yet key investment in the future. A pattern emerged: I'd target the coaching situation with the most potential, wrangle my way onto the staff, and start picking everyone's brains. I was a sponge. I observed everything, focused on theory and fundamentals, and pushed hard to develop my sideline skills. In this way, both my confidence and my resumé grew. I never tried to hide my ambition.

The Climb Begins

Late that spring I read where an ex-Tiger teammate of mine had been hired as the high school head coach in Joplin, Missouri. Ron Taylor was the quarterback who led Missouri to the 1961 Orange Bowl win over Navy. I'd always regarded him as extremely bright and competitive. I wrote him a letter, telling him I'd be interested in joining his staff if he was interested. He was, and Lyndi and I were soon headed to Joplin. It was bittersweet saying good-bye to Coach Rash and the other assistants. I know if I'd remained under their influence, my character and our marriage would have greatly benefited. But the career had become an impatient taskmaster. I would never again find myself working around those kind of willing, capable role models.

Lyndi was nine months pregnant when we arrived in Joplin; she gave birth to our first child, Michael Shawn, on September 8, 1964. We felt as if our lives had taken a dramatic upswing. My salary jumped from $5,100 annually in St. Charles to $6,200 in Joplin—a huge raise in those days for an assistant high school coach. And from living in a Quonset hut, the school set us up in a pretty stone house in a swanky part of Joplin (it was actually the servants' quarters for a mansion up the hill). The rent was only eighty-five dollars a month, but it felt like a castle.

I was working alongside a much younger—you might say *high-spirited*—group of coaches. Ron Taylor brought in Morris Watts, a bright, energized, likeable offensive coordinator. These young, cocksure ex-athletes were friends, not mentors. For a town of about forty thousand, Joplin had one big high school, impressive facilities, and a stadium with lots of bleachers. We competed in the Springfield, Missouri, conference, which meant we played an extremely competitive schedule with lots of big games. For a young staff like us, it was all very novel and exciting. We were brash, confident, and capable. We immediately installed a new system. Our inexperience showed through at times, but the team tasted some good success and sparked a lot of excitement in the community.

Lyndi liked Joplin and made some good friends. But it was a test for me. Working alongside Ron and Morris was, in certain respects, like being back in college. It wasn't uncommon for us, after a tough practice or a big game, to head into town for a cold pitcher or two. Though I can't recall any unduly embarrassing incidents, I know I probably crossed the line a few times. It was a less cautious environment. Working and socializing with younger guys saw me frequently tip-toeing the edge of good taste and civility.

The Cursillo

Throughout our time in Missouri, I faithfully attended the local Catholic church. In this respect, nothing had changed. I still considered myself a devout Catholic and ranked faith at the top of life's priorities. I prayed daily and participated as much as possible in the life of the church. I didn't spend a lot of time studying Scripture, but reading the Bible had never been heavily emphasized. In my heart, every day, I earnestly sought God. When I showed up at church on Sunday morning, it wasn't to chat or look around. I was there to do business. I went before the Lord with real focus and intent. I felt God's blessing and mercy on my life and wanted to do everything I could to be in right standing before Him.

Things were going well in Joplin. We had no immediate plans to leave. It had been a good career move. We were enjoying our lifestyle and newborn son. I was able to keep my drinking in check the majority of the time, and it just felt like a healthy, balanced family experience. I was prepared to stay put for another season or two. Early in the spring, however, a fellow from our church approached me. He said he and some others had been observing me and could see I was serious about my faith. "I have a proposition," he said smiling. A special type of Catholic event called a *cursillo* was being held in Kansas City, and he would pay my fifty-dollar registration fee, as well as that of another young coach in town, if we would attend the three-day conference.

Most Catholics understand *cursillo de cristianidad* to mean "little course in Christianity." It's really a three-day period of spiritual renewal or spiritual awakening that helps people focus on the dynamic aspects of their Christian walk. It's for Catholics who want a richer, deeper appreciation of their faith—*exactly* the kind of thing that pumped me up. The other young coach, Ron Toman, coached at the local junior college. Years later he would go to the University of Notre Dame as an offensive coordinator and help them win a national football title. Ron and I left on a Thursday night for Kansas City and a three-day spiritual wake-up call that would transform our lives.

The *cursillo* revolutionized my thinking about what it means to be spiritually *zealous*. It seemed as if this were the first time I'd been around people who were *more* intense about their faith than I. We spent the entire weekend lost in worship or on our knees in prayer. We heard speakers who called us unashamedly into a radical lifestyle of devotion to God. It felt strange and uncomfortable at first. I'd never knelt on my knees for thirty minutes at a time to pray; I'd never raised my hands in worship; I had simply never spent so much concentrated time just contemplating God and seeking His will. It made me realize I wasn't as devout as I'd thought, but I just lapped it up. I couldn't get enough. Surrounded for three days by such unabashed, rigorous, wholehearted devotion sparked something in my spirit to a new level.

The big moment of the weekend came shortly before the *cursillo* ended on Sunday. The organizers said that within seventy-two hours *something* would happen to each of us to irreversibly alter the course of our lives. Then it ended. On the drive back to Joplin, my imagination leapt with possibilities of what God was going to do. I had no doubt that within three days God was going to show up and rock my world.

I returned home, spilled my guts to Lyndi about it all, then waited, full of faith. The phone rang. It was my brother Tom calling to say he'd been hired as the head varsity football coach at Holy Redeemer High School in Detroit. He wanted to know if I'd be his assistant. I nearly dropped the phone. *This is my call!* I thought. *Just like they said at the cursillo*. I didn't hesitate.

"Yes!" I said, hanging up the phone. I told Lyndi to start packing. "We're leaving for Michigan." My hands were quivering from excitement.

I'm not sure this is what the elders at our church had in mind when they paid my way to Kansas City. But within the hour we were on the road to Michigan. Lyndi was stunned and bewildered. "Why the rush?" she wondered. "Don't we even have time to say good-bye to our friends?" It was indeed an abrupt decision, but to my way of thinking, when you get a direct call from God, you don't twiddle your thumbs. I sensed it was the beginning of big things.

Chapter 7
Slipping into Overdrive

WHEN IT COMES TO CAREER moves, the move back to Michigan turned out to be strategic. Suddenly I was back in the invigorating orbit of big-city high school and big-time college sports. The benefits of proximity it would afford me over the next decade were impossible to calculate but paid off handsomely many times over. Lyndi, however, was crestfallen. She was eight months pregnant with our second son, Tom, and had terrible memories of the summer we lived with my parents after college. For her it meant I was back in my old stomping grounds, faced with all the temptations *that* afforded. She wasn't keen on the unlimited pool of card-playing, beer-drinking cronies who would now be minutes from our doorstep. From her vantage point, we'd been rudely and prematurely uprooted from our pastoral Joplin lifestyle. In a matter of days, we'd been transplanted back into a threatening, unpredictable environment. And she was right—I was immediately exposed and vulnerable to the same old temptations. But I didn't see it. I was electrified with anticipation, almost giddy that, finally, with God at the helm, my coaching career was about to blossom.

It was indeed a dramatic turning point. Everything to do with coaching kicked into maximum overdrive. I was back in the city, encompassed by all the tradition, all the great schools, coaches, and teams. What's more, we lived practically next door to Michigan State and the University of Michigan. For a local kid, these were the Mt. Rushmore and Washington Monument of college football (Notre Dame, of course, being the nation's capitol). As a source of inspiration, as a training ground, these were rich local resources. I began to live and breathe coaching, viewing my career much like a chess match: Each move had to count.

That first year I assisted Tom in football and also served as Holy Redeemer's head basketball coach. From then on, I rarely stayed at the same school for two consecutive years. I did continue on as Holy Redeemer's head basketball coach for a time, but I began hop-scotching around the Detroit area, pursuing assistant football coaching jobs at different schools. It was a crazy period—I began juggling a series of afternoon coaching jobs with a revolving assortment of day-time teaching positions. I taught third grade students, coached P.E. classes, whatever a school needed. Between coaching and teaching, I made enough to support a family that had now grown to four: Lyndi and me plus Michael and Tom, our two sons.

Being an ex-linebacker, my goal always was to focus one day solely on football. But at the age of twenty-five, I'd been handed the unexpected title of "head basketball coach" at Holy Redeemer. The school had a lengthy *winning* basketball tradition; it was a high-powered, high-profile situation for an inexperienced coach. I'd been a good high school player, but I knew as a coach I was in over my head. In order to survive, I'd have to get up to speed *fast*. I approached it as a challenge, and with characteristic resolve. My approach hadn't changed—if I was going to learn the game from someone, I may as well learn from the best.

Back then, Adolph Rupp at the University of Kentucky was the premier offensive basketball coach in college; Army's Bobby Knight was an up-and-coming genius on defense. I began attending clinics by both, often driving great distances to hear them speak.

Learning the finer arts of basketball became for me an almost religious enterprise: I became a Rupp disciple on offense, a Knight convert on defense. I remember once approaching Knight at a clinic with a question about some principle he'd just shared. He snapped back, "Hey fella, I didn't come here to *debate* it." That stung. It wounded my pride because I was wholehearted. I sincerely wanted that answer, because I knew it would make me a better coach. In this way, I transformed myself into a devoted student of the game; I loved nothing more than to spend hours going over offenses and defenses by myself, devising new plays, game plans. Within a short time, my basketball teams were quite competitive in the Detroit Catholic league.

The Subtle Seduction

It all looked very conscientious and admirable on the surface—this incredible zeal I brought to the job. But this dutiful, almost childlike ambition had now taken on an overbearing, distorted dimension. Coaching was beginning to dominate—no, *consume*—my time, thinking, and energy. It verged on supplanting even my sincerest affections for God, marriage, and family. During one exhausting span in the late 1960s, I found myself serving triple-duty: I was the head basketball coach at Holy Redeemer, a third grade teacher in Taylor, Michigan, and an assistant football coach in Dearborn—three jobs in three different cities. I shake my head now, trying to recall how I juggled, much less *excelled* at, each of these jobs.

One stretch that year saw me rising daily at 5 A.M., driving to Melvindale on the way to Detroit, picking up some basketball players, and holding an early 6:30 A.M. practice at Holy Redeemer. Then at 7:45 A.M. sharp I'd hop into my car and drive (over the speed limit) twenty miles south to Taylor, just beating the tardy bell at my full-time teaching job. When the day was over at 3 P.M., I'd jump back into my car, race fifteen minutes back to Dearborn, and spend the next two hours coaching football. As soon as the final whistle blew, I'd run to my car—parked strategically near the edge of the practice fields—and hastily dispatch myself back to Detroit, where my basketball players were waiting for an evening practice. I never thought about getting home before 8:30 or 9 P.M. If I happened to stop off somewhere for a cold one, it was much later than that. A typical twelve-hour span required me to hold two basketball practices at opposite ends of the day, teach a full day of third grade, and participate in a full football workout—all in different cities. I never counted it a hardship. It didn't bother me in the slightest. This was my passion, my calling. I was a *coach*. These were my *teams*.

What this one-track mind cost me at home is difficult to fathom. While I was cheerfully crisscrossing Detroit every day from sunup to *way* past sundown, leaving every ounce of my creative energy on the hardwood or practice field, it fell to Lyndi to keep things happy and functioning at home. We'd been on this treadmill for a few years. I'm sure she wondered if this routine was ever going to end. *Was it worth it?* Always made to feel like a distant second or third fiddle to the teams I coached, I know she secretly regretted ever marrying a coach, or at least one as obsessed as I was. Our daughter, Kristy, was born during this time frame, on September 12, 1968.

Even when I was home, my mind was often distracted, scheming up some new pass formation or full-court press. I was blind to her sense of pain and separation. I figured if my coaching was hitting on all cylinders, well, the universe was in order. Everything else, family included, must be faring well too. It's no consolation. I wish I had it to do over. But back then, the fact is, for all the disappointment my obsessive nature fostered in our home, the results on the field were hard to dispute.

I've rarely met another young coach who willingly subjected himself to such a non-stop grind to make his mark. It was my whole plan. It was the only way I knew to claw out a career, taste some success, and feel good about myself. It had always worked. As with athletics in my youth, *coaching* now defined my identity. Self-confidence? Sense of acceptance? These came from my won-lost record. If we won, life had meaning. If we lost, the world turned gray and rainy. Brute determination ultimately paid off. I was gaining a reputation as a young coach on the rise, applauded by both parents and peers for my teams' character, for their gritty tenacity. The first obvious, attention-grabbing breakthrough came while coaching high school basketball and football teams at two different schools. When both teams went on to win their respective Detroit city championships, it raised eyebrows around town.

By 1969 I'd hooked up with one of the best high school football coaches in the country, Tony Versaci. As the head coach at Divine Child High School in Dearborn, Michigan, Tony had lost only fifteen games in fifteen years. He was definitely someone who could mentor me to the next level. When Tony Versaci left Divine Child to take a job with Michigan State, having given me everything I needed, he recommended me as his replacement. I was hired to take over the school's football *and* basketball teams—an unusual combination at any level. The school also, interestingly, named me Dean of Discipline.

At last I'd achieved a long-term goal: I was a high school head football coach at one of Michigan's premier programs. Determined that we wouldn't falter with Versaci's departure, I began attending college football camps and frequented the film rooms of some of college's elite programs. Living near the University of Michigan was auspicious. On occasion I traveled to the campus, getting acquainted with their coaches, watching practice, studying film, and essentially learning Michigan's system. My teams at Divine Child were soon patterned after the Wolverines. When the University of Houston began using what's known as the "veer offense" to blow their opponents off the field, I caught a plane to Texas. Houston offensive coordinator Billy Willingham personally taught me the veer, and shortly thereafter, I installed it at Divine Child. We won all nine of our regular season games with that system and captured the mythical state Class B Championship. That same year, with the spirit of Knight and Rupp coursing through its veins, our basketball team at Divine Child also won the state championship.

My career was taking off. I was gaining a measure of notoriety locally. It wasn't long before some area colleges started calling. The chess match had turned in my favor.

Monkey on My Back

My drinking was a sore spot. It was a wedge in my marriage *and* in my personal life. Throughout my time coaching Michigan high schools, alcohol continued to exert its damaging influence—it was a source of profound discouragement to Lyndi and me. Let me make one thing clear: Coaching, not alcohol, controlled my life. They had become dual addictions, but I wasn't about to let *anything* compromise my career. While at work, I was *always* energized, intently focused, and, if anything, *over*-prepared. I *never* showed up with alcohol on my breath. If at times I suffered the ill-effects of a late night pub stop, it didn't stop me from getting up early and dutifully going to mass. I was never disciplined or warned about sketchy conduct; none of my employers ever pulled me aside and said, "Mac, you'd better cool it with the booze," or frowned and whispered, "You might consider keeping a lower profile." Just the opposite. I would have frankly been astounded if any player I'd ever coached, or any parents or administrators who knew me, ever even *suspected* I had a problem. So far as I could tell, they all regarded me as a positive role model, highly motivated, *more* than dedicated, *more* than an encourager. I was a good, young prospect who was fast developing competence.

Outward appearances told of a robust, passionate life filled with honest ambition and promise. At home, our life was not a horror story. It was probably like most homes where you'd find a six-pack in the ice box. I liked to patronize an occasional saloon, but my sons didn't think of me as a problem drinker. They were proud of their father. *He's a coach!* Lyndi brought them to my practices, and I would call them over to stand by me, make them ball boys. That excited them. They loved sports and accepted my frequent absences and distraction as the price an important, busy coach had to pay. They knew I loved them. Lyndi, who probably suffered more from my casual emotional neglect than from my drinking, always tried to put a happy face on our home life, in spite of what she felt inside. When it came to drinking, I was my own worst critic. I alone knew the extent of the battle.

There were brief reprieves when my drinking subsided or stopped altogether. These were times of great relief for Lyndi, times when she allowed herself to believe I was changing. In these blissful intervals, I was more attentive, less temperamental. I have reason to believe she enjoyed marriage, enjoyed *me*, and felt affirmed as a wife and mother. But I couldn't sustain it. Inevitably, I'd get together with friends for a couple of beers and typically have great difficulty stopping. Sitting in a bar, I used to marvel at those who'd get so wrapped up in a conversation that they'd let their beer get warm, or forget which glass was theirs. I *always* knew whose beer was whose. And my beer was as frosty cold at the last drop as it was streaming from the tap.

After a long, hard day, I'd often feel the need to unwind, to relax. Those days I looked forward to a quick stop by the local pub, intending, almost to a fault, to have *one* quick beer and head straight home. It rarely happened. Some friends or coaches would invariably wander in; we'd get into a high-spirited discussion about sports, our teams, players, and our stirring triumphs. I'd drink a couple of beers. It would have the desired calming effect. But unless the whole party just got up and left, or Lyndi was there and could prod me away, I rarely left it at that.

I was one of those guys who'd say, at a quarter till nine—fifteen minutes before I had promised to help Lyndi put the kids to bed—"Oh, all right, I'll just have *one* more. Hey, bartender! Just *one* more." I might be walking toward the door with car keys in hand,

and someone would chirp up, "Ah, c'mon Mac, let me buy you one for the road." I'd do an about face. No one *ever* had to twist my arm. "Okay, only one, then I gotta go." *One more.* Always one more. Usually, I'd have *several* more. Then with a thick tongue and guilty conscience, I'd limp home and try to sneak in without a confrontation.

One night Lyndi called and asked me to bring home dinner. I drove instead to the saloon, making it a point to drink *fast.* Four or five quick beers later, remembering my promise, I bolted toward the exit. I sped over to Kentucky Fried Chicken and bought a family-sized bucket. Between KFC and home, however, I decided to gnaw on a thigh. Polishing it off without blinking, I reached over and plucked out a leg. By the time I pulled into our driveway, I had devoured the entire bucket. All the chicken, *gone!* With my family waiting patiently in the kitchen for dinner, I showed up late, beer on my breath, holding a greasy bucket of bones. Realizing what I'd done, rather than fessing up, I crept in the back door, tiptoed to the bedroom, and crawled into bed. What was I thinking? Heaven only knows. The larger question is, what did my family think? What went through their minds? *Dad ate our dinner?* To this day, Lyndi chides me about that one.

Well into my season of local coaching notoriety, I was all too capable of this type of behavior. It was robbing Lyndi of her joy. Rarely a full, active partner at home, I was making it hard for her to love me. Our family, with the birth of Marc in 1972, had grown to include four children. They were my pride and joy, but I didn't adequately express it. I rarely had *time* to express it. When I was home, it was too often on the unsightly side of happy hour. Without realizing it, I was chipping and hacking away at the fragile foundation of our family.

Even as some nights vanished in a boozy fog, and my family weathered some fresh new disappointment, my coaching star was on the rise. Neither alcohol nor marital strife ever intruded into this sacred realm. For a time, it was heady and satisfying. It didn't last. It had stopped being much fun. The victories weren't enough to buffer the unnerving turn my personal life had taken. I was now afraid. It was only a matter of time, I knew, before my drinking would cross that blurry line and get me into real trouble. If I didn't get a handle on it soon, it would destroy everything I loved. My family was already frayed around the edges. I was caught up in, sold out to, and lost in a dream that was draining my youth and stealing the life from Lyndi's countenance. Moreover, I was flirting with a devilish addiction that clouded my soul and laid bare the foundations of our home. A silent, sinking desperation stirred within. I feared everything I loved might simply slip away.

Lyndi: A Man of Many Conflicting Passions

If a man could "have it all" by sheer force of will, my husband should have been able to do it. Each area of life that he deemed worthy was given his complete devotion. From early on you can see his passion for God, his passion for sports, his passion to excel in his chosen profession, and even a passion for drinking to the extreme. He couldn't stop when the drinks were gone; no, as he said, he headed for the medicine cabinet in search of Old Spice!

Like many men, Bill kept the various compartments of his life separate. He never let his drinking interfere with his career. When he was focused on football, it was as if all else disappeared and reappeared when the season was over. While at mass, he gave God his complete devotion. But as life went on, the passions Bill kept compartmentalized in his mind began to conflict in reality, sometimes in humorous ways. For example, early on Bill didn't tell me about guzzling the Old Spice—that was in the drinking compartment, so what did that have to do with me? For years after we were first married, I couldn't figure out why he never wore the aftershave I bought him as gifts. I thought he liked Old Spice!

While Bill's religious devotion was sincere, it didn't necessarily connect with the other parts of his life. He was sold out to his ideals and his Catholic faith, so much so that he told one of his college roommates, who happened to be the son of a Protestant minister, that he was going to hell because he was not Catholic. Bill was sincerely concerned for his friend's soul. It never occurred to him, at that time, that his friend might be a true Christian. However, while he was sold out to his faith, there were glaring contradictions between what he did in the pew and what he did with his pals. Recently he was describing this phase of his life, saying, "Many men I knew at that time went to mass every single day, as I did. It was a show of true devotion." I had to chime in, "Yes, and those same men who went to mass every day, went to confession every Monday!"

His religious zeal during this phase of his life didn't directly influence how he behaved as a husband either. While his religion made him revere family in concept, it seemed to have little effect in making him conscious of my needs as his wife. I saw this most blatantly when he uprooted us to move from St. Charles to Joplin, Missouri, in late August of 1964. I was nine months pregnant, after having a miscarriage in my first pregnancy. He was offered a better job; so he packed his dog and his wide wife in the car, and we were off on a new adventure.

I was scared to leave my doctor, who told me our baby was due in one week and that I should take it easy. But I also wanted to please my husband and make the best of it. We arrived in Joplin, unloaded the car, and within the hour the other coaches arrived to pick up Mac. They were excited and chatty. After introductions, they said, "Bye, Lyndi! We're off to go hunting for the weekend." Mac jumped into their car, and they all drove off into the woods, where I couldn't reach him. I didn't even know Mac was a hunter!

I stood there in total amazement and shock. I was left alone to unpack. This man, who considered himself a model Catholic family man, had dumped me—the mother of his soon-to-be-born child—in a strange city, without a phone, without knowing a living soul, without a doctor or anyone to take me to the hospital if I should go into labor. The only way this makes sense is to understand that, once the coaches arrived, it was time for Mac to focus on his career. He had to please the head coach; and if that meant going hunting, so be it.

Mac was highly respected within the church, but his religion was *his* religion. We went to mass together on Sunday, but he didn't share his spiritual pursuits with me. When our first son was eight months old, and I was pregnant again, Bill went to the *cursillo*, the little course in Christianity. When he got home, I was swept along in the whirlwind of his enthusiasm. He received a phone call just minutes after arriving home. Twenty minutes later we were in the car headed for Michigan, with me trying to figure out why. Mac went on talking about the retreat as I waited patiently for him to get to the point. He explained that if we would devote our entire lives to the Lord, our lives would never be the same. He further explained that he had been told at the retreat that a drastic change would occur in his life within days of his return home. Ah, that must have been why he reacted so strongly to the telephone call he received just moments after he walked in the door. It must have been something miraculous. The call had been from his brother Tom, with news of a great job opportunity in the Detroit area—his old stomping grounds.

When he told me that, I leaned back in the seat and dropped my head in my hands as tears streamed out. To me, this meant leaving the stability we had established for our family; it meant Bill leaving the church that meant so much to him; it meant him coming under the bad influence of all his old friends again; it meant the possibility of a more demanding job that would take him away even more.

Lord! Lord! Lord! I prayed silently. *I am pregnant! We have an eight-month-old baby and a good life. Now my husband has lost his mind. He is taking us back to hell.*

I was looking at how all the compartments might be affected; Bill had a single-minded focus, with a direct call from God to back him up.

That was the moment Mac became Bill to me. Mac had been an affectionate name, and I lost my affection right then and there. He went on talking excitedly for hours, but I didn't hear a word he said. I was lost in my own worried thoughts, but I don't think he noticed. You see, his spiritual life, family life, and career were in separate and unrelated compartments. At that moment, I felt like his hundred percent devotion to his religion and his career left nothing for me. In my estimation, he had sold out, but not in a positive way.

Men tend to compartmentalize their lives, just to cope with the real and conflicting pressures put upon them by our society. This is especially hard if you try to be sold out in every area. It's just too much. And if your passions conflict or are not as God intended, you too will end up selling out your family along the way.

When a man is the kind to sell out to his endeavors, it isn't long until something has to give. In Bill's life it was his marriage and family that had to operate at a deficit because he was missing. He knew I was committed to him for life. I guess he figured I could handle the family compartment. I did the best I could, but I don't think he realized what *he* was missing and what his kids were missing *of him*.

Men, I pray you are reading this while your children are still young. Bill said it well when he said that his one-track mind on the career track cost him more than he can fathom at home. You will never realize the value of your children's childhood until it is gone. I've heard it said, "If you want to be in your children's memories tomorrow, you have to spend time in their lives today." If you still have that time, grab it and make the most of it. If that time is already past, God can still redeem the time you lost; but it will help if you acknowledge your losses and the value you place on them to your children and your wife.

Women, if this describes your husband, there is hope! If God could help my husband bring his passions into some sort of harmonious balance, he can change any man! If your husband's passions are controlled by the Holy Spirit, that's great, but I know how disheartening it can be when his passion is being spent in compartments of his life outside of marriage and family, leaving little for him to give to your needs and the needs of your children.

You can't force a man to put his family first, or even to bring his passions into agreement with God's design. But if he is a Christian and calls himself a promise keeper, you're ahead of the game. He wants his passions to be in agreement with God's design. If you see the conflicts that he cannot see, you can gently bring any disparity to his attention. Just be sure to affirm your love for him and your appreciation that his life is not easy to balance. Pray for God to help him integrate his passions with his commitment to his family and his faith. Let him know you are on his side. Then, let God do the rest.

Chapter 8
Where Is the Power?

IT HAD BECOME THE GREAT contradiction of my life—the polar extremes of my nature that didn't add up. On the one hand, I was a devout Catholic, conscientious to a fault, ultra-dogmatic, theologically unbending, the guy who never missed Sunday mass. I had a love for the beauty of the ritual ceremonies of the church. They spoke to me of the grandeur and might of God; I had an insatiable zeal to *know* God. As a younger man, I attended mass every day. Later, as a high school coach, inspired and transformed by my Kansas City *cursillo*, I literally went ten years without missing daily communion.

My reverence toward God was the constant theme of my life since early childhood. Pleasing God was what mattered most. To me, that meant going forward every day to receive communion, kneeling at the altar, receiving the bread of life, confessing my sins, and sharing in the holy sacraments. Wanting to draw near to Him, hoping to be cleansed, I poured out my heart, repented, lingered on my knees, and left feeling absolved. My zeal was such that I was willing to embrace any religious exercise offered by the church, if I thought it would bring me into God's presence and imbue me with some of His wisdom and power.

Yet behind it all there was a profound paradox at work. In spite of an ever-growing faith and a thirst for religious discipline, there was a disheartening disparity huddled in a corner of my personality that would, if allowed, prove to be my undoing. In my dread battle with alcohol, I was at an absolute standstill. God, church, ritual devotion, prayer, faith: These all spoke to me of *power*—power to change, power to heal—of transforming power and blessing from on high. I knew of Christ's sanctification so that God's glorious holiness should be vibrantly displayed in His children.

Where *was* this power? There came a crushing point, while coaching high school in Michigan, when I knew I was never going to quit drinking on my own. I was simply too weak in the face of temptation. If I was ever going to harness this menacing side of my nature, I knew I needed God's power to do a deep work within me. I had prayed for it, *pleaded* for it. I had confessed my drinking in the confessional, denounced it before the priest, and repented for my weakness more times than I could ever count before God Almighty on my knees in my bedroom. Still no power. No breakthrough. No sense of hope whatsoever. It was confusing and discouraging in ways I couldn't articulate. It stirred in me overwhelming sensations of guilt.

I was drawn to bars. The places I frequented were well-lit, noisy pubs that provided a congenial, captive atmosphere where coaches could gather, throw the peanut shells on the floor, get the napkins out, and start scribbling plays and formations. Coaching is like any other profession. Coaches like to talk shop with their peers. At the neighborhood bar I patronized, a handful of local high school coaches would drop in most nights before heading home. We'd buy each other a round or two, laugh, talk about special plays and players, brag about our brilliant coaching decisions, rehash the week's highlights, and talk about upcoming opponents. It gave us a chance to unwind, release some pressure, celebrate each other's victories, and commiserate the losses. By the time we were ready to leave, we remembered why we were in coaching in the first place.

I used to sit in the bar in these groups, eyeing the crowd, observing how others would drink. I'd notice with great fascination that most didn't have a problem setting their glass down after one or two beers and walking away. They were very nonchalant about it; the alcohol hadn't taken control. They were able to enjoy it, relax, and let it go. It was a mystery to me. I'd always fought to control my drinking; their control over alcohol didn't make sense. I wanted what they had. I wanted to drink like normal people drink. I wanted to know that when I stopped in for a beer with the guys, I could get up and leave before I was stone cold drunk. Virtually every time I stopped for a beer, my genuine desire was that I would *not* drink to excess. So why couldn't I stop when I wanted? Left to my own common sense and will power, why did I always carry it to an extreme?

It affected how I socialized. When I was around others who were drinking, I would become fixated on the drinks themselves: who's drinking what, whose beer is whose, who's drinking as fast as I am, who's drinking slower, how many drinks has each person consumed? I learned to manage my cravings in very discreet ways. During my high school coaching days in the Detroit area, I played on a pretty good slow-pitch softball team during the summer. After games, most of us would head to the bar. I hadn't usually eaten dinner, yet I knew that if I was going to drink, I needed food in my stomach. Before even sitting down at a table, I'd very deliberately flag down the waitress and carefully give her my order. Before anyone else had even thought of eating, my burger would arrive, I'd wolf it down, and then, satisfied I was duly fortified, I'd get down to some purposeful drinking.

Always, my drink of choice was beer. On any given occasion, any night of the week, that's what I'd order. The taste was OK, but I liked it because I could drink beer in fairly fast, hearty quantities without suffering immediate side effects. If I needed a quick, post-game pick-me-up, an icy mug was the perfect prescription. If I was stressed out after a long day, beer was my choice. If my softball team had played well, and I wanted to celebrate, roll out the foamy suds. Occasionally I'd have a glass or two of wine. That was mostly for special occasions. Wine was for *sipping*. Beer I could drink all night and still feel like I was able to get in the front door of the house without making a scene.

Then there were those rare nights—I can probably count them on two hands—when I drank hard liquor, mixed drinks, or cocktails. Manhattans were my cocktail of choice; sometimes gin and tonic. Those nights, all bets were off. I was looking to get drunk, plain and simple. It may not have been a conscious choice or desire, but something in my mind would just click in. In spite of the mountain of evidence screaming, "Don't do it!" some cognitive quirk in me would reason that nothing else but a stiff shot or a cocktail would suffice.

I knew better. Nothing even remotely tolerable had ever resulted when I drank liquor. Since that first time back in Columbia, when I ended up at the medicine cabinet with a mouthful of Old Spice, liquor had, without exception, unleashed a side of me that was best kept under tight lock and key. From that night on, there was never any excuse for me to go near hard liquor, no matter how rough the week had been or how badly I wanted to let off steam. Motives were inconsequential. An alcoholic doesn't exercise good judgment, period, when it comes to alcohol. The drink itself is boss. For this reason alone, my hard-and-fast rule on any night out was *stay away from hard liquor*. It required no guesswork. My track record was conclusive.

Beer was a more temperate tyrant, but a tyrant nonetheless. As most of these nights got underway, I would mentally pre-calculate how many beers I could drink in a given amount of time to give me the best chance of leaving under my own power. I'd read the studies that said you could have one drink an hour without getting inebriated. As the night progressed, I was zeroed in on how many drinks I'd had. If I'd had three beers in the last hour, I knew in my mind I should slow down. But I found it almost impossible to moderate. Does the word "chug" ring a bell? Inevitably, I'd give up, quit counting, and all my good intentions would fly out the window. I'd banter and toast until closing time.

Other nights, bored or just plain thirsty, I'd call a friend under the pretense of inquiring whether his softball team was playing that night. (I knew it was.) If he said yes, I'd casually suggest, "Why don't I meet you down at O'Riley's Pub afterward?" It was very shifty, very pre-planned. If I felt like drinking, I would leave nothing to chance. If I wanted company, I'd find a drinking partner. If I needed an excuse, I'd make one up.

These mannerisms didn't surface overnight. I was an alcoholic, and had been to varying degrees since college. The very qualities that made me so intense and ultra-zealous about life in general were probably of the same seed that contributed to my radical, over-the-top drinking patterns. I was ready for it to stop. I knew my life would be much simpler, my family life much healthier, probably even my coaching more effective, if I could simply stop or develop moderation. Whereas I had always confessed my trials of excess, I now began to seek God with renewed intensity; I prayed for deliverance.

Over time I developed a sort of mechanical routine. If I drank too much and got home late, I'd kneel at my bedside and ask God for forgiveness and deliverance before I went to sleep. The next morning I'd rise early, go to mass, and confess my sin. And while it made me feel better and relieved my guilt, I experienced no change, no transformation, no deliverance. Nothing seemed to make a difference. I frequently ticked off what I knew to be true: I loved God and wanted to serve Him; I knew Christ was the Son of God; I faithfully confessed my sins, expecting to be forgiven; I desperately wanted, and thought I knew how to merit, His cleansing power. All who knew me clearly saw that mine was a *radical*, sincere, outward longing for relationship with God. But when mass was over and the prayers had been said, none of it provided much peace or power. I was the same Mac. The facts spoke louder than my petitions: I could not stop drinking and hurting my family. And beyond what it was doing to my marriage, I knew my style of drinking was wholly displeasing to God. The implications were grave.

Did God really hear my prayers? Was God angry at me? Had I stepped over the line one time too many? Many times I fell to my knees and cried out: "Lord, give me victory over this. *Heal me of this drinking! Please God, I don't want to take another drink.*" I'd beg Him with pangs of remorse; then, a night or two later, I'd go out drinking again.

While going through the motions of religion made me feel as if I were doing things right, the horrifying evidence of ongoing failure said I was, in fact, *separated* from God. I had to face it: All my spiritual fervor, heartfelt genuflection, and solemn, ritual prayer had somehow failed to endear me to the *only* One who could stop my drinking. In fleeting moments of despair, I was forced to admit I was a slave to a demon master named "alcoholism." I didn't see any way out. If I couldn't exactly see that I was headed for destruction, I simply couldn't see where it was headed, period! I was on a speeding treadmill, unable to get off, unable to stop. And to my increasing alarm, God remained silent.

Chapter 9
Transition to Hope

SOMEONE ONCE SAID THAT no victory in life—no professional advancement, no championship trophy, no monetary reward—will compensate for failure in the home. Today I believe no truer words were ever spoken. Unfortunately, this awareness came to me late in life. It is a godly principle by which to guide one's life. Yet it poses a tricky question: How do we live out such an ideal in a culture that promotes success at work over success at home, that emphasizes performance in career over performance in marriage? Early in my coaching career, I was scarcely aware of the tension between the two. I was merely a compliant product of the culture, in ambitious pursuit of my own unbending dreams.

As a young man climbing the coaching ranks, I can't recall the number of times I was boisterously encouraged to go the extra mile, put in the extra hours, make that extra sacrifice, for the good of the team. I willingly . . . no, *eagerly*, complied. It was what I enjoyed most. It's what made me feel alive. And the hard work paid off. Yet, I honestly cannot recall a single instance in all those years when I was ever prodded by an employer, one of my players' parents, or a peer to *ease up a little* at work so I could spend more time with my family or on my knees in prayer. It simply wasn't done. To this day it's an unspoken *rule*, not an exception, that marriage comes second, that family is expendable. In a society that, from early childhood, measures much of a person's worth by his job performance, career choice, material wealth, physical and intellectual prowess, it's no surprise that a person's spiritual vitality, emotional health, and family balance are regarded as peripheral, secondary issues to one's value as a human being.

To me, one of life's great mysteries is how God allowed a man whose personal life was so out of kilter to bear such fruit in the workplace. God's hand over my career was obvious, unquestioned. I knew my success was the direct result of His blessing. But as my record proves, it's also obvious that God's power, peace, and blessing were absent elsewhere in my personal life. Try as I might to gain spiritual victory over a slew of compounding weaknesses, I was spinning my wheels, running on fumes. Unable to foresee His plan in all this pain and inconsistency, I might have gained some consolation in realizing these ugly blemishes would one day glorify God; my unsettling past would ultimately train the spotlight squarely on His transforming power, and on His ability to heal and redeem one so lost as I.

In the early 1970s, I didn't give much thought to such sublime possibilities. As a high school coach I was riding high. And as a studied observer of the game of life, I'd concluded that this is what mattered most. I was thirty-three years old, brimming with confidence and promise. When I coached both the 1973 Divine Child football and basketball teams to respective state championships—something no other coach in Michigan had achieved in a single year—it caught folks' attention. Suddenly area colleges were curious: "So, what's the story with this McCartney fellow?" The turnaround was dramatic. I'd nurtured some friendships among a handful of college coaching staffs and suddenly found myself weighing flattering offers. At one point I'd been asked to join the coaching staffs of three different universities: the University of Michigan, Michigan State, and Eastern Michigan. Any one of these jobs would have been a dream come true. But in March 1974, at the personal insistence of Bo Schembechler, I signed on with the University of Michigan for $19,000 a year. It was a feeling of gratification similar to what I felt earning a college scholarship. Not only was it a chance to prove myself at the next level, it was a ringing affirmation of who I was as a person. It reinforced everything I wanted to be: accepted, successful, celebrated. As the only high school coach Bo ever hired in his twenty-two-year career at Michigan, I'd arrived through the back door at the "big time" of college football. It was indescribable, exhilarating. My self-esteem was soaring.

My promotion to the college ranks gave me reason to hope I'd be more available to Lyndi and the kids. Recognizing the wear and tear my year-round high school coaching schedule had imposed on our marriage, I'd made up my mind that if I didn't get a college job in the coming year, I'd drop basketball altogether. It wasn't necessary. Lyndi was genuinely excited for me, but she was wary about moving our family again and skeptical about how severe the demands on my time would be. I think I just assumed the entire family viewed the promotion as a merciful pay-off for the heavy toll they'd paid to launch my career. Though I knew she would never say so, I assumed Lyndi privately considered it some measure of compensation for her quiet forbearance. But as I later discovered, she simply didn't know what to expect and carefully guarded her emotions for the worst. I was excited to end my year-round juggling act. I'd been unsuccessful trying to coach multiple high school teams *and* be a fully-engaged husband and father. Now, I thought, I would at least have a chance to do it better.

Settling into my campus office after a decade of doing double and triple duty in prep sports, it was an unusual luxury to have just one job to concentrate on. Lyndi was cautiously upbeat. She'd persevered through some tough years. She'd long wondered where marriage and family fit into a coach's chaotic lifestyle. With four young children at home now, she was tired. She *needed* me to come alongside her, and she had every right to expect I would now be able to be a more attentive, full-time husband and father. Lyndi deserved a partner who would build security and contentment into her life. She knew coaching would always exact a steep price, but she still longed for a partner who would willingly put her and the children first.

As I got acclimated at Michigan, I made what seemed a legitimate effort toward Lyndi and the kids. We bought a home a mile from Michigan's athletic offices, freeing me to actually come home for lunch and spend a quick hour with my wife. But the career was a powerful rival, and I allowed it to quickly shove itself to the forefront. As I saw it, we finally stood at the brink of *real* success; we were on a roll. This is what *we'd* been working toward since I graduated from college. Now wasn't the time to hold back. Lyndi was hopeful for change, but I was ready to shift into high gear. I didn't find myself looking back at our lives with a lot of remorse. Sure I'd made some mistakes—some *big* ones—but they were in the past. Time passed, life kept screaming past at 100 miles per hour, and I'd subconsciously blocked much of it out. Now, on the cusp of a giant breakthrough, I wasn't harboring grim fears that I'd missed the mark with my family. I'd only done what I was *supposed* to do to get ahead. Now God was blessing our diligence.

Back to Square One

My elation at being promoted to the college coaching ranks was a short-lived euphoria. It was more like another rude awakening, very similar to showing up on the Missouri campus as an undersized freshman and being bowled over by the size and talent of the upperclassmen. Almost from the minute I stepped onto the Michigan campus I was back to square one. As far as my new employers were concerned, my former achievements in high school coaching were *small potatoes*. Now I was at "Michigan!" where the attitude was "Let's see what you can do *here*."

This manifested itself in several ways: Instead of leading the staff meetings as I was accustomed, I was now the greenhorn student. There was a lot to learn: Colleges prepare harder, teach more, and implement much more technical offenses and defenses than at the high school level. The terminology was like learning a new language. Each college has its own terminology. Bo's came out of his experience in Ohio. Furthermore, a primary aspect of my job was recruiting. I had to learn from scratch what it takes for a high school athlete to play at the highest level in college at each position. Like any new job, it takes time to become accomplished in new skills. I was being stretched in every area from day one; it was a painful period of adjustment. The thought of having to prove myself all over again in an elite environment dredged up the sickening feelings of inferiority I'd always battled: the fear of failure, doubts of not quite measuring up.

It's both sad and ironic: Having experienced wonderful good fortune throughout my coaching career, I never completely got out from under the paralyzing fear of not being valued or accepted short of exhibiting surpassing excellence in all respects. I always compared myself to others, ultimately a no-win proposition. As such, I was never satisfied that, since I had done my best, I could simply leave for home after work and, with a clear conscience, spend quality time with my family. The job was never done. It was a poisonous mind-set that turned my focus inward in a way that was already proving toxic to those around me. Outwardly, it looked like I was working hard. Inwardly, my insides were often tied in knots. Yet I'd developed an incredible capacity to dig my heels in, grit my teeth, roll up my sleeves, and, by sheer hard work and tenacity, tackle whatever challenge stood in my path. True to form, being the new coach on the block at Michigan, I set about my new duties with clenched jaws, steadfastly refusing to fail. I had scratched and clawed my way up through the high school ranks. No one was going to outwork me *now*.

Like an old veteran linebacker, I flung myself into the fray with abandon, with nary a nod to self-restraint or maintaining a balanced lifestyle. Over time, I elevated my performance to these new surroundings. At last satisfied that I'd made some strides toward validating Bo's confidence in me and thinking I'd proven my mettle, or at least demonstrating that I was a solid worker and loyal team member, I was able to settle down and start over feeling good about myself.

What Was Missing

The move into the college coaching ranks afforded us professional opportunities we'd only dreamed of. But it also brought changes that would interrupt and transform our lives. The most profound of these came shortly after being hired. I met a young player named Chuck Heater. He was a fast, strong young fullback from Ohio. What made him stand out in my mind was his unabashed sincerity; he made no attempt to hide the fact that he was a Christian. He intrigued me. I kept my eye on him. His consistently gentle manner, poise, and integrity set him apart. I was curious about what he, a professing Christian, had that I, a professing Christian, *didn't*.

One afternoon after practice I approached Chuck, sized him up, and bluntly asked, "What is it about you, Chuck? You really seem to have it all together." His smile made me feel as though he expected the question. We chatted briefly; then he invited me to an event being held in Brighton a few days later—a Campus Crusade for Christ conference. Having had no experience with the organization, but eager to learn more, I readily agreed to go. I showed up with few expectations. I wasn't prepared for what happened.

Several Michigan athletes were on the program. It was a small gathering. One by one they shared from their hearts about their Christian faith. Their words and faces reflected genuine joy as they spoke of a deep, personal relationship with Jesus Christ. They described an intimacy and inner peace I couldn't easily understand. As each person shared, my heart began to beat faster. They offered up free-flowing prayers filled with hungering adoration. As I listened, I realized something which, frankly, had never before crossed my mind. If their words were true, then I did not really *know* Jesus Christ. I knew *all about* Him, but I did not know *Him*.

They spoke of the Bible, too, as something with which they were very intimately acquainted. They each expressed a deep love for God's Word. It was to them the living, breathing Word of God, and they delighted in and cherished it. This, too, caught me off guard. In all of my years of church upbringing, the Bible had always been interpreted for us in church by a priest. These athletes, however, talked of the Word of God as something practical and relevant to their everyday lives, something they continually studied and used, and which helped them live out their faith. I was surprised to learn that it was written over a period of fifteen hundred years by thirty-six authors; that it had been historically and archeologically authenticated, containing over three hundred prophecies spanning eons, all culturally relevant, all in perfect accord. I saw how each word, chapter, and book were interwoven into an epic, remarkable tapestry identifying Jesus Christ as the world's chosen Savior—and as the *only* path to God. Authored under the infallible inspiration of the Holy Spirit, I began to see how God gave mankind His Word so that all might experience the joy, love, and power He always intended for His creation. That day I came to see that the Bible was not only for priests and pastors; it was God's personal Word to *me*.

I thought I knew what it meant to be a Christian; I thought I *was* a Christian. But that day I saw that there was more. I saw, laid out in Scripture, how Jesus Christ does not merely require my allegiance to His pure, uncompromising gospel. He desires something much more valuable—a personal relationship with *me*. I had never entered into a personal relationship with Him or invited God's Holy Spirit to take up residence in my heart.

As these athletes continued to share, I suddenly understood that while I loved God, knew Jesus Christ was His Son, and certainly considered myself *saved*, I needed to make the simple request, "Jesus Christ, please save me." I needed to personally surrender my life to Him: "Jesus, I give my life to you." I needed to invite God's Holy Spirit to take over: "I invite You in, Holy Spirit, to provide me the power to live a holy life." I had been working and striving and doing my best to do the right things and live a good life, but I was floundering. I had been doing it without that critical *relationship*; I was trying to do it without the empowering presence of the Holy Spirit. That day in Brighton, I realized I had to be deliberate about it—like the Word says; I had to make the choice; no person or church could make it for me. It was personal, between God and *me*.

It was a very subtle shift from where I was to where I needed to be, though it made all the difference. It was not like being struck by a lightning bolt; nor did it come as a spontaneous burst of divine insight. I wasn't jolted from my chair or shocked into a higher state of spiritual awareness. This new way of relating to God came gently. My new understanding of who I was in relation to Jesus Christ came very simply, very sweetly, like a soft, subtle twist to what I already knew was true. I had known since childhood that a Christian's primary duty is to know, love, and serve God. But I saw now why there had been no power in my endless quest to obey this command. I had known for some time that something was wrong, but now I saw what it was. There was a critical, priceless ingredient missing from my life that all the zeal, piety, and earnestness on earth couldn't overcome.

That day I had what Catholics call an "adult conversion." I asked Jesus Christ to come into my life as both my Savior and my Lord. I was *born again* and granted new life by the very Spirit of God. In so doing my faith underwent a drastic turn that rerouted my eternal destiny. All my life I had been doing the external things, cultivating a childlike faith in God, trying to obey all the rules, embracing all the structure of the church, all of the habits, all of the *religion*. But from that day I began to cultivate a tangible, hands-on, heart-to-heart relationship with the person of Jesus Christ. From that day I began to actually *feel* His overshadowing presence guiding me and helping me grow. More precisely, what I immediately began to experience, which I'd never experienced before, was the indescribable *power* of God. *Power* came into my life in the form of the Holy Spirit. It was exactly what had been missing, and it changed *everything.* My life was revolutionized, altered irreversibly.

The contrast could be summed up in one word: *Power!* It was like night and day. I *knew* I had been changed. Before I asked Jesus Christ into my life, I was sold out, devout, zealous for God. But the real spiritual power needed to live out my most heartfelt convictions was lacking. All of the striving, all of the painful failures, all of the maddening addictions that I found impossible to overcome were due to a chronic power shortage. I needed God's healing *power* to fight off that craving for alcohol. Instead, I was pinning my hopes on a *program.* A static routine. A passive ritual. What I needed was a *relationship.*

How could the truth have eluded me for so long? Why had I now been privileged to discover it? Thank you, Chuck Heater. Thank you, Dennis Painter. Thank you, Campus Crusade for Christ. Thank You, God, for orchestrating the events of my life to bring me to that auditorium on a day my heart was ripe to hear the truth. The days to come would prove that I had been granted God's own *power* to overcome the sin that had bound and neutralized me. It was a tender, miraculous moment. I went home bursting with excitement, buzzing with new life. Not since I was child, when God answered my prayer for a five-dollar wallet and made Himself *real,* had I felt such penetrating joy. God had once again reached down and touched me, this time claiming me forever as His own. Jesus Christ had been knocking at my door for many years. Now, with benevolent warmth and gentle reassurance, He had come in and given me the power to finally do what I knew was right.

Chapter 10
Disciplines of a New Believer

IT'S HARD EVEN NOW TO fathom the profound developments that were swiftly recasting our lives. A fascinating, two-pronged scenario had begun to unfold: As a coach, I was living out a lifetime dream, immersed in the heady atmosphere of college football. Each day I was working alongside the best coaches and athletes in the nation, competing against the top programs in the country. In my personal life, I was a new Christian. And while this development by far held the most exciting prospects, I still wasn't entirely sure what this new status before God encompassed. Initially, what it implied was a radical, unadulterated transformation of my beliefs, behavior, and identity.

The great Christian pastor and teacher A.W. Tozer describes the natural, instantaneous transformation that occurs when a person enters into relationship with the person of Jesus Christ. He writes this in *Of God and Men:*

> If redemption is a moral restoration to the divine image, then we may expect one of the first acts of God in the Christian's life to be a kind of moral tuning-up, bringing into harmony the discordant elements within

> the personality, and adjustment of the soul to itself and to God. And that He does just this is the testimony of everyone who has been truly converted. The new believer may state it in other language, and the emotional lift he enjoys may be so great as to prevent calm analysis, but the gist of his testimony will be that he has found peace, a peace he can actually feel.[1]

I did. I felt this peace—sensed it deep down. Nothing had ever penetrated so deeply. While I had trouble describing what was taking place, this *sense* told me everything I needed to know. More concrete was the moral tune-up Tozer describes. It kicked in almost from the moment I prayed, "Jesus, I am Yours. Come into my life . . . take control. . . . " He began to refine my jagged edges and realign my shrill components. It was as if I'd turned a key and opened the door to a vast, unsearchable freedom. What transpired in coming weeks and months can only be described as a complete turnaround in my outlook; measurable reform would come a bit slower. Good things, nonetheless, were beginning to happen.

In a very condensed time frame my attitudes about life in general, and about Bill McCartney in particular, came under furious assault. I was about to undergo a battery of bedrock adjustments, tied not so much to new theology or spiritual perceptions as to my newfound power to *act* on my convictions. For example, for years I had been living with a heavy conviction to make a more sincere effort at home as a husband and father. But since I would allow nothing to interfere with coaching, it remained just that—a sincere conviction producing little more than a nagging sense of guilt and inadequacy. Now, bursting in the door from my Campus Crusade conversion, I couldn't contain my ecstacy at my new commitment to Christ. What was my family—Lyndi especially—to make of this? What did Dad's new commitment mean to them, when Dad had rarely included himself in the orbit of their lives? There was ample opportunity for confusion.

This time, however, I had a new Resource. With Christ at the helm, I took what turned out to be my first shaky steps to honor my convictions. A couple of nights a week, I began to lead the family in devotions. As I could find time, I started opening the Bible at home and reading it with Lyndi and the kids. It was a beginning. Fortified by a budding liaison with the Holy Spirit, I began to pray daily over each family member, laying my hands on the children before they went to bed, asking for God's protection and blessing over them. It was a new point of connection; it didn't suddenly make me the ideal father. That's *still* a ways off. I realize now that I didn't fully grasp what an ideal father even was, or what he was supposed to do. Thankfully, God did. And at His insistence I took a few baby steps in the right direction. I carved out more time to spend with my family. Some of it was genuine *quality* time.

Lyndi wasn't sure what to make of it all. On the one hand, she welcomed the time I now seemed willing to invest praying with the kids and reading the Bible. Instinctively she knew it was a positive development. She had, after all, grown up in the church. The content and the heart behind the change was wonderful, encouraging. But the way I approached it was not. I still left her out; I was my typical hard-charging, follow-or-get-left-behind self. I never took the time to nurture her along, to ease her into this new passion of mine. From her vantage, I'd simply replaced one overbearing obsession with another: *Things have changed now, and this is how we're going to do things from now on!* One of her friends told her it was just a phase that would soon pass. One thing was clear to all: Something had happened to Dad. While they couldn't put their fingers on it, I was different and, from what they could see, a far sight more promising than the old model. I'd been born of the Spirit of God. A personal transformation was underway, whose end is still uncertain. But no one would have argued with the fact that our home was being forcefully impacted.

Power from Above

It's almost humorous. Before Jesus Christ came into my life, I wasn't consciously aware that I had no power. At the time, I wasn't even able to explain what was happening. The fact is, before I met Jesus, spiritual *power,* in *any* form, was a foreign concept to me. So I wasn't actively looking for it. If I had gone out the night before and drunk too much, or acted irresponsibly, I understood the steps I needed to take the next morning. I went to confession, asked to be forgiven, and partook of holy communion—I'd done my part. I'd made it right with God and my priest. I'd come clean and could, therefore, forget about it until the next time. And there was *always* a next time.

Through years of this ritual confession of pleading for God's forgiveness and on occasion begging for deliverance, I never felt an empowering Presence, or anything that might cause me to believe these strongholds could be broken. There was a certain degree of guilt-management occurring in my prayers, but they had produced no discernable power. As I continued to confess and pray with great diligence, I grew resigned to two possibilities: Either it was God's will that I would always struggle, or perhaps I was just plain unworthy of such a healing. If anyone had ever asked me, "What exactly did you expect from all those years of exacting religious exercise?" I would have had to confess it had more to do with covering my bases than seeking a miraculous deliverance. Captive within my frail, puny world view, God remained distant and unknowable. His Spirit was absent from my life, and with it the power for deliverance.

If I had only known the truth. Everything I now know about God has to do with His power to convict, restore, and transform. Something dramatic had changed. A veil had lifted. I had invited Jesus into my life and found myself suddenly in partnership with the great I Am—the All-Powerful God. God's Holy Spirit now dwelt inside of me. God's own Son saved me from the pit. I had been granted a new eternity, and with it, a new today. I was no longer reduced to repetitive prayers and wishful thinking. I was living proof of Jesus' words in John 4:14: "Whoever drinks the water I give him will never thirst. Indeed, the water I give him will become in him a spring of water welling up to eternal life."

A fountain of God's presence surged within me, restoring me. It was a fountain of faith. I simply *expected* to stop drinking now. Could there be any doubt? Life in general would take a major upswing. Things would be different—*better*. With Jesus in my life, I knew I would begin to operate on a higher plane. I was *that* certain, that supremely confident, that abounding in faith. The living, pulsating force of Jesus Christ coursed through me, tended to me, brooded over me, rested upon me. I was so excited. My Lord gave me unbridled hope and courage where before I had none.

Of course it didn't happen overnight. The morning after Brighton I didn't wake up miraculously healed of alcoholism. The urge to drink wasn't gone, never to return. It would take time. It would take diligence. It would take true effort. But whenever I took one step toward God's promise to heal, He lifted me on His shoulders and carried me the rest of the way. It would be a number of years before I took my last drink. But I had received instantaneous deliverance from the heavy, out-of-control drinking that threatened to destroy me and my family. The days of losing control were over, and I found myself going for weeks, months, even years, without taking a drink.

God freed me from the chronic pattern of abuse. Almost from day one of my salvation, I was able to take a more measured approach in every walk of my life. The times I stumbled were in the unexpected, unguarded moments. In naïve lapses of overconfidence, I thought I could now handle an innocent beer or two. I would revert back, stumble, and have to start over. I arrived at a point when I realized I simply could not be around alcohol. Through it all the cry of my heart remained the same: *Please, Lord, deliver me from this addiction*. But unlike before, these prayers didn't vanish into thin air. They were spoken with authority and assurance, granted me by the One who had been given "all authority in heaven and on earth" (Matthew 28:18).

God's Word says, "Come near to God and he will come near to you" (James 4:8). As I came near, I had access into the Father's presence and entitlement to His power through the free gift of Jesus Christ. Jesus said, "I am the way and the truth and the life. No one comes to the Father except through me" (John 14:6). For the first time in my life I was in biblical alignment with God through His Son. I sought God in prayer, sent out my requests. And He met me there. My cries of deliverance were being heard and answered with *power*.

The Power of a Witness

A touch from God can do many things. Sometimes what's needed is for God to simply touch a man's eyes, to remove the scales and allow him to see himself in unadorned, horrifying clarity. This was the touch I received; I glimpsed myself from His perspective—a truly unsettling sight—and saw with brutal transparency the inconsistencies and mistakes I'd been making. Without the Holy Spirit, I'd never been able to fully grasp the damage I was doing to my life and my family, or even to see the opportunities I was squandering to minister to others. With the Holy Spirit now shining a light into my spirit, I could see myself from God's viewpoint. It was shattering.

It was with this new ability to see reality that I began to experience something quite unusual. Within a matter of days after Brighton, I found myself feeling an almost overwhelming, inexplicable passion for anyone who didn't know Jesus; I'll go so far as to call it an evangelical anointing. From nowhere, I was literally seized with a yearning to tell others the good news of Jesus Christ. Erupting from inner quadrants unknown, I had a burning *need* to spread the gospel, and tell others what Jesus was doing in my life. I suddenly began to see everyone in terms of what Jesus could do in their lives. I found myself telling anyone who would listen (and, I'm sure, many who tuned me out) about the power and love of Christ. It was a compulsion wholly separate from my nature. I couldn't contain my joy or keep my mouth shut. *Everyone* needed to know. And I was ready to do it by myself if I had to. "Do you know Jesus? No? Let me tell you about Him. He'll change your life." To this day that craving has not subsided.

What this did on a more personal and private level was to effectively bring my behavior into better moral alignment with Christ. Jesus says in Matthew 5:16, "Let your light shine before men, that they may see your good deeds and praise your Father in heaven." I realized that I couldn't rightfully tell people about Jesus if I was living erratically, or still abusing alcohol. God's Word told me I couldn't continue to live like that. In the Word, I'd read how Jesus told His disciples, "Be perfect, therefore, as your heavenly Father is perfect" (Matthew 5:48). How could I testify to the power and wonder of Jesus if I wasn't aggressively appropriating His power for my own perfection?

Ultimately, this compulsion to witness for Jesus resulted in my eventual, *total* abstinence from alcohol. I didn't want damning lifestyle contradictions to destroy my witness. I was desperate to have a clean testimony for my Savior. The Holy Spirit showed me my need to clean up this area of my life first, and then we'd move on to others. No longer motivated by guilt or shame, I was now able to respond to Christ's irresistible call on my life. It was my heart's desire to glorify God and tell others of the beauty and glory of Christ. It left me one option: I must make a change. And as I walked it out, His healing power was there. God had birthed in me an insatiable desire to share Christ, and wouldn't you know it, it was the breakthrough I'd been looking for in my battle against alcohol.

It was my miracle. In partnership with Jesus Christ, I found both the conviction and the power to turn from this besetting sin. *Jesus* is the only explanation. Mine was an uninterrupted record of failure, but Jesus proved He could do "immeasurably more than all we ask or imagine, according to his power that is at work within us" (Ephesians 3:20).

It was a process that required my full cooperation, but, as Tozer explained, "There is a remedy for inward evil. There is a power in Christ that can enable the worst of us to live lives of purity and love. We have but to seek it and to lay hold of it in faith. God will not disappoint us."[2] Mounting personal victories proved I could, indeed, "do all things through him who gives me strength" (Philippians 4:13). Within one year, the moral and physical tune-up of my life was well underway. I had made lifestyle changes that would move me away from alcohol altogether. I had quit a three-pack-a-day cigarette habit. With these breakthroughs, a measure of balance was restored to my life that paved the way for even greater changes.

Chapter 11
New Gifts Begin to Surface

The acts of the sinful nature are obvious: sexual immorality, impurity and debauchery; . . . hatred, discord, jealousy, fits of rage, selfish ambition . . . drunkenness, orgies, and the like. I warn you . . . those who live like this will not inherit the kingdom of God. But the fruit of the Spirit is love, joy, peace, patience, kindness, faithfulness, gentleness and self-control.

—GALATIANS 5:19–22

WHEN A BABY IS BORN into the world, he possesses natural gifts and talents. These areas of God-given ability—it might be athletic ability, musical skill, intelligence, even business aptitude—develop as we grow and mature. Properly nurtured, they provide direction for our lives and, hopefully, blessing and service for others. But when men or women are *born again* by the Spirit of the living God, they're granted new *spiritual* gifts—new talents, longings, and special aptitudes and, perhaps, a sense of "calling" for a particular area of ministry. These gifts are supernaturally bestowed by God for use in advancing His kingdom on earth. There is nothing more exciting or awesome than to see these hidden, untapped treasures spring forth in a new believer.

From early childhood, I knew what my *natural* talents were. By both disposition and ability, I was a natural coach and athlete, someone who could instinctively lead and motivate others. Yet the gifts that surfaced in me after asking Jesus Christ into my life were without compare. The "fruit of the Spirit" was obvious. Guided by my old nature, my life was just as the Word says we are without the Holy Spirit—a sinful jumble of impurity, debauchery, idolatry, sexual immorality, envy, and drunkenness. Yet solely by God's sovereign Spirit working *His* nature into my nature, previously unknown qualities of peace, patience, joy, and self-control began to manifest themselves. And as I matured, God kept chiseling my natural gifts into tools He could use, which brings us back to the inexplicable burden I had for the unsaved. My heart broke for those who hadn't heard the good news. So, according to my bent, I went for it with unrestrained fervor and boldness. For a time, some people around me thought I'd lost my mind.

The point is, this was a new gift. Beyond the confidence I felt on the football field, my *nature* was to be chronically insecure, painfully self-conscious, likely to compare myself unfavorably with others, and maniacally driven to perform for others' acceptance. My natural bent was to never quite feel as if I measured up. Now, through this spiritual gift, I was gaining a new identity. I saw myself for who I now was in *Christ.* I could tell it was a spiritual gift because it was illogical, irrational—utterly contrary to everything I'd ever been.

Suddenly, I was willing to be rejected by countless numbers of people in the hope that a few might be saved. Beyond the realm of common sense, I was bold, unashamed of the gospel. If the truth of Jesus was at stake, I gladly weathered sharp criticism, even public humiliation, in His defense. If, as it says in 1 Corinthians 1:25, "the foolishness of God is wiser than man's wisdom," I was a happy fool for Christ's sake. If God indeed chose "the foolish things of the world to shame the wise; God chose the weak things of the world to shame the strong" (1:27), then He chose well in me. He picked the weakest, most foolish, most unlikely and undeserving candidate to go out there and tell people about Jesus. With these new spiritual gifts, and armed with a new identity in Christ, I was making waves, but having the time of my life.

Chapter 12
Power in Discipline

SO IT WAS, WITH ALL THIS inexplicable power to resist old temptations and the emergence of an evangelical gifting, I pursued God with greater zeal and intentionality than at any time in the past. In my desire for a deep, abiding relationship with Jesus, I longed for more knowledge, carved out more time for prayer, yearned after a deeper familiarity with God's Word. In the process, I saw how deeply rooted I was in old habits. It taught me the cost of becoming a disciple of Jesus—the difficulty of embodying in one's nature qualities of meekness, humility, generosity and obedience, which the Word says are the *evidence* of our salvation. I quickly discovered how longstanding carnality in my life ran contrary to a life of faith and devotion. My personality was the biggest roadblock I encountered to my spiritual growth.

For instance, my yearning to know more about the Bible was effectively neutralized by pre-existing behaviors. While I knew the Bible was God's divine blueprint for a victorious, well-balanced life, other interests crowded my time. Trusted mentors shared with me the importance of not only *reading* the Word, but of *memorizing* Scripture. I'd read that Jesus said, "Man does not live by bread alone, but on every Word that comes from the mouth of God" (Matthew 4:4). It just fueled my excitement to become well-versed in the Bible. But I found it difficult to get started. My new responsibilities at Michigan were more demanding and time-consuming than ever. The only time slot possible for me to catch a few minutes in the Word was first thing in the morning, before I left for work.

Therein lay the problem. *That's* when I read the morning sports page. In fact, since I was a young lad in catechism dreaming about sports, it was my unvaried morning ritual: I'd retrieve the newspaper from the front stoop, yank out the sports section, and pour over every inch of it while I ate breakfast. Football, golf, baseball, bowling, horseshoes—it didn't matter. I'd read about it, start to finish. Now that I was a Christian, that chronic habit didn't suddenly vanish. Quite the contrary—now, as a college football coach, there was an even greater reason to read the sports: I needed to be apprised of the day's events. Every morning I'd wake up full of curiosity about what an opposing coach might have to say about next week's game. Maybe one of our own players had been quoted in the press; I wanted to know where his head was. Perhaps I'd even been quoted; I wanted to see how I sounded in print. The point is, sports still captured my imagination.

It may seem silly, but it left me with a troubling dilemma. Weeks and months of brushing off the Word of God so I could read the sports page before rushing off to work left me empty, miserable. It forced me to take a hard look in the mirror. I saw how my actions didn't match my convictions. It seemed such a small matter, but the Holy Spirit showed me how it's the small choices we make each day that prove our passion for God. My sports craving was an unmistakable tip-off: Outwardly, I was on fire for God; inwardly, I wanted the mental vacation the sports page offered. Still, I knew I needed to be reading and memorizing God's Word a lot more than I needed to be memorizing every nuance of the sports page. I knew I was *supposed* to love the Word more than the morning news, but I was finding old habits hard to break.

At an early stage of my Christian growth, it was a stern test of my true intentions. I began to pray, asking God, "Please, increase my love for Your Word more than anything else, *including* sports." The answer came in an intensified hunger for the Word, but the first step was mine to make. After many frustrating false starts, it came down to a do-or-die decision. One night on my knees, I made a personal promise to myself and to God that I would refuse to read the day's newspaper until I'd spent meaningful time in the Word. In my heart, it was settled. I never broke that promise to God. Twenty years later, I don't pick up a paper until I've read the Bible. It was a major breakthrough that had a far-reaching impact on my growth. It was a choice that helped determine my spiritual temperature and what kind of Christian I would be—lukewarm or sold out.

Within a short time my appetite for the Word began to grow. My appreciation and love for Scripture soon dwarfed any appeal the sports page once held. As I began to learn the Word, I kept praying, "Lord, I want to love Your Word. Jesus, I want to *know* You in the Word." I began to memorize the Word of God. And as my hunger and discipline for God and His Word continued to grow, God's power in my life grew proportionately.

Fasting

> I wait for your salvation, O Lord, and I follow your commands. I obey your statutes, for I love them greatly. I obey your precepts and your statutes, for all my ways are known to you.
>
> —Psalm 119:166–68

My Christian apprenticeship got a boost from a keen fascination I developed for the practices and disciplines of some of history's great Christians. How did they live their lives? What did their relationship with Christ look like? I sought out books that recounted the lives of revered martyrs, the great revival preachers, men and women who'd made godly sacrifice a part of their daily lifestyle. I found I couldn't get enough of the testimonies of Christians who lived lives of celibacy or deprivation, or who willingly endured hardship in order to press in closer to God. I loved reading about people who eagerly turned their backs on the ways of the world in order to serve the Lord more freely.

An early mentor of mine told me about the great eighteenth century preacher John Wesley. Fondly called the "little man" by his adherents, Wesley helped spearhead England's greatest spiritual awakening in the mid-1700s. I picked up his biography and was fascinated to learn how rigorously disciplined he was in all aspects of his faith. His *methods* for spiritual growth (thus the name, "Methodists") saw him rise each day by 4 A.M. for prayer and study of the Word; he kept meticulous track of his time so as not to waste a moment that could be better used in God's service; and he took heavy precautions against idleness, rich foods, shallow talk, and unedifying literature. His heart was hot after Jesus, and that stirred me. For more than twenty years, Wesley fasted every Wednesday and Friday from 8 A.M. to 4 P.M. It was a Spartan biblical regimen that brought him greater authority in prayer and a hint of lowliness to his gait.

I thought to myself, *Here's a guy who was really after God's heart. God used this man greatly. Wesley paid the price*. I was convinced. I wanted to be used by God; I wanted deeper intimacy with Christ. I knew I could do much worse than to emulate a devoted servant like John Wesley. So twenty years ago, shortly after I was saved, I started fasting every Wednesday and Friday from 8 A.M. to 4 P.M. It was an exercise in self-denial I knew would help me become more like Jesus, and would help me overcome my self-centered nature. Over the years, it helped me learn to say no to my carnal appetites, and yes to the things of God. If you've never fasted, you haven't truly discovered how powerful your flesh is; the Bible says it continually "wars against the Spirit."

These small acts of discipline were the first of many I would embrace in coming years. Each, in their own way, helped me settle any doubts about where God stood in my life. Each was instrumental in proving the intent of my heart toward Jesus. Through each I gained a greater measure of self-control; denying self helped me set parameters for living out the new principles I learned. Patterning my disciplinary habits after some of Christianity's great saints brought power and vibrancy to my own walk. Denying my body brought greater appreciation for Christ's sufferings on my behalf. Each act testified to my true first love.

There was still much to learn. My endless search for balance—in my family, in my career, in my spiritual devotion—had entered a new phase. It would be a lifelong battle. There was no turning back. Christ's love and power had come into my life. I was in the game for keeps.

Pangs of regret were never far off, surfacing frequently to remind me of what I'd been and how far I'd come. I chose to walk forward in the forgiveness Jesus offers to those who call on His Name. I made a definite choice, as the Word counsels: "Forgetting what is behind, and straining toward what is ahead, I press on toward the goal to win the prize for which God has called me heavenward in Christ Jesus" (Philippians 3:13). Life had taken a miraculous turn, and I knew it. I moved on with all the joy and gratitude of a death-row inmate who had received a second chance—a full *pardon*. I graciously accepted His breathtaking mercy.

Lyndi: Bill's Conversion and Its Influence on His Family

Before receiving Jesus, Bill was on a quest to prove himself to God and everyone else. Bill was raised in church, but he took the biblical teachings he received to mean "Do it right or else!" His drinking made him realize he couldn't do it right—even though he wanted to. Bill had to see a problem he couldn't tackle before he'd receive God's solution.

To Bill's surprise, God's solution wasn't found in a list of things to do or rules to follow. Bill loves lists, and he thrives on rules that impart discipline. Every part of his life had rules. He was taught to believe that if you followed the rules and took steps 1, 2, and 3 in order, you could expect to win. That's the way it was in football, and that's how he had approached every other area of his life too, including his religious life. He knew the rules and the rituals to follow, exactly, step by prescribed step. He set out to follow the rules and expected to get the ideal result. This is what he described when he said, "going through the motions of 'religion' made me feel as if I were doing things right." The frustration arose when Bill had to admit his sincere efforts didn't produce the expected results. God used his frustration to prepare his heart for what he heard at that Campus Crusade for Christ rally.

God's solution came in a person, the *person* of Jesus Christ.The guys shared how they experienced the results he wanted, but *not by keeping the list and following the rules!* They got results by admitting they *couldn't* follow all the rules and inviting Jesus into their hearts so *He could* follow the rules *through them*. They quoted Jesus saying, "I stand at the door and knock. If anyone hears my voice and opens the door, I will come in and eat with him, and he with me" (Revelation 3:20). This was a new concept for Bill. He'd been trying as hard as he could to *endear himself* to God by *doing it right*. Then these guys showed him he was already dear to God; that's why Jesus was knocking at his door. Bill had been *out there* trying his best to please God, only to discover that what he was seeking wasn't to be found *out there*, but rather by allowing Jesus to *come in* to his heart.

It seemed to me that Bill was always chasing God, and I was always chasing Bill, choking on the dust. God was important to me, too, but I felt as if I couldn't keep up with Bill. When he announced that he'd been born again, I thought, *Here we go again*. I also thought of the verse from the Book of Ruth: "Don't urge me to leave you or to turn back from you. Where you go I will go, and where you stay I will stay" (1:16). That was my commitment to Bill, even though I didn't understand what had come over him.

Bill brought the reality of a personal relationship with Jesus home to his family. This upset my cart! I had learned to cope and live one way with a measure of contentment. Suddenly all I knew was stripped away and replaced with unfamiliar people and events. Bill surrounded himself with godly people. Meanwhile I was left to make the adjustment alone. I felt like a lady standing there with hands on hips, frantically calling out, "Excuse me? What happened to my life?" At first, I was confused and uncooperative because I was mad. I felt helpless, but I tried to go with the flow.

Soon I noticed real changes. Jesus began to deal with the various compartments of Bill's life he'd managed to keep separate. His faith started to be applied to his drinking, his career, and our family. Before his conversion Bill looked at his family life with a nagging sense of guilt and inadequacy. With Jesus *in his life* Bill seemed to have hope that God would empower him to become a good father and husband, and to find balance at home.

Bill's conversion had a positive influence on our whole family in many ways. God empowered him to go for long periods of time without drinking, which blessed us greatly; he read the Bible to us and prayed over each of our children; he showed sincere efforts to make up in *quality time* what he could not give in quantity, like having family baseball games and play wrestling with the kids. There was one other benefit that I must admit we enjoyed, perhaps more than these. Bill started having his quiet time with the Lord before he read the sports page in the mornings. That left only five of us to fight for reading rights of that coveted sports page!

Within a year of Bill's conversion, I followed his lead by receiving Christ in my own quiet way. Shortly thereafter, each of our children heard God's call and opened their hearts to Jesus at different times. Our family enjoyed a new sense of harmony by becoming one in Christ. This is not to say that our family problems disappeared.

Bill grew spiritually, but neither of us dealt with the serious problems and pain that his alcoholism had caused to our relationship, nor did we make any attempt to repair the damage. Bill was a press-on-and-don't-dwell-on-the-past man, while I was a drag-it-along-with-you woman. He wanted to forget the past, and I wanted to have the past problems *resolved*. Although each of us made concentrated efforts to do loving and good things, we both turned away from our marriage. Bill turned to the Lord, and I turned toward the children. The unresolved issues were simply put away.

Recently, Bill and I discovered a wonderful booklet called *My Heart—Christ's Home* by Robert Boyd Munger.[1] It describes how each human heart is like a home, into which Christ is invited. He's first invited into the front room—the *presentable* part. But soon Jesus wants to go into other rooms: the study of the mind, the dining room of appetites and desires, the living room where He waits for daily fellowship, the work room, the rec room, the bedroom, and the hall closet—wherein are hidden things we consider unpresentable to Jesus. (Maybe that's where Bill and I put our unresolved issues.) The book concludes that Jesus doesn't want to be just a guest, He wants the deed of ownership! He wants access to every door and to go with us to help us deal with whatever is in there.

While discussing these ideas, Bill mentioned that most people think Jesus' words about knocking at the door were written to unbelievers, but they were written to the church. He pointed out that we all tend to keep some doors closed. Then Jesus knocks on one door after another until we are willing to let Him in to each area of our lives.

Bill described this when he said, "The Holy Spirit showed me my need to clean up [the drinking] first, and then we'd move on" to other areas. This is another picture of how we become sold out to Jesus little by little. This applies not only to besetting sins, like

Bill's drinking, but to letting Jesus help us control every area of our lives. Bill invited Jesus into his heart in 1974, but his sanctification has been an ongoing process of Jesus' knocking on door after door asking to go in with Bill to help him put an area of his life in godly order.

Bill's conversion and its influence on his family has lessons for all of us. The first lesson is that zeal, piety, and earnestness—even when you're a sold-out kind of person—will never be enough to give you fully the kind of life God intends. Bill was raised to do the right thing. In the past, he *was* always trying to do the right thing. He made mistakes, but he always knew what was right and kept trying. In the present, Bill *is* trying to do the right thing. And in the future, I believe he *will* always try to do the right thing. That's my Bill, a good man who tries his best to do what's right. But, as sold out as he is, he still misses the mark whenever he tries to do it in his own strength. The fact that he falls short encourages me, because I don't have the energy he does. I figure if someone as sold out as he *is*, *was*, and *will be* to doing the right thing can't live the life God intends by his own strength, nobody can!

Bill kept mental lists of all the ways he tried his best to reach his ideals. That's what he would use to defend himself against his guilt, but the list of good deeds couldn't accomplish God's will in Bill's life. Only Jesus could do that. What a relief to know that admitting what we can't do is a step toward letting Jesus do what God wants in and through us. Once we admit our shortcomings, we can trust Jesus to fill the gap between what we know God wants and what we are able to do.

Men, I also want to encourage you that your shaky efforts to lead your family in prayer, Bible reading, and the things of God will be honored. God will use you if you let Him. To the women married to men who are trying, I say, *Don't get discouraged.* If your husband has Jesus in his heart and agrees with God's Word, even if he isn't living it yet, take heart! When he asked Jesus in, *Jesus Christ came in!* This has gone beyond your husband's best efforts. If

Jesus has been invited in, don't worry. It won't be long before He starts knocking on those doors. Yes, your husband has to open the doors, but Jesus won't go away. I believe the promise of Philippians 1:6 applies here: "He who began a good work in *your husband* will carry it on to completion" (adapted). So don't worry about what's going on within the doors of his heart. Rather, focus on where Jesus is knocking within your own heart. And let Jesus take care of transforming your husband. He will!

Chapter 13
Faith Revolutionizes the Career

BY 1977 OUR LIVES WERE STILL undergoing radical transformation. It was the year I was promoted to the position of defensive coordinator at the University of Michigan. It had been three years since I had committed my life to Christ. In that time I had experienced repeated, irrefutable proof of the power of the Holy Spirit. The Lord had released me from forms of bondage that once held me in a death-grip. When I put my trust wholly in Him, God never once failed me. Beyond this ongoing radical *personal* transformation—which had swept up the entire family—my faith was impacting and innovating my approach to coaching.

To grow professionally as a coach, I had always depended on long hours of hard work, rigorous preparation, and a methodical off-season program of clinics and in-depth study. It was a regimen that led to a lot of my early success. The routine wouldn't vary much throughout my career, but recently the Lord had gently begun to teach me how to trust more in Him for the solution to a problem—even for football-related strategies. It was sacred territory, an area of my life I held on to firmly with both hands; I rarely relinquished a speck of control. To trust some of the details of my job to God was a major leap of faith. But at His persistent prodding, I was learning.

Time after time I'd seen that whenever I simply did my best and put my trust in Him for the outcome, He always came through. It happened a small step at a time, from faith to faith, and from glory to glory. As my reliance on God grew, so did my confidence in the results. Almost imperceptibly, over time I surrendered control to God in every significant aspect of my career and livelihood.

For instance, recruiting the nation's best players was a huge part of my job at Michigan. Out on the road, where it counts, I began putting my faith to the test, no longer trusting solely in all my old ploys and powers of persuasion. Before I'd leave home, I'd simply ask the Lord: "Lead me to the young men you want; help me identify those who will fit in at Michigan; bring me into contact with only those who have solid character and a great work ethic." Before I'd enter a young man's home, I'd pray for wisdom, discernment, and favor. "If this is the player You want, Lord, grant me favor with him and his family." It led to some amazing recruiting coups. And as the returns began to multiply, I started to see every phase of my job as God's sovereign domain. I knew that with God in charge, the outcome would be far superior to anything I could muster. Handed a particularly difficult assignment, or some lofty goal to meet, I'd *begin* by boldly asking God for His discernment. And I found that as I went about my day connected to Him in prayer, solutions to tough situations would just materialize. God would provide the answers, sometimes in quite unusual fashion.

The "Six Penny" Defense

An incident in 1980 dramatizes the point. The University of Michigan was preparing to play Purdue, at the time the hottest team in the country, sporting a six-game winning streak. Boilermaker quarterback Mark Herrmann was the engine behind a sleek, pro-style offense that was blitzing opponents for more than forty points a game. As our game with Purdue approached, Herrmann had established himself as the most prolific total offense leader in college football history. His ability to break down opposing defenses with his laser-accurate passing struck fear in the heart of a defensive coordinator. No team had come close to slowing Purdue. That was our job.

Any Division 1 college coach will tell you that work schedules during the season are grueling. Days last from dawn to way past dusk. Michigan's game-week regimen frequently began Saturday night and kicked into full-swing Sunday morning. By that time each coach had graded film and completed a detailed post-game evaluation. The players arrived that afternoon for an intense film-grading session; then the coaching staff would settle in for the night (often until past ten o' clock), devising next week's game plan.

Mondays always meant long hours. We'd spend the day gauging the opponent's strengths and weaknesses, running through a light afternoon workout with the team and drafting a rough game plan. Monday evening saw the offensive and defensive staffs split up to study film and zero in on their respective game plans. Tuesdays and Wednesdays were rugged practice days, highlighted by full-speed, two-and-a-half-hour afternoon practices. Afterward the staff would work late into the night revising and polishing the game plan. Thursdays were tune-up days capped off with a brisk afternoon practice and one last, hard look at practice film. The team would taper off on Friday—plug in minor tweaks and adjustments, and make sure the team was rested for Saturday's game.

It's an unforgiving schedule; there is no room for miscues. You can't afford a single wasted moment of preparation time. Yet late into our preparations for Purdue, I was stumped. I didn't let on. But the truth is, I didn't have a clue how to stop their passing attack. It employed a revolving platoon of fleet receivers exploding off the line and executing elaborate, slashing crossing routes in the secondary. Monday came and went: no plan. Tuesday arrived—I was tinkering but still had no plan. While the offensive staff was busy finalizing their schemes, we were going through the motions. We'd installed our basic "vanilla defense," knowing it would be about as effective as a hairnet against a charging bull. I began to pray: "Oh Lord, I need Your help. This could be ugly. Give me a clue, a plan . . . *something* to go on!" Throughout the day Tuesday I continued to pray. With each passing minute that I didn't have an answer, I became more anxious.

By nine o' clock Tuesday night, I was sitting in our defensive meeting room scratching my head. It looked helpless. I knew we couldn't cover all of their receivers because they also threw to their backs coming out of the backfield. I thought, *We're not even going to slow them down*. Our linebackers would be sitting ducks against those running backs. And then, without any warning or build-up, *I had it!* A detailed picture of the strategy formed in my mind. It was perfect; *it was the game plan!* Without a moment's hesitation, I rushed down the hall and burst into Bo Schembechler's offensive meeting room. He was having an intense dialogue with his assistants. I butted in. With great theatrical inflection I laid out the "six penny" defense. It would utilize *six* defensive backs instead of the normal four to muddle the secondary and jam their receivers. As I intricately explained the strategy, Bo listened patiently. He heard me out, rubbed his chin, and then, without a word to me, turned to his assistants. He rolled his eyes and said, deadpan, "We're going to have to outscore them."

Game day arrived. Our defense worked to perfection. We beat Purdue 26-0, stuffing their vaunted passing game. And in a sort of bizarre twist, I was named the Big 10 "Player of the Week" by the conference sports writers. It was the first time in conference history a *coach* had been so honored. It was almost comical, completely unheard of. But as unorthodox as it was, and the way the week had unfolded, it simply confirmed what I already knew: Only the Lord could have orchestrated such an outcome. I knew, from the moment that wacky scheme popped into my head, it would work. Why? Because it was from God. Coupled with Bo's reaction, the margin of victory against the hottest team in the country and the slapstick absurdity of being named Player of the Week all pointed to God's handiwork. *And* to His subtle sense of humor.

Some scoff at the notion of God orchestrating the outcome of a football game. But this story really has little to do with football. It's merely a simple testimony of God keeping the promises He makes in His Word: "He answered their prayers, because they *trusted* in him" (1 Chronicles 5:20, emphasis added). And as I trusted in Him, this sort of thing was becoming par for the course. Eleventh-hour rescues as I waited on Him to clear a path were becoming a predictable pattern—almost the rule of thumb—even if the answer was an eccentric, unheard-of pass defense. I had learned that I could depend on God without fail.

The Old Man Versus the New

God's hand over my life was becoming *that* real to me. Jesus Christ was a person I could reach out and hold on to. With Him, every day was a new adventure—exciting, educational, personally edifying. Each day the Holy Spirit drew my attention to areas of my personality that were in sharp contrast to His own. It usually had to do with how I related to others. I was self-centered and I had a tendency to shut others out of my life or to simply dismiss their feelings. In revealing these areas to me, the Lord was sometimes subtle, sometimes harsh. I always had ample chance to ponder what I'd done. But whether I responded by apologizing, or repenting, it seldom had the effect of softening my obstinate, inflexible behavior.

Even as I grew spiritually, in many respects I was the same old Mac. There was still serious imbalance in my life that I hadn't yet identified. The wiring of my personality was still the same. Even the new power in Christ that was helping me to quit drinking hadn't transformed who I *was*. Substantive change comes slowly. I had been granted God's raw power to resist certain forms of temptation, but in other respects, I was not a changed man. My wife was concerned that I was still a fairly insensitive, emotionally distant, mostly unavailable husband and father.

This manifested itself in peculiar ways. For instance, when I began to experience deep conviction in my battle with alcohol, I immediately, perhaps even callously, cut ties with some very good friends of ours. These were people with whom Lyndi and I used to drink and socialize. My explanation to Lyndi was, "I just can't be around alcohol." I didn't take into account how this might strike her. There was no discussion to it.

Lyndi hadn't yet made her own decision for Christ. So our sudden involvement with my new circle of Christian friends left her sad and alienated. I thought she would be happy with my new resolve to stay sober. But as painful as my drinking had been for all concerned, Lyndi had no warning; she wasn't prepared to leave our old life behind cold turkey. She missed our old crowd, still enjoyed a casual drink with friends, and would have appreciated some input into this abrupt social transformation. We'd still host BYOB parties at our house on weekends, but now it meant "bring your own *Bible*," not "bring your own beer." Lyndi used to joke that we'd switched from booze to Bibles, with little change in our relationship.

There is no doubt, my relationship with Christ *was* dramatic *and* life-changing in ways I'm still just beginning to understand. It was noticeable. I had received His Holy Spirit. In Christ, I was, as it says in Scripture, "a new creation; the old has gone, the new has come" (2 Corinthians 5:17). I was in the process of shedding the old self and putting on the new self; I was being renewed in knowledge in the image of Christ (Colossians 3:10). But my old nature was waging a fierce battle. My deep love for Jesus was not a panacea for our marriage; it hadn't automatically transformed me into a great father. My priorities, all the ways in which I spent my time, my lifelong behaviors, were being transformed, but not quickly. The indwelling presence of Christ had filled my life with power and compassion for the lost; it had given me a zeal for God's Word; it instilled in me a hunger for prayer. I loved to be around other sold-out Christians. But Christ's presence in my life had not tempered my voracious appetite for coaching.

I was experiencing something every young Christian must endure.

The apostle Paul describes this agonizing process in Romans: "For in my inner being I delight in God's law; but I see another law at work in the members of my body, waging war against the law of my mind and making me a prisoner of the law of sin at work within my members" (Romans 7:22–23). Yes, I was in stages learning to identify myself with Christ. In small doses, aspects of His character were melding with mine. But if sheer time invested in a single pursuit says anything, my life still revolved around coaching. I was still serving a system blatantly at war with my love for God and my responsibilities to my family.

Chapter 14
Searching for Balance

WITHIN A YEAR OF MY OWN CONVERSION, Lyndi, in her own quiet way, made her own decision to follow Christ. However, wary of the possible ambush of enthusiasm I might send her way, she kept it to herself for a time. Each of our four children in turn made personal commitments to Jesus. Our home was like a young Christian incubator. We had begun to read the Bible and pray together as a family every night. Even if company was over, we'd stop what we were doing, kneel, and hold hands; I'd read the Word and then lead us in family prayer. Twice a year I'd take the entire family off to a Fellowship of Christian Athletes camp, where we learned more about Christ and about each other.

Lyndi was paying close attention. She saw the hunger I had for the Word and the way I would spend personal time on my knees with the Lord. I was attending Bible study groups around Ann Arbor. Lyndi and I were meeting with other Christian couples every other Saturday for prayer and Bible study. There was no denying it, God was breathing life back into a stale marriage. Jesus Christ was having a major impact on our family. But a fundamental problem remained: I was still out in front of the pack several lengths, charging out ahead of our family and rarely looking back in a full-throttle, solo sprint to the finish line. Lyndi saw what I couldn't—the pendulum had swung to yet another extreme.

Needless to say, all this time my coaching career was *gaining* in intensity. As the Purdue game confirmed, my relationship with Christ brought more favor, more success at work. Now, however, a not-so-subtle shift had occurred. As I used to travel distances to attend workshops by great coaches, I would now travel practically anywhere to hear great men of God speak. I took immense delight in listening to a humble preacher who could divide God's Word. I surrounded myself with mentors willing to teach and disciple me. Michigan's area director of Athletes in Action, Dennis Painter (who presided over the Campus Crusade meeting where I got saved), took me under his wing. We began meeting in the mornings at an Ann Arbor Denny's, where he helped me take my first baby steps into an exciting but unfamiliar world.

By 1977 I was getting up three mornings a week before dawn for prayer meetings and Bible studies. A new prayer partner, Charley Kennedy, and I would meet at 5 A.M. for an hour of prayer and Bible study. We'd watch the sun come up together. Then I'd hurry back to my office for a full day of football. The other days I'd drive to Taylor or Ann Arbor for men's prayer breakfasts, where we'd challenge each other in the Word, pray, and encourage one another.

All the while, a pattern was emerging. Here I was, utterly consumed by coaching, working long hours, giving my all for the Wolverines, completely energized by success. But now, I'm also up before dawn three days a week in hot pursuit of God in the company of godly mentors. I was out there fighting the battle, proclaiming the gospel, growing as a coach, building into the lives of young athletes—by any criteria a rich, challenging daily routine. It seemed a life of growing significance, a *dream come true*. I was making a difference, sacrificing for God *and* career.

But it came at my family's expense. My spiritual fervor rarely equated with more quality time at home. Most of these enriching experiences took place *outside* of my home. Working sixteen hours a day, six and seven days a week, ten months out of the year doesn't leave much time for anything else. When the day was done, I had spent the bulk of my time with someone *else's* kids. I had had my most engaging conversations with Christian men. My wife and children were on the outside looking in. They needed me to be *in* their lives, but my focus was turned outward.

I tried. Even if it meant picking up donuts on Saturday morning and taking the boys with me to practice, I made a conscientious effort to include them. My kids loved me. We had fun when we were together. My sons especially loved Michigan football, loved standing with Dad on the sidelines during a game or a scrimmage. These were healthy, bonding interludes.

Still, the demands on a coach at this level conspire against family bonding. Lyndi shouldered the burden at home. And because of her sensitivity to my workload, she went to absurd lengths to shelter me from the mundane details. If she needed something done—home repairs, painting, plumbing, fixing the lawn mower—she'd buy a fix-it book and do it herself. Those times I changed coaching jobs, Lyndi handled our moving chores herself. I would essentially leave for work from our old house in the morning and come home to our new home in the evening. That was the extent of my involvement in the move. I never really considered the pressure and hardship my schedule inadvertently dropped in Lyndi's lap. Except for one month out of the year, when I was on vacation, I simply wasn't around to help. Understandably (though I remained clueless), all of it caused Lyndi to harbor a deep-seated resentment toward me.

Yes, to Lyndi I was in many ways the same old Mac. I always insisted that my priorities were God first, family second, and coaching third. But if you'd asked them, my family would have told you they were bringing up the rear by a sizable margin.

In 1980 I was named among the top five defensive coordinators and recruiters in the nation; it was a rare double citation in college coaching. I was elated. It meant I was succeeding in the big time. It only distorted reality for me. The same principle was at work: Success at work spawned in me a cloudy sense of well-being that all was running smoothly in life. It was a blind spot that would haunt Lyndi for years to come, but it was a weakness I chose not to quickly address. Accomplishment and coaching recognition were dual demons undermining the fabric of my family.

It was an odd dynamic at work. Enthralled by the hoopla of big-time sports and captivated by youthful adoration for Christ, I was now obsessively focused on two parallel tracks. I was an aggressive warrior for the gospel, a devoted disciple of Christ. But coaching stirred in me a root attraction to what some term the "culture of success." The intoxicating challenges of coaching combined with my full throttle approach to faith effectively removed me from proper headship over my family.

It breaks my heart to think of it. My wonderful, beautiful wife, my three handsome sons, and my beautiful, sensitive daughter deserved the passion and energy I selfishly lavished on coaching. And Jesus? I now see that He never condoned such overwrought discipleship at the expense of those He placed in my life to love, serve, and protect. He can only be revealed and glorified in the radiant, full-flowering health of one's primary relationships. Thankfully, God is so invested in *my* life—so thoroughly committed to the proper growth and care of His children—that He did not allow me to remain in this lopsided predicament no matter how I wrestled Him.

Chapter 15
CU: A New Season

He will not always accuse, nor will He harbor His anger forever; He does not treat us as our sins deserve or repay us according to our iniquities. For as high as the heavens are above the earth, so great is His love for those who fear Him; as far as the east is from the west, so far has He removed our transgressions from us. As a father has compassion on his children, so the Lord has compassion on those who fear him. . . .

—PSALM 103:9–13

THE LORD DID NOT TREAT ME as my sins deserved. He did not repay me according to my iniquities. I walked as a new man in the full freedom and forgiveness of His love. But not because I deserved it. Most days, I disappointed those closest to me. For too long I blindly inflicted pain on others. Yet, because I loved the Lord, because I trusted Him as my Father, He kept loving me, working with me, refining me. In spite of myself, God promoted me and furnished me His power. God unexpectedly held out a growing platform from which to declare His salvation and sing His praises. These are what the Lord will do for a man—*any* man—who fixes his gaze adoringly on Him.

Yet one thing must be made clear: If my life attests to nothing else, it's that I've done absolutely nothing to merit God's grace and favor. I embraced all that this new relationship offered. Now I walked in unspeakable freedom; I enjoyed a remarkable new adventure; I reveled in the knowledge of my eternal fellowship with Christ. I did all of these things, but I could take credit for none of them. They were not my doing. It wasn't by my keen insight that I chose to know Christ. It wasn't by my deep sensitivity to His gentle touch that I *earned* the power, mercy, and healing that flowed into my life.

And when I found healing deliverance from alcohol, I couldn't even claim to have been seeking it. The power to resist and the conviction to quit was not my own. It was a majestic miracle of God to spare a marriage, a career, and a life created for His glory. It was a gift. Power, love, healing, forgiveness, rebirth, rejuvenation—the sum of my revitalized life in Christ—were free, unsolicited gifts.

Jesus told His disciples, "You did not choose me, but I chose you and appointed you to go and bear fruit—fruit that will last. Then the Father will give you whatever you ask in my name" (John 15:16). Jesus *chose* me, as He does everyone who receives Him as Lord and Savior. He knew me and my ways from before the womb. It's Jesus who chooses; it's He who tenderly guides us by the hand and hand-tailors each twist, turn, and event that brings us to His feet. And this is the incredible mystery: Sublime gentleman that He is, Jesus grants us the respect and dignity to exercise our free will. He allowed me to choose what He alone set in motion before I took an infant's breath.

And now I submit to you: If you find yourself contemplating these words, I suggest He's also choosing *you*. What will your answer be? Will you freely choose that which has already been decided? Will you exercise your free will and accept His free gift?

"For he chose us in him before the creation of the world to be holy and blameless in his sight. In love he predestined us to be adopted as his sons through Jesus Christ, in accordance with his pleasure and will" (Ephesians 1:4).

He Chose Me

Oswald Chambers suggests that the sovereign call of God on a person's life is too grand to fathom, and becomes even less clear as we grow and mature. "We are not taken into a conscious agreement with God's purpose" when we are saved, Chambers begins, "we are taken into God's purpose with no awareness of [our purpose] at all. We have no idea what God's goal may be; as we continue, His purpose becomes even more and more vague. God's aim appears to have missed the mark, because we are too near-sighted to see the target at which He is aiming."[1]

I was far too nearsighted to see God's long-term plan when I accepted the head coaching job at the University of Colorado in June 1982. But it was much in keeping with this vague, brooding sense of God's purpose and mystery over me that I packed up my family and moved to Boulder. Just like my walk with Jesus, I had not chosen the CU job—it chose me. And when I least expected it. Had I a clue of what lay in store for my family over the next thirteen years, I would have been torn between uncontrollable excitement and the gnawing urge to stay put in Ann Arbor.

When Chuck Fairbanks resigned as Colorado's coach on June 1, 1982, Colorado's football program was down. *Way* down. The timing was bad for a coaching change. Spring training was already over, and fall practice was about to begin. Most college head coaches wouldn't float their names in connection with the CU opening. It certainly wasn't a job you wanted to pursue and *not* get. Life would have been pretty embarrassing back home for the failed candidate.

As Michigan's defensive coordinator, however, I toyed with the thought of applying for the CU job. But the timing seemed wrong, so I opted out. At Michigan, we were preparing for a critical 1982 campaign. I didn't want to seem disloyal.

Destiny intervened. God evidently had other plans. My old friend and mentor Tony Versaci called me, insisting that I enter the CU derby. He asked my permission to contact CU on my behalf. I gave Tony the OK. As it turned out, Tony talked me up so highly to Colorado's athletic director Eddie Crowder that I was granted an interview extremely late in the game. Crowder was on the verge of offering the job to Drake University's head coach, Chuck Shelton. Bo Schembechler gave me the green light—in fact, he exhorted me to go.

I flew to Colorado. I told everyone exactly what they could expect if they hired me. I then bluntly informed CU's president and board of regents that God and family—*not* football—were the two most important things in my life. And I won the job. It was the classic case of an unheralded underdog coming in through the back door.

Crowder later explained that what turned the tide in my favor was potential and pedigree—the dual advantages of having played and coached on a major college level, in highly competitive, nationally-ranked programs. As always, the way everything fell into place at the eleventh hour told me God was in total control. This was confirmed when two Christians I'd never met, and have never heard from again, contacted me and told me that God intended me to be "His rock in Boulder." That's the God I'd come to know. I flew back to Ann Arbor, received my family's unanimous endorsement, and accepted the post at CU. In so doing, I bit off the challenge of a lifetime and inherited a floundering program.

In hindsight, the order in which I recited my priorities to the board of regents that day was misleading. Precious little in my day-to-day behavior supported it. But it provides some insight into the fact that I *believed* they were the correct priorities—God, family, *then* football. I didn't say it lightly. I had every intention of honoring that commitment at CU. But it's also true that nothing I'd done so far *demonstrated* it. Did family really come before career? And given the time and energy I poured into work, could I have convinced God that He was Number One.

Still Striving, Still Imbalanced

Coming to Colorado as head coach gave me a new lease on life. I wanted the unseemly disparity between my oft-stated convictions and day-to-day reality to end. I was determined to change my priorities to match my beliefs. By the time we left Michigan, I knew Lyndi was running out of steam and enthusiasm. She'd consistently gone the extra mile to compensate for my frequent absences, and I knew it. If I genuinely hoped to one day represent Christ's selfless love and sacrifice to my family, it would require some drastic changes.

There was reason for optimism. Now, for the first time, *I* was the head coach. I was finally in a position to decide how the program should be run. I was determined to end the tyranny my career had imposed on our personal life. At Michigan, I was the subordinate. I wasn't allowed to set meeting times. I was there to serve the schedule. Now I was in a role of authority. I decided to use it to free up the Colorado coaching staff to honor the Sabbath.

Scripture speaks very clearly to the blessings to be realized by keeping the Sabbath holy. In Isaiah 58:13–14, the Lord said through Isaiah, "If you keep your feet from breaking the Sabbath and from doing as you please on my holy day, if you call the Sabbath a delight and the LORD's holy day honorable, and if you honor it by not going your own way and not doing as you please or speaking idle words, then you will find your joy in the LORD, and I will cause you to ride on the heights of the land. . . ."

My first official act at CU, therefore, was to ban Sunday staff meetings. I intended it solely as a way to enable the coaching staff to spend time with their families, something unheard of in my coaching experience. Too much gets done on Sunday. Yet knowing I needed to somehow carve out some more time with my family, I was trusting God to redeem the lost time. By honoring the Sabbath, I hoped for even greater productivity when we came back to work on Monday. It was an earnest, sincere idea. But it didn't pan out.

Becoming a major college head coach is something you can never be completely prepared for. As a rookie head coach in Division 1, I was instantly swept up in the enormity of the job. It was compounded by the fact that CU was a rebuilding program, where losses would be coming fast and furious at first. I quickly learned the monumental differences between being an assistant coach and being a head coach. In addition to the initial copious tasks of installing your system and imparting your vision, the head coach is personally responsible for everyone in the program—from the players on the field, to the assistant coaches and managers, to each high school recruit. He must give a constant accounting of each player's academic record as well as his behavior on and off the field. He oversees team deportment and is indirectly responsible for how his players conduct themselves in the community. All of these things were now under my surveillance. As an assistant at Michigan, I had no understanding of how this must have weighed on Bo.

Family Football Sundays

Taking Sundays off under such a load isn't all it's cracked up to be. For a time, I instigated informal Sunday gatherings in our home called Football Family Bible Study. The coaches and their families would come over, and we'd serve a potluck. Lyndi would get out the guitar and we'd worship and read the Bible. It was an honest attempt to promote some quality family time among our staff. The problem is, when you enter into a football season, you enter into a rigid, twenty-four-hour-a-day mind-set. Week in and week out, it's like preparing for war. You don't just vacate that mentality when Sunday rolls around.

The day after a game, there are always a thousand details to attend to: personnel issues, film review, player injuries, getting focused on next week's opponent. It's a continual bombardment. And then there's the matter of dealing with defeat. Humbly swallowing lots of blowout losses had never been part of my coaching experience. In the early days at CU, it was a way of life. Not surprisingly, it had a chilling effect on family bonding time. Let me give an example. During my second year at Colorado, we played the University of Nebraska in Lincoln. Our players fought valiantly and accumulated a lot of yards by half-time. The score at the start of the third quarter was 14-12, Nebraska. We came out in the third quarter full of fire. The CU fans were cheering wildly, eager for an upset. Then Nebraska ran us over. They racked up an NCAA record 48-point third quarter. It was a humiliating experience for the entire state. Most coaches I know don't quickly get over something like that.

Imagine going home after an embarrassing blowout like that and trying to sit down to a nice family meal. Your mind is deliriously ticking through a check-list of things that went wrong, rehashing in fine detail all the miscues that might have slowed the rout. I'd get up on Sunday morning, still wincing from Saturday, and take the family to church. It's just pure suffering on days like that. Folks are eyeing you with pity from across the sanctuary. Yet, because it was Sunday, I'd try to let it all roll off my back and lead the family into a day of quality togetherness. All I really wanted to do is go to the office, blow off steam, and figure out a way to avoid another debacle next Saturday.

Sundays also meant taping my weekly television show. For a first-year coach, it was a rare treat to go before the entire state and try to hold out some hope for a brighter tomorrow. You've heard it before: A coach's life is lived out under a microscope. And it's true. Everybody has an opinion about your value as a human being. The so-called experts are quick to critique. Your face and name are all over local and national television. It was the life I'd chosen. I saw it coming. But I'm not going to try and pretend it fostered an intimate family Sunday.

We ended up abandoning the Sunday day off. As I later learned, Lyndi was hoping we'd get back to work. The thirty-person potlucks in our home were less than restful for her. And the conspicuous *lack* of quality family time made us all wonder why I was insisting on it. Sadly, if my character had been of a higher caliber, even in those first seasons, I suspect I could have endured the losses and not allowed them to detract from our Sundays.

But the primary reason for abandoning them was that it just wasn't working out from a coaching standpoint. Our staff was always playing catch-up, always behind in our preparations. While an entire state waited for us to turn things around, we were wrestling just to get our work done on time. When Monday rolled around after a Sunday off, we simply weren't prepared. It created frustration. The coaches, needing every spare minute to prepare for another week that would undoubtedly stretch us to new limits, started coming in on Sundays on their own. Family was again placed on the back burner. But the consensus was, it's OK, for now. At least the work was getting done.

Dry Sprig in a Parched Field

In hindsight, much of the chaos could have been avoided. My stress level, the inability to get over a loss, even Lyndi's and my lack of marital intimacy at a time I'd set aside especially to bless my wife, were due in part to the stress my new responsibilities waged against my quality time with God. Psalm 1 says, "Blessed is the man who does not walk in the counsel of the wicked. . . . But his delight is in the law of the LORD, and on his law he meditates day and night. He is like a tree planted by streams of water, which yields its fruit in season and whose leaf does not wither. Whatever he does prospers."

Since becoming a born again Christian, that verse had always described me. Meditating on God's Word was my delight. It's not God making a passing suggestion to thumb through the Word in one's spare time. It is the key to finding peace and calm in the midst of turmoil. We are instructed to read and meditate on the Word day and night—all day, all night. We are to be so familiar with God's Word that Scripture slips off our tongues in silent prayer every moment of the day.

Study and meditation on the Word was my lifeblood. It was my daily fuel for living. Trying to handle the scope and intensity of my daily obligations, however, rarely afforded me the restful times of simply dwelling in God's presence that I craved and needed. During the season, I would grab them when I could. They sustained me, but things were moving fast. When I'd go before the Lord, I'd often leave feeling guilty that my prayers weren't more focused, or that my heart and mind weren't more fully engaged. It was a tension I would battle the duration of my career—how to carve out the uninterrupted time I needed with the Lord when the demands of the football season were buzzing about me like angry hornets. Thankfully, I was still feeding on God's Word, disciplining myself, fasting, and centering myself in prayer. I had met some strong Christian brothers who supported me and regularly prayed with me. That fellowship equipped and empowered me to weather those trying early years at CU.

But I also know that if I had been intimately abiding in Christ like He commands, with a heart uncluttered and a mind unfettered by the agitating thoughts and mounting tasks of the day, I would have been like that tree whose roots drank deeply from refreshing streams. *Whatever* I would have done would have prospered, including family Sundays. If I had been able to delight in and meditate on God's Word day and night, continually drawing on His perspective, I would have been better able to strike a healthy balance between work and home. I would have had more to offer my family during their difficult adjustment to a new environment.

Chapter 16
Lean Times in Boulder

THE NEXT THREE YEARS were lean. From 1982 to 1985, wins were scarce. I came under sharp criticism. Some called for my ouster. Others questioned my coaching ability. At times, I questioned myself.

What buoyed me through the rough times, however, was my ability to project into the future. I have always been somewhat of a visionary, and at CU, formulating a strong vision for the future allowed me to endure the present. I firmly believed we were laying a solid foundation at CU. One day it would provide us the leverage to push over the hump. Each week at our Buff Club luncheons, usually after another disheartening loss, I'd roll out the vision anew. It was part of my job to reassure the boosters that Colorado was indeed building toward a fruitful harvest, even though they couldn't see it yet. "We are building a solid foundation for this team around quality individuals," I explained. "We're recruiting dedicated competitors, young men who are hungry to win, who will pay the price. You can't see the evidence yet because the structure—the *foundation*—is below ground. It's invisible to the eye. But trust me, it's rock-solid, deep and broad. One day soon you'll see this program back on its feet."

Few knew how deep the foundation was. Proverbs 16:3 says, "Commit to the LORD whatever you do, and your plans will succeed." On June 10, 1982, the very day I was hired at CU, we laid what I still believe was the enduring foundation for the program's long-term future. We consecrated the football program to Jesus Christ. We got down on our knees and offered it up to Him. We surrendered any personal motives or agenda we might have and then committed the entire program to His glory and honor. "Lord, may Your perfect will be fulfilled in this program."

It was the single act I credit most for CU's ultimate rise back into the national rankings. Though it would take time to see, installing God of Creation as the cornerstone of our program had an unfathomable impact. As we continued praying for and consecrating our work and plans to Christ, we purposefully retrofitted the program with a permanent spiritual base, and built a program on the only foundation that lasts—the Rock of Ages. I believe its legacy endures today.

Building on the Rock

Of course, there were other practical matters to attend to: like mending fences with Colorado high schools, reestablishing recruiting networks in the big football states of Texas, California, Louisiana, and Illinois, and instituting an adequate year-round conditioning program. It was required legwork to reconstruct a team capable of competing in the rugged Big 8 Conference. I knew I had three, maybe four years, max, to achieve it. A man in my situation gets only one chance to be a head coach at a major university. When CU hired me, I knew . . . it was *my* chance. If the team didn't make significant improvement within that three- or four-year window and I was fired, it was probably my last opportunity to be a head coach at the Division I level. These were the rules of the game. I lived with them every day. The stakes were high. Either the rewards would be considerable or the fall would be hard.

I can still recall, with a bit of a nervous tic, a letter I received from CU president Gordon Gee one August as the team reported for preseason workouts. At the time, CU had appeared in two consecutive bowl games—the first since the mid-1970s. We'd demonstrated consistency. There was optimism in the air. Gee's message, however, stated in no uncertain terms that he *expected* us to win our home opener in late August. It came just short of being a veiled threat. It had that "you'd better win or else!" undertone. I had real mixed emotions about it. It filled my heart with unrest and anxiety about my job even before our first practice.

Don't misunderstand. Gordon Gee was one of my strongest supporters during his tenure at Colorado. He signed me to an unprecedented fifteen-year contract and helped find the funding needed to upgrade our facilities, pushing CU's program into the upper echelon. But that's the whole point—that's *life* for a coach. I served a very demanding system that was never satisfied. It's a system that constantly asks, "What have you done for me lately?" Even after CU established itself as a perennial national contender, I never failed to get the message loud and clear that dead fish are wrapped in yesterday's newspaper. We could coach the team to its biggest win in decades on Saturday, but by early Sunday morning the pressure was on again. I would be up early, watching film, trying to muster the energy to do it all over again.

In 1984, my third year at CU, the Buffs went 1-10. One of our best players, sophomore tight end Ed Reinhardt, suffered a life-threatening brain injury in our second game against Oregon. It looked like the bottom had dropped out at Colorado. Some fans, even some players, questioned whether I could lead the team back to respectability. Incredibly, in the middle of that dismal campaign, CU athletic director Bill Marolt awarded me a contract extension. Though many thought it an irresponsible move on Marolt's part, he understood that continuity was a big part of the answer to CU's long-term future. It bought us the time we needed to finish setting the foundation.

I felt we were about to break out of the Big 8 cellar. And, as I had hoped, the next year we rebounded. In 1985, CU went to the Freedom Bowl, losing 20-17 to Washington. It was the first bowl game CU had played in since the 1976 Orange Bowl. Around the state, there was guarded optimism that the program was back on its feet.

Expectations were sky high to start the 1986 season. But we squelched them quickly enough by jumping out of the blocks with a 0-4 preseason start. It was our much-hyped breakout year, and we'd laid an egg. The winless start included a particularly distasteful loss to Colorado State University, CU's intrastate rival in Fort Collins. The mood around campus turned surly. All of a sudden, it looked like the solid foundation we'd been building had vanished. All the progress we had made in my fourth season—the bowl game, the respectability, the national attention—was down the tubes.

It was my all-time low in coaching. I didn't have to read the newspapers or listen to the radio. I knew what people were saying: McCartney's time at CU has about run its course. The bowl appearance was a fluke. Being a head coach, it seemed, was not Bill McCartney's strong suit. It felt like the beginning of the end. The way I felt, I would have to die to get better.

Fortuitously, after that start we had an off week before facing Missouri. In the days following our fourth loss of the preseason at Arizona (we lost the final three games by a total of eight points), I staggered into my prayer room at home and fell on my knees. What proceeded from my lips was a true blue, heavyweight-caliber whining session with the Lord. I held nothing back. I cried out, "Oh, Lord . . . please, Lord, help me. You've got to rescue me from this . . . How could this be happening? Where are You, God? I can't take it anymore. What have I done to deserve this . . . ? Rescue me, Lord."

This went on for some time. When I finally stopped for breath, I sensed the Lord's presence in the room. In a calming whisper to my spirit, He spoke. There are times in a Christian's life when the Lord clearly speaks—now one way, now another—and this was one of those times. Into the stillness of the moment, He made His will known: *Why are you acting like this? . . . Why are you whining? . . . Do you not have a great big God? . . . Have I not been faithful to you time after time? . . . Do I not support those who love Me?*

Do I not work all things together for the good for those who call on My Name? . . . Now stop whining. . . . Stand up and be counted. . . . You're a man. . . . Be the leader I brought you to Boulder to be. . . . You're not leading, you're whining. . . . Do not fear, for I will go before you. . . . This battle belongs to Me!

I left that room a changed man. That was on a Tuesday. Our staff reconvened on Wednesday after three days of recruiting trips. We called the team back together. I was upbeat, refortified, braced with steely resolve. The team heard it in my voice, saw it in my face. Our next game was at Missouri. We had ten days to prepare.

"Let me tell you what's going to happen at Missouri," I began. "We've just finished the preseason. Now we're heading into the *real* season. And I assure you, we *will* rebound. We *will* respond. We *are* built on the right character and substance. We're going to turn this thing around. We're not losers. We're *winners!* From this point on, things will not be the same. We're going to stop losing and start winning."

I turned to face the entire offensive line. The offensive line on any football team usually consists of the most unselfish, unsung players. They're the guys most willing to lay it all out there for the team. I told them, "I hereby entrust the entire football team to you guys. I'm putting the team in your hands. From now on, every time the ball is snapped, you're going to SURGE! You're going to SURGE forward and blow your man off the line. Do you hear me? You're going to SURGE! You're going to EXPLODE!"

For the next ten days we worked almost exclusively on getting the offensive line ready to detonate off the snap. You've never seen a team take such advantage of an off week. Our offensive line rose to the occasion. We marched into Columbia and scratched out a gritty victory. It was a huge win, even though we'd beaten Missouri in

Boulder in 1985. For most of the past decade the Tigers had totally dominated CU, particularly in Columbia. We celebrated that win as if we'd won the Big 8 title. Our confidence was rekindled. The following week we played better and aggressively in beating Iowa State. We were reignited. Next up was third-ranked Nebraska.

The importance of the Nebraska game to CU at this crucial crossroads cannot be minimized. Colorado hadn't beaten the Cornhuskers since 1967. Shortly after I was hired, I targeted Nebraska as CU's number one rival. People laughed outright. I know the folks out in Lincoln, including their distinguished coach, Tom Osborn, weren't too concerned. For CU, however, it was put-up-or-shut-up time.

CU never trailed in the game. We beat them 20-10 at Boulder's Folsom Stadium. Our defense held their vaunted running attack to 123 yards. The entire state of Colorado was electrified, relieved—*stunned.* It was as if the entire weight of the Great Plains had been lifted from our shoulders. We left the scoreboard lit in Folsom Stadium until Sunday night, with that cathartic 20-10 score ablaze for all to see. Our team went on to finish 6-5, losing only once more in the regular season, to third-ranked Oklahoma in our last regular season game. We were invited to play against Baylor University in the Bluebonnet Bowl. We lost 21-9 to perhaps one of the best teams Baylor has ever fielded. There was no doubt, Colorado had turned a corner. Maybe not *the* corner. But appearing in two consecutive bowl games was a milestone that served notice to all that the program was back on solid footing.

To think, CU began 1986 with a 0-4 record. But with God putting His hand on me in my pitch black despair, I was able to gather myself and rely solely on the Rock upon which we'd built our future. It allowed me to communicate hope and resolve to a team that could have gone either way. That landmark season helped us attract our first blue-chip recruiting crop. Though we only signed about thirteen players after the 1986 season, half of them turned out to be All-Americans. A handful are still playing pro ball. It was that class that eventually powered Colorado to the top of the national rankings. They led CU to two consecutive Big 8 titles and two consecutive Orange Bowl appearances in 1989 and 1990. That's the class that earned me Coach of the Year honors in 1989, and brought Colorado its first national title in 1990. The Rock was indeed deep and solid.

Chapter 17
Raising the Standard

WHEN I FIRST ARRIVED AT CU, I was, frankly, distressed at the condition of the program. I predicted it would take seven years to reestablish CU as a ranked contender. The most difficult challenge I faced, after working at Michigan, was getting the team to see that playing at Colorado did not automatically make them big-time college players. I had to get them to stop comparing themselves with one another and deciding that they were working hard enough. It was an easygoing attitude that had brought the program to its knees. At our first conditioning workout, for example, I asked the team to jog one-and-a-half miles. Nearly a dozen players collapsed or stopped before the finish. A handful of exceptional athletes reported in good shape. But there was no strength and conditioning program when I arrived—no strength coach at all—and it showed in the team's overall performance.

What had happened at CU was not all that uncommon. When a player looks around and all he sees are a bunch of guys no better or worse than he, it fosters complacency. Once a heavyweight in the Big 8, Colorado had lost its sense of football tradition, and with it a true standard of excellence. I wasn't prepared for what I found, and it was too late that first season to do anything about it.

It's like a creeping virus—it can suffocate a football program. Athletes boastfully comparing themselves to one another on a team that has no real competitive standard are prone to deluding themselves into thinking, "Hey, I'm working as hard as that guy. I must be in pretty good shape. I don't need to push myself any harder."

What this lethargic attitude fails to consider is that the Michigans, Southern Cals, Nebraskas, and Notre Dames are churning out squadrons of players who've been immersed in rich tradition and are fire-tempered by ferocious competition at every position—*every day*. At Michigan, for instance, our players were involved in rigorous year-round conditioning programs and were expected to become astute students of the game. Our coaching staff rarely rested; we were constantly evaluating players, drafting new schemes, refining our systems. It was a year-round, ultra-intense regimen. Practices were conducted with greater intensity than most CU players had ever tasted in a *game*. The rebuilding process would take every bit as long as I thought.

Tradition: The Secret Weapon

It was a lesson I learned early in my career. In the mid-1960s a good friend, Wayne Gorman, asked me to be his assistant coach on a young football team in Southgate, Michigan. It was a new school called St. Thomas Aquinas Catholic School. It was so new, in fact, that there was no junior varsity or varsity team—only a freshmen squad. Wayne and I arrived at our first practice certain we stood at the threshold to a prep football dynasty. For good reason. Wayne and I both had major college-playing experience; we each had already served as a high school head coach. We fancied ourselves as a rare combination of youth, talent, and experience. We were confident.

Furthermore, Aquinas, located in the suburbs of Detroit, drew from a vast pool of young families. It was a football-rich territory. There would be plenty of young, raw talent, not to mention financial resources, flowing into the program for years to come. It was a blank canvas. An ambitious young coach could paint a masterpiece and make quite a name for himself at the same time.

Wayne and I took this sprout-green squad of freshmen and whipped them into quick shape. By the week of our inaugural game, they'd rounded into a crisp, tightknit unit. We had home field advantage that game. Our kids sported new uniforms, new helmets, new shoes, new pads—everything new. On game day we suited up a full contingent of forty-five players and made a big splash as we sprinted on to the field under bright lights. The bleachers displayed proud, cheering parents. Our pre-game drills were sharp and precise—our pass routes executed with flair and precision. The stage was set. We turned to watch our opponents amble on to the field.

Our opponents were the freshmen team from Redford Catholic Central in Detroit, an excellent school with a lengthy athletic tradition. It was known for its consistently good sports teams. This freshmen team, however, was comprised of freshmen who hadn't made junior varsity. They looked a bit shabby. Their uniforms were old, and some didn't even match. Except for a few parents, their bleachers were empty. Their pre-game drills were erratic—it seemed like they could barely hike the ball from center—and their coach, while fired up, certainly didn't have the major college pedigrees Wayne and I had. We were practically salivating. We shot each other a glance. Our eyes said, "Let the dynasty begin!"

The whistle blew. The rout was on. It was a stunning performance. Redford trampled our behinds up and down the field all night long. They beat us to a pulp, left us dazed and scattered all over the turf. The game was effectively over before halftime. Our stands were like a morgue. Our promising young team with its new uniforms and snappy drills had been thrashed and humiliated on their home field, in their inaugural game. Redford's kids, ragged as they appeared, had handed us our heads still quivering in their helmets.

After the smoke cleared, I stood for a long time on the sidelines, trying to make sense of it. We seemed to have had every possible advantage—a new school, the home field, great enthusiasm, coaching prowess, a big crowd, high emotions, even new uniforms and equipment. Our freshmen had been drilled and conditioned. We thought they were ready to rumble.

Then it hit me like a Redford off-tackle sweep through our porous interior line. Our team had no *history*. No legacy. No tradition. Our kids didn't know *how* to win. They had new shoes but no game experience to draw upon. We'd judged Redford by their appearance, but Redford's kids were being groomed in a program with great players and even greater tradition. They'd been taking hits all preseason against older, tougher sophomores and juniors. They knew what it was like to get popped and hop back up. They were chomping at the bit to get a crack at someone their own size. Our kids didn't know what hit them. When they took that first big lick, they wilted. Redford's freshmen had endured trial and hardship together. We just *looked* like a team. As the season wore on, our kids got better. But the lesson stuck with me.

The Bienemy Factor

We faced a similar type of situation in my first years at Colorado. It wasn't until we began successfully recruiting players with a winning pedigree that significant victories started to follow. One such player was a young, 5'6", 195-pound fire-plug of a freshman named Eric Bienemy. I'd never seen a kid like that. It was by the grace of God, and some excellent recruiting by assistant coach Oliver Lucas, that he signed with us. Bienemy stalked the sidelines like a coach; he was excitable, combustible. He radiated a defiant rage that elevated the play of even the older players on the team. He had such a thirst for victory, such a competitive zeal, such an uncompromising spirit, that he simply ignited everyone around him—even the coaches. Bienemy raised the standard for our team. He was part of that breakthrough class of recruits that turned CU into a contender. He was the caliber of player who regularly signs on with Notre Dame and Nebraska. Bienemy had a great career at CU and was on the field in 1990 when we won the national championship.

David in the Cave

I believe the same principles apply in our spiritual lives. We need people in our lives to challenge us, to inspire us to greater depths of passion and greater heights of commitment. In the same way that CU players justified their mediocrity by comparing themselves with their teammates, I see far too many Christians today who think and say they're OK with Jesus. They're comfortable spiritually. And why wouldn't they be? Looking around at all the other Christians, they see folks much like themselves. They see them and conclude that "Hey, I spend as much time in prayer as that guy," or "I read the Word more than most," or "I attend church faithfully." And they delude themselves. They have measured their walk against someone else's standard of mediocrity. It's rampant in the church today. Much like athletes in a middle-of-the-road program, the church of Jesus Christ today is filled with self-satisfied, lukewarm Christians—folks who are enamored with the trappings of culture and the comforts of conformity. They don't even know what being totally sold out to Christ *looks* like.

King David provides us with a perfect example of a man who single-handedly lifted those around him to new heights. As a young warrior, enjoying his reputation as a "giant slayer," David incurred the jealous rage of King Saul and was forced to flee for his life. Over the next fourteen years, he lived off and on in a cave. During that time, many of Israel's disenfranchised, frustrated loners aligned themselves with David and came to live with him in his cave. This rag-tag crew was never the same. David's passion for God, his discipline as a psalmist, his hunger for God's word, his courage in the face of God's enemies, revolutionized their lives. Once an unsavory, complaining lot, these vagabonds came to be known as "David's mighty men." Their years with David had made them fearless warriors, united in spirit, undefeated in battle. They were, like their leader, on fire for God, and they formed an impenetrable phalanx around their nation. In proportion to their numbers, they became the most fearsome army the world had yet seen.

My David

I have a friend like that. Within a week of being hired at CU, the president of the CU Buff Club, Colorado Springs businessman Jerry Rutledge, hosted a booster dinner to introduce me to the other prominent CU supporters. It was a festive atmosphere. There had been a golf tournament; people were drinking and laughing. All the CU coaches were there to give a report. When I got up to speak, people were very curious about who the new coach was, what he looked like, what his plans were. I stood and gave a very forceful, Scripture-laden description of who I was and what could be expected of me as CU's coach. I'm told it surprised everyone. The mood in the room changed dramatically. Few probably knew what to make of a rookie head coach with such bold convictions. Few, perhaps, besides Jerry Rutledge. Jerry was a strong Christian himself, and was evidently deeply touched by my remarks.

In the weeks and months that followed, Jerry really came alongside me as a friend and a brother. I've known Jerry now for fifteen years. He has become my "David." This guy has stuck by me closer than a brother, in good times and bad. He has been my prayer partner, my confidante, a relentless encourager, unwavering in his support. Every Saturday morning before a game, he would come to Boulder and we would just walk, talk, and pray for an hour or so. When everyone else was calling for my head, Jerry would calmly assure me, "You're God's man. You came to Boulder for a purpose. Keep your eyes fixed on the Lord. It's going to be OK."

Because of my time with Jerry, I have become a more faithful, wholehearted Christian. He's challenged me to live out the principles I preach. He's held me accountable in my marriage, to how I'm treating Lyndi. He has exhorted me to be a better father, to spend more time with my kids. He's made sure that I spend regular, quality time in the Word and in prayer. I shudder now to think how many times I might have fallen if Jerry hadn't been there, always on my side, phoning me every day to pray, pointing me back to the Lord.

Throughout my Christian life, I've tried to find Davids to surround me, godly men who were more serious about their faith than I. I delight in men who are on fire for God—being around them lights a fire under me. I've always needed that. I've always needed a David to challenge me, inspire me, point me back to what God's Word has to say, uplift my spirit, and continually encourage me in my faith and love and discipline. It saddens me that so few see or understand this need. Spending consistent time in a mentoring relationship is a critical ingredient to one's spiritual growth. Jesus shared His character and disciplines with His disciples through the time He spent with them. He walked with them, taught them, and exhorted them. He breathed His life into theirs, and they revolutionized the world. It's the model for the church. In an age of rampant, passive indifference to the things of God, every Christian *needs* a David. Tarying long in the cave of a godly mentor, one finds his heart becoming inflamed for personal godliness and deeper intimacy with the Lord.

Chapter 18
All that Glitters Is Not Gold

FINALLY, THE CU BUFFS had turned the corner. My prayer closet encounter with God in 1986 ignited in me a faith that surged throughout the team. It saved our season. The program was now entering a period of unprecedented prosperity. We had built the program on the Rock of Christ; the program had withstood many storms and was now standing firm. Spiritually and professionally, I was growing. The success of the football program had enlarged the platform I had to share Christ. I was being sought out as a speaker at a growing number of Christian functions. I felt that my faith was growing by leaps and bounds, that I was growing in my relationship with the Lord.

But all that glitters is not always gold. Amid this host of professional and personal triumphs, I guess the best you could say was that our family was bearing up. A bright spot occurred in June of 1988 when I began taking our family to a new church, the Boulder Valley Vineyard. After fifteen years of living as a born-again Catholic—eight of them in a very Spirit-filled Catholic church in Ann Arbor—our move to Boulder in 1982 landed our family in a church environment that proved very tedious for our children. They were not flourishing spiritually. Lyndi and I could see they were becoming apathetic, frustrated in their faith. After struggling for six years under this burden in Boulder, I decided it was time for a switch. Now, under Pastor James Ryle, an outstanding preacher who became a good friend, Lyndi and our kids really began to blossom in their faith. And after years of missing her Ann Arbor women's Bible study, Lyndi finally tapped into a great women's group. Their support and encouragement was a healing balm.

If anything, I was spending more time in prayer for my family. I daily sought God's blessing and protection over them, and was blessed that each seemed to be experiencing his or her own deepening relationship with the Lord. I knelt down each morning and prayed a blessing over Lyndi. Before my sons and my daughter left the house, I would rest my hands on their heads and ask God's blessing, power, and healing over them.

These were brief snapshots in the day that made me feel like I was doing my part as the husband and father. But I was not fully connecting; I was not entering into their lives. I was sharing Christ, telling them that all they needed was in their relationship with the Lord, but I wasn't spending that close, individual bonding time with them. I wasn't taking my daughter Kristy out on father-daughter dates and letting her into my heart—or hearing hers. I wasn't taking my sons on those summer camping trips and spending special times with them. I wasn't sitting down with Lyndi on a regular basis and really talking with her, listening to her. I wasn't entering into her world and trying to meet her where she really needed me. I was including them, to the best of my ability, in my life—in the things that captivated *me*—but they needed me to enter into their lives, on their terms, to know and love them where *they* lived.

Work was always there, and the prayers that frequently filled my head pled with God to extend His favor on CU the next Saturday. But there were more pressing priorities closer to home. Oh, that these had been the impassioned objects of my prayers. I believe God would have eagerly helped me right the nagging imbalances.

He would have given new vitality to our marriage and brought my often tortured focus on career into proper perspective; He would have opened my eyes to all the ways I was avoiding intimacy with my kids.

Underlying it all, I was still motivated by insecurity, by that need to win, to succeed. As the Buffs continued to advance, my identity became tied more critically to our won-lost record. While I had allowed God to oversee my coaching success, I had not yet allowed His cleansing Spirit to touch these other deep-rooted areas—the *heart* issues. I had unknowingly kept them off limits. And, for that reason, I wasn't hearing what my family was trying to say; I was still largely oblivious to Lyndi's pain—to how she continued to shoulder most of the baggage, stigma, and hardship of being the head coach's wife while enjoying relatively few of the benefits.

I wasn't in touch, a fact demonstrated by my failure to realize how deeply Lyndi suffered when the media attacked our family and my character, or how deeply protective she was of our privacy. Being the head coach's wife, she had become emotionally isolated from her traditional support networks. Out of her concern for my reputation, she was stifled from being herself. I was unaware, for example, of the little stinging sleights that regularly undermined her self-esteem.

One day, for instance, a local reporter called Lyndi to ask her if she would consent to an interview in our home. She was thrilled. Lyndi rarely received much attention, even though her role in my success was incalculable. The thought of a special profile on her in the local paper really propped her up. The day of the interview, she spent all day cleaning house. She prepared a sumptuous dinner and a dynamite dessert. She put on a new dress and looked absolutely radiant. All she told me was that I was supposed to bring the reporter home with me. When we walked in the front door, the reporter said hello to Lyndi. Then he spent the entire night interviewing *me*.

Though she didn't let on, Lyndi was crushed. The reporter had simply used her to get at me. I was too dense to catch on. While it caused her to retreat further into a shell of angry mistrust toward the media, it had other consequences. That anonymous swipe, and untold others, simply confirmed to Lyndi that she was an insignificant afterthought in my high-profile life.

My Real Team

Yes, I thought I was doing my best to nurture my family. But the simple truth is, Colorado football—like every other coaching job I'd had—was firmly installed in my heart as an idol. It was a consuming force. It dredged up all the glaring contradictions I'd always glossed over. My natural giftings had paid off: I'd made a nice career fashioning unselfish, well-oiled teams with athletes who had come together from all parts of the country. I'd done it from the grass fields of Dearborn to the fake turf of Boulder. Yet, even with all of the spiritual tools now at my disposal, I'd never learned the secret of forging a dynamic team in my own home. I'd never learned what it meant to be a full-fledged team member to my wife and kids. All of the advanced theory I'd studied, all of the workshops I'd used to charge to the top of a profession, had done nothing to help me realize that my *family* was the team I should have been laying it all on the line for all along. I'd bought into a lie.

Our ability to create team togetherness at CU was celebrated. We learned to inspire sacrificial love and respect among athletes. Yet my efforts to love and affirm my family were flimsy and off target. My best efforts came up short. While making myself endlessly available to those who called me *coach*, I'd casually neglected my higher ministry to those who called me *Dad*, and *honey*.

When God wants to do a powerful work, He often uses the foolish things of the world to confound the wise, the weak to frustrate the strong. Little did I know what a prime candidate I was for the job. God was about to unfold a wonderful mystery in our midst. The stakes were about to rise again. My dream opportunity at CU had peaked beyond my wildest expectations. Now the axis of my life was about to shift. Who could have predicted that from this imbalanced picture of modern manhood God was setting the stage for radical changes? And not just for me—for an entire nation of men.

Chapter 19
The Truth About Team

Team: a group of people constituting one side in a contest or competition; a group of people working together in a coordinated effort.
—WEBSTER'S DICTIONARY[1]

ONE OF THE FASCINATING EVENTS in sports is the Ryder Cup golf championship. Like the Davis Cup competition in tennis, the Ryder Cup pits the best golfers from one country in a patriotic duel with rival teams from other nations. Throughout my coaching career, I was always intrigued by the team dynamics of these Ryder competitions.

The first thing that always caught my attention was the caliber of competition. All competitors are typically top money winners or tour leaders in their respective countries. Second, the Ryder Cup isn't as financially lucrative as most tour events, so the players have little monetary incentive to compete. They could make *much* more money staying home, playing in any number of minor tour events or corporate-sponsored tournaments. Be that as it may, earning a spot on the Ryder team is far and away one of the most coveted, hotly-pursued honors in sports.

Why is this? Golfing is an *individual* sport. If you were to look at a personality profile of some of the best professional golfers, you'd find that they are "lone rangers" in the classic sense—solo artists who have learned to thrive in a high-stress, patently individualistic sport. Even though it's billed as a "gentleman's sport," many are cautious about passing on a strategic advantage to a foe. From the time they're small children taking lessons at the public links, up through the amateur ranks and into the pros, they've learned that they're dependent on no one but themselves for the day's score.

Accustomed to big crowds and paralyzing pressure, the very best players have ice water in their veins. They can drive a ball straight as an arrow through a fifteen-yard-wide fairway lined on both sides by a mob of spectators; they can pitch it from deep in the sand to the lip of the cup. They're that good. Yet place them on the Ryder Cup, a *team* consisting of their *peers*—with their country's honor at stake—and watch what happens to these seasoned veterans. Suddenly everything changes. The pressure goes through the roof. Each hole becomes a heart-stopping drama. Often wilting under the relentless intensity, tour champions choke and fade while unsung underdogs ride the adrenaline tide to heroic heights. Short chips and putts strike terror while seemingly impossible shots settle softly on the green or backspin to within inches of the flag.

In 1995, Curtis Strange did what many thought was impossible to let the Ryder Cup slip from America's grasp. A single par by Strange on any of the last three holes of the tournament would have won it for the United States. One single par. Pros make par in their sleep. Instead, Strange made three straight *bogeys* to seal the next-to-impossible defeat. An article in *Sports Illustrated* struggled to capture the near comic magnitude of the collapse: "It was Bill Buckner letting three straight balls go through his legs. It was Jackie Smith dropping three straight in the end zone. It was unthinkable, not possible. Yet, it happened."[2]

It simply proved that anything can happen in such an electric-charged team environment. Players who wouldn't nod to one another on tour now are seen cheering and back-slapping one another. Cool rivals are suddenly best pals. Why? Because there's something about being part of a *team* that draws this out of us. Players certainly enjoy the personal glory and pay-off of individual trophies, but the spirit and comradery of a team victory are impossible to match. No one wants to let their *teammates* down. The burden of coming up with their best performance for the *team* is what makes the Ryder Cup so much fun to watch. The team spirit elevates play to epic proportions.

Pat Riley, coach of the NBA's Miami Heat and former coach of the NBA champion Los Angeles Lakers, said, "Great teamwork is the only way to find our ultimate moments in life."[3] It didn't take winning four NBA titles for Riley to understand that belonging to a team spurs individuals to greater commitment and performance than they could ever achieve on their own. Human potential, set within the framework of a team, is somehow multiplied; individual power and effectiveness increases, concentration is heightened, the senses are amplified. The bottom line is this: "Team" brings out our best.

Understandably, and sadly, it's in the sports arena we're most likely to see this principle modeled. When Michael Jordon crawled from his sickbed to score thirty-eight points in a momentum-swinging Bulls' win over Utah in the 1997 NBA Finals, what kept him from collapsing when he could barely stand? "I didn't want to let my teammates down," he said without hesitation. Team does something to us. Participating in something greater than ourselves raises the stakes dramatically. I've seen it too many times: With the game on the line, seconds ticking down, the most unlikely candidates come through with lifetime performances. How do they do it? Like Mike, they don't want to let their teammates down.

My old boss Bo Schembechler, the great former football coach at the University of Michigan, spent his career convincing athletes of the virtues of *team* over *individual*. He describes a team as "a code of conduct and a job description for every single player. Everyone's role is to help the team. Nothing is more important than the *team*, the *team*, the *team*."

Nebraska coach Tom Osborne, who has the most wins of any active coach, and whose teams have won two national titles, noted this about his 1995 national championship squad: "This group illustrates how a *team* of athletes can accomplish much more than the separate members working individually. That's what many coaches call 'synergy.' The whole was truly greater than the sum of its parts. There was excellent individual talent, but it was their ability to pull together as a team that helped them perform at the highest level possible."[4]

We live in a culture that encourages independence and self-reliance, but the facts speak for themselves. Giving one's mind, talent, and energy to a team beats anything we can do by ourselves. "Two are better than one" (Ecclesiastes 4:9). Joining together with another multiplies our joy, brings out the best in us, raises our commitment level. But teams aren't just for sports. Far from it. The fact is, you, too, belong to a team—or *teams*. In your daily life, wherever you're linked with others in pursuit of a shared goal or belief, that's your team.

Our lives consist of a series of teams. For many it's marriage and family—for others it's associates at work or the men in your weekly Bible study. Maybe it's your local church, or your Neighborhood Watch, or even the Elks Club, or VFW. Perhaps it's the members of your community service club. When you come right down to it, it's almost impossible *not* to be part of some team or another. It's why so many are drawn to sports: We're all inclined toward teams.

So why don't we exercise the same team synergy, passion, and commitment on these real-life teams? Why is it that Ryder Cup golfers or Magic Johnson or Larry Bird can tap into this potent dynamic in the athletic arena, while the rest of us regard our teams with passive neglect or indifference? Shouldn't all of us, athletes or not, invest the same consuming passion in our families, partnerships, and worthy pursuits?

How much healthier would the average family be if each member exhibited the same focused spirit of teamwork, affirmation, and cooperation as golfers chasing a bronze-plated trophy? Wouldn't our homes be more loving and nurturing places? If we continually exhorted and supported our workmates as we do members of the company softball team, wouldn't our work places be more encouraging and productive environments? And our churches, special interest groups, and cherished friendships—wouldn't they each take on heightened significance and yield sweeter returns? If we viewed them all as crucial, high-stakes enterprises, worthy of our noblest effort and enduring loyalty, it's difficult to imagine how much richer our lives might be.

Whose Team Are You On?

Where does God fit into this equation? He fits in at the very foundation. He is the root and the cornerstone of every worthwhile endeavor, but even more of our key relationships. For no matter how successful a team may seem to be, in whatever context you choose, it's probably not performing up to standard. If God isn't involved in each of our teams as a full-fledged member, it's simply not performing anywhere near its potential. For without the Lord personally involved in every aspect of our lives as a fully-invested, wholehearted Partner, our most brilliantly inspired efforts will remain a hollow husk of what they might have been. When we invite God to participate in our lives, we have the supernatural power of Creation backing us up. God says to His people, "I will do whatever you ask in my name" (John 14:13).

Christian scholar L.T. Jeyachandran writes, "[Jesus Christ] defined all virtue only in terms of relationships. He always linked vertical relationship with God with horizontal relationship with fellow human beings. By putting the first commandment [Love the Lord your God. . . . Love your neighbor as yourself (Mark 12:30–31)] first, Jesus made it clear that we can selflessly love others only when our self is dealt with adequately by our relationship with God. At the same time, He also made it clear that our selfless love of others is the only demonstrable evidence that we truly love God."[5] In other words, before we can impart life to another, life must first be imparted to us. Before we can heal and fulfill our marriages, families, and friendships—our *teams*—we must first be healed and made whole. Nothing blossoms or grows into something meaningful or enduring until it has received God's empowering blessing. There simply is no thriving or true vitality apart from full-fledged membership on God's team; He is the very Source of wholeness and healing.

Jesus said, "I am the vine; you are the branches. If a man remains in me and I in him, he will bear much fruit; apart from me you can do nothing. If anyone does not remain in me, he is like a branch that is thrown away and withers" (John 15:5–6). The point cannot be overemphasized: If we are not first in vibrant relationship with God, we will never taste the full joy and sweetness of kinship with our wives, children, and other loved ones. Severed from the Vine, our once-promising future fades; the incomparable richness and potential of these incredible relationships will become as lifeless branches bound for the bonfire; our once-worthy passions will end in decay. What's more, on God's team there is no striving, worrying, or competing. Performance is not the measure of success. When we have done our best, God does the rest. Jesus says, "Apart from me you can do nothing" (John 15:5). Left on our own we may do what *appears* to be good, but what is genuinely, eternally *best* for our lives and those around us will forever escape our grasp.

Team Is God's Idea

It's not my aim to reduce one of life's most profound principles to a sports metaphor. Still, I don't think it's a stretch to say that *team* began with God. We're *naturally* drawn to teams. Something in all of us was meant to contribute to the greater good of a team. Look in the Bible—team is *everywhere*. "It is not good for the man to be alone" (Genesis 2:18) is the first team principle on record. It led to the sacred institution of marriage—the original team. "Two are better than one" (Ecclesiastes 4:9). "If one falls down, his friend can help him up" (Ecclesiastes 4:10). With few exceptions, as we study the Bible we see that God looks to the team to carry out His plans. The Bible is God's Play Book to instruct His people how to live, work, and minister together as a vital, empowered, efficient team.

In the Old Testament, a breakdown in team principles always invited disaster. God's protective covering vaporized whenever the Israelites compromised team goals by turning to idols, fraternizing with pagan nations, or busying themselves with worldly concerns. *Team* is God's idea. His eye is always on the quality and consistency of our teamwork. Frankly, it is why the church today remains weak and powerless—sectarian walls and cultural and racial disunity have destroyed this fragile team dynamic. His church is divided, competitive, and, therefore, neutralized.

In the Book of Exodus, as Israel was preparing to enter the Promised Land, God provided His people everything they needed to be a well-nourished, smooth-running, victorious team. The Israelites were to take the land as a united, God-fearing nation. But at the moment of truth, the team fell apart, torn by strife and dissension. The result? They were forced to wander forty years in the desert until every mutinous dissenter had perished. When Israel finally entered the Promised Land and found itself enjoying an unprecedented winning streak, it was only because the *team* was together in harmony, hitting on all cylinders. Today teamwork remains the guiding principle of the church; God's blessing is bestowed in fullness and power only when His people are truly together. Unity, harmony, and togetherness in the church equals courage, faith, miracles, and new believers.

Our Home Teams

So how are we to regard these rare jewels that comprise our inestimable "home teams?" What of these treasures from God that are our families? Are we really taking to heart our key roles as integral members? If not, something is horribly wrong. The evidence tells us that even Christians, whose relationship with God will one day be measured by the quality of the love, care, and intimacy cultivated among our precious loved ones, have neglected to courageously contend for the health, balance, and success of our closest kin.

In life as in sports, the teams that come closest to reaching their potential rely on the selfless, sold out, united effort of the whole team. No amount of individual talent or self-interest can compensate for a lack of teamwork. It's a principle that transcends ordinary human experience. At crunch time, when the heat is on, when fierce opposition and steady pressure would otherwise cause one to crumble, the individual draws strength and encouragement from his mates. It is exactly the same with our families, with our marriages. The strength of the whole is greater than that of its parts. Each member reaches his or her full potential by drawing deeply from the team's well of pooled resources, and by locking arms in a united front to meet the larger goal.

Please understand: Our marriages, families, and friendships are heavenly prizes whose health and vitality are worth our laying down our lives daily. Our marriages and family face potent opposition. In an age of plummeting morality and rampant godlessness, our wives, husbands, children, brothers and sisters, friends, and relatives are being beset by destructive influences at their points of greatest exposure. *These* are the flesh and blood ties that give meaning and depth to our lives. These are our true "home teams." Don't be misled—they require *greater* teamwork, energy, effort, and enthusiasm than anything we see so passionately celebrated in the sports arenas of our day. The fact remains: The health and success of *your* team depends on the quality and consistency of *your* contribution. It requires a long-term vision and specific steps to carry it out. The rewards are incomparable. And the stakes are higher than you can imagine.

Almost Too Late

I came to this sense of understanding almost too late in life. It took me too long to discover that, aside from coaching, I've been a member of *several* teams throughout my life, the most important one being my own family. More often than not, I either casually declined or blatantly ignored my role as a member of these teams. As a coach I poured out my very lifeblood to teach team principles and acquire a deeper understanding of what makes a championship-caliber team tick. Through rigorous study and an iron-man work ethic, I came to understand what it takes to meld a close-knit, unselfish team from a high-spirited group of individuals. More than most, I understood what it took to be a sold-out coach.

But as a man—a husband, father, and friend—I simply didn't pay much attention until it was almost too late. My own marriage started out sick and imbalanced because I didn't see my wife as my *true*, number one teammate, given to me by God as a precious gift to protect and shepherd. For years I permitted this crucial teammate—by God's own definition the most accurate reflection of my true love for Him—to lie dormant, without clear leadership or direction. I did not realize until much later that if my marriage wasn't healthy and blossoming, all my other teams, dreams, and successes were a house of cards, an illusion. By allowing myself from an early age to become focused almost exclusively on ideals and pursuits that competed with my true team, my heart became numb. My eyes became clouded to the urgent needs and subtle hopes of the team that needed me most of all.

What's worse, I cannot say that it ever even crossed my mind that I was supposed to let Lyndi be *my* teammate, to be *my* helpmate. I thought I knew what my role was, but I did not appreciate *her* value to the team, her talents, strength, and stamina—my incredible need for her. I missed out on so much because I did not enter our marriage seeing Lyndi as a teammate to listen to me, or as someone I could share my weaknesses with. My pride, my deep-seated, rugged individualism, got in the way of seeing what God intended for the marriage partnership—"I will make a helper suitable for him" (Genesis 2:18). It implies that I need help. It took me a long time to realize that.

Lyndi: A Member of the Team?

This concept of a man seeing his wife as a teammate is a recent revelation for Bill. You'd have to find another analogy to fit how he viewed our relationship during most of our thirty-four years of marriage. He may have seen me as a loyal cheerleader, which I was; or perhaps he saw himself as the coach and me as someone desperately trying to make his team but never quite making the cut; or perhaps I was a member of the team, but when it came to important plays I was left on the bench while Bill ventured into the fray alone.

This is not surprising. Men of my husband's generation were raised to believe that a man was expected *always* to do things right and have all the answers. A boy's working class upbringing in the 1950s left no room for tears, fears, or admitting that he needed help from a female. These were clear signs of weakness, of unmanly and unacceptable behavior that was "Sissy Award" material.

Likewise, it is not surprising that women of my generation did not consider themselves likely teammates with their husbands. We were raised to believe that a woman's role was to serve the man in her life, but never in terms of being an equal or a valued member of his team. We were raised to believe that whatever men do has value in life. A woman was supposed to find her value in subordinating her life to her husband's work, his dreams, his will. That was the unwritten law for a woman of my generation. To breech this unwritten law was to fail as a woman, a wife, and a mother.

Therefore, it's no wonder I saw myself much more suited to be Bill's cheerleader than his teammate.

However, I did long to experience the kind of synergy Bill described in this chapter. I wanted to help him—especially in his battle against alcohol. But, back then, we didn't conceive of ourselves as teammates. Over the years, I had grown resentful and bitter, not just over the drinking, but because I felt completely closed out of most of his life. I grew weak and fearful, then antagonistic and hostile. My reactions contributed to his closing me out, but, also, he didn't realize that God meant us to be teammates.

Bill believed his struggle against alcohol was his exclusively. It probably never entered his mind to share his pain or the intensity of his struggle with me. We were both Christians, but he didn't see me as a source of spiritual support; so he never asked me to pray for him or even with him so we could combat this stronghold of the enemy together.

We were fighting the same opponent, but not together. We battled the pain and consequences of his drinking independently, unaware that the other cared in any way. He was unaware of how much I wanted to help. I was unaware of how hard he was fighting to maintain his sobriety. The combination of his self-sufficiency and my animosity created a division in the ranks that blocked any hope of oneness in this battle, any hope of victory. That is, until God and Bill gave me a tiny way I could help, my chance to get in the game.

It happened on a Caribbean cruise. Each February from 1986 to 1995, we joined eighteen or twenty other coaches and their wives for a four-day holiday hosted by Nike. In 1990 it was a cruise. I cherished and looked forward to this trip each year with great anticipation. I would join the coaches' wives, the Nike wives, and some of the coaches during the day for shopping, sight seeing, or fun in the sun and lots of laughter. Most of the coaches—Bill included—played golf all day. Each evening there was a beautiful theme party with incredible food and lots of fun, planned activities. I prepared for months for those theme parties.

While we were on a cruise in February of 1990, we were finishing dinner while the other couples made plans for the evening. As they discussed the show with all the glitz and glitter and talented singers, I prayed Bill was listening. Finally, I couldn't contain myself and said, "Oh, honey! Let's go." Bill just smiled and gave me that look that says it's not for us. We were the ones who usually went back to our room when the fun started. If we did get to stay, Bill would talk football while I watched other couples laughing, dancing, and having so much fun. It hurt. I, too, wanted to have fun like that with my husband. This particular evening we left the table and headed back to our little cabin, while the other couples left to go have fun. I felt so down and disappointed.

I asked Bill again, "Honey, why can't we go?"

He looked at me seriously. "Lyndi, whenever I go into a room where people are drinking, I hear a certain buzz in the air. Whenever I hear that buzzing sound, it makes me weak. It makes me falter in my resolve not to drink."

That bit of information was exciting to me. I couldn't stop drinking for him, but I could help by not asking him to take me places that would lead him into temptation. This was a breakthrough for me. Not only could I now understand, but more importantly, I could be on the same side with Bill. Now *we* could choose wisely where not to go, instead of Bill choosing and me trying to get him to change his mind. We could enjoy our times at home together after declining such an invitation because we shared the same opponent and the same goal. I'd caught a glimpse of what it meant to be teammates.

At the time, my discovery didn't seem to make a major difference, but at least I wouldn't unwittingly work against Bill. However, in retrospect, I wonder if his allowing me to be on his team didn't have greater significance than we realized. From our wedding, until he accepted Christ in 1974, Bill had been drinking for twelve years. He felt guilty afterward, but he knew no victory. Once Bill accepted Christ as his Savior, *and Deliverer*, his battle changed dramatically. He had long periods of time between falls, going months without touching a drop. But once he took one drink, he was out of control again. God was giving him victory, little by little, but the battle was still hard fought and he was still fighting alone. This went on for sixteen years, from 1974 until July of 1990.

I honestly don't know how much having me on his team gave Bill a source of strength that kept him from being overpowered by alcohol. But, in fact, Bill took his last drink just five months after he allowed me to play a tiny part on his team in this fight.

Bill mentioned Ecclesiastes 4:9–10: "Two are better than one, because they have a good return for their work: If one falls down, his friend can help him up. But pity the man who falls and has no one to help him up!" This passage goes on to say, "Though one may be overpowered, two can defend themselves. A cord of three strands is not quickly broken" (Ecclesiastes 4:12). Could it be that this describes the synergy of a husband, wife, and God working together? A three-strand cord has multiplied strength over a single- or double-strand cord. So, too, will husband, wife, and God—working together on the same team—create a strength unknown to a man who battles alone, or even with just God on his side.

Men, I appeal to you to consider your wife as your teammate, not just as someone to protect, direct, and lead, but also as someone who can help you. Didn't God give Eve to Adam as a helpmate in Genesis 2:18? This implies that God created men with a need for their wife's help. And God uniquely designed women to be able to help their husbands. If you leave your wife on the sidelines, you may struggle longer than necessary.

You may have to overcome your pride to treat your wife as a valuable teammate, especially if you and your wife are of the same generation as Bill and I. However, if you must humble yourself to do so, you can take heart in knowing that God gives grace to the humble. Think of any team sport you like; a player whose pride keeps him from handing off to his teammates will cause the team to lose. The same holds true in marriage.

Bill also said to see your Christian brothers as members of another team. This is certainly true, as attested to by the upsurge of participation in small groups where men encourage each other and hold each other accountable. However, be careful not to turn to your support group *instead* of turning to your wife. Make her your first line of support, then she won't resent your relationship with the guys in your support group.

To wives, I say, respect your husband. But also respect the role God has given you to play on his team. While you cannot force yourself onto the field of his life, you can pray and live as one who is on his side against the world, the flesh, and the devil, instead of acting as if you are his opponent.

I must admit that while the Lord is showing Bill that I am his teammate, we're still growing into this reality, little by little. I think it's hard for Bill to see himself as anything other than the coach. To be teammates means he has to see himself as a player on the field with me, not the coach pacing the sidelines wearing the whistle. The more he lets the Lord wear the whistle, and sits down on the bench of life beside me, the more we will go out together and win.

Chapter 20
Priceless Testimonies

SIX YEARS AGO, A YOUNG WOMAN we'll call Mary called home to tell her parents that she had met a young man at college. "Mom, Dad, I've met someone," she began. "He's really great, and I'd really love you to meet him."

Mary's mother expressed excitement for her daughter, but her father was reserved. His first question was, "Is he a Christian?" As if expecting the question, Mary timidly replied, "No, Dad, he isn't. But he's wonderful—very kind and gentle and . . . and I love him. Can't I please bring him home for you to meet? I know you'll like him."

Her father's mind was made up: "We've been through this before," he said. "We're not going to condone your dating a non-Christian. Don't bring him home." Mary hung up the phone in tears.

She and her boyfriend were married some months later. Her parents did not attend the wedding. The daughter and parents did not speak again for a long time. It broke Mary's heart to think her father had rejected her and her husband. She kept praying for her husband's salvation and a joyful reconciliation with her parents. Six years passed.

In May 1996, Promise Keepers held a conference in San Diego.

At the invitation of some of his friends, Mary's husband reluctantly agreed to attend. On the first night of the conference an evangelistic message was given and an invitation made for men to receive Jesus Christ as Lord and Savior. Among the hundreds of men who streamed from their seats at Jack Murphy Stadium was Mary's husband. Praying in unison with all the others, he surrendered his life to Jesus that night. An evangelistic counselor came to stand by him, guiding him through the principles of the gospel, answering questions. Afterward, he asked, "Do you have any questions?"

The young man hesitated, then finally confided, "Yes, I guess I do. . . . This is the biggest moment of my life. I can't tell you how good it feels, but . . . there's something that worries me." "What is it?" the counselor asked. "Well, my wife is a Christian," he explained. "We were married six years ago without her parents' consent. I've never met her mother and father. Now that I've accepted the Lord, I want to meet them. I've wanted to for so long. But I have to admit, I'm kind of nervous about how they'll receive me."

The counselor stared at the young man. "What's your wife's name?" he asked. "Her maiden name is Mary Thompson." The counselor was silent. All expression drained from his face. Seconds later he broke into a broad grin and said softly, "That's my daughter." The two stood staring at each other, stunned. Then the tears came. The father and his new son-in-law embraced, a living portrait of God's handiwork on the floor of the stadium.

How I would have loved to have seen that family reunion. Can you imagine Mary's joyous smile when she saw the two most important men in her life standing together not only as awkward in-laws, but as new brothers in Christ?

A Man's Man Is a Godly Man

In seven short years, Promise Keepers has been blessed beyond compare, but has also weathered its share of storms. It has taken some shots from some very obvious sources, but also from some very unexpected ones. Yet whenever anybody points a critical finger at Promise Keepers, I always refer them to the testimonies. "Thus, by their fruit you will recognize them" (Matthew 7:20). In moments of uncertainty, or when personal doubts arise, I find strength and inspiration in the testimonies. "A good tree cannot bear bad fruit, and a bad tree cannot bear good fruit" (Matthew 7:18).

Since Promise Keepers' inaugural conference in July 1991, it would be impossible to count all of the testimonies from women just like Mary. At our Denver headquarters are boxes stuffed with literally thousands of letters detailing every imaginable type of healing—from marriages brought back from the brink, to father and son reunions, to testimonies of men freed from lifelong addiction to alcohol and drugs, or from bondages to pornography, lust, or extramarital affairs. The pattern is almost always the same. Most relate somehow to a man falling under heavy conviction at a Promise Keepers conference, then—in weeks and months to follow—being supernaturally transformed by the sovereign hand of Jesus.

And there is no shortage of testimonies chronicling instances in which a dead or slumbering church was jolted awake and revitalized by the prayers and good works of men returning from a conference—or of pastors rescued from burnout, renewed in their spirits and re-charged in their calling in the aftermath of a stadium event. God alone knows how many spiritual and cultural walls of mistrust and division have crumbled inside a football stadium as a result of God's easing—sometimes even erasing—long-held prejudices between men of various colors, backgrounds, and denominations. These are the testimonies. They are the backbone of the ministry, the evidence of God's stern, tender heart for the men and families of this nation.

Undeniable Irony

No one appreciates more than I the irony—the absurdity, really—of how God suddenly takes a man with so much baggage and thrusts him to the forefront of a national ministry spotlighting the very issues I was wrestling with. It's a mystery: a college football coach fighting to achieve balance in his own life, unexpectedly blessed by God with a vision to fill stadiums with men who love Jesus Christ. I'd always believed that if you brought men together in great numbers to celebrate and exalt the Name of Jesus there would be a tremendous outpouring of God's power. But I had no idea. To actually stand before thousands of men, calling them to raise the standard of godliness in their lives and take seriously their all-important ministry to family, is something I was not particularly qualified to do, and would have never imagined.

I certainly did not foresee the cultural phenomenon that has resulted. But today there can be little doubt that God has used Promise Keepers to help redefine the term *masculinity*—a man's man is a *godly* man—and foster a long-overdue role reversal among the sexes, whereby *men* are now beginning to assume greater responsibility for spiritual and servant-hearted leadership in the home.

The International Coordinator of the Rutherford Institute, Pedro C. Moreno, poignantly captured this radical new dynamic among men in a recent letter to Promise Keepers. He said, "America need not fear. Women need not fear. Politicians need not fear. The fact that thousands upon thousands of men are getting serious about their manhood is, if anything, a positive development. I have found I am at the height of my manhood when changing my children's diapers. I am at the height of my manhood when helping my wife with the dishes. I proudly bear the marks of fatherhood—the drool left on my shirt by my six-month-old son. I feel the most 'macho' by being faithful to my wife and making her feel secure and appreciated."

David Hansel of the Word of Life Church in Iowa puts it more bluntly: "Some guys are wimps. A wimp is a guy who doesn't take responsibility to be a good husband and father." By this definition, I have been a wimp most of my life. So for God to involve me in

His project is truly using the foolish things of the world to confound the wise.

How Did We Get Here?

So how did we get here? Who does God use to effect such an unlikely paradigm shift in male notions of masculinity? To a large extent, He has assembled an incredibly anointed and gifted spiritual SWAT team of speakers to inject truth into the hearts of men at Promise Keepers conferences—teachers, evangelists, writers, and pastors who have walked humbly with their God and fulfilled their promises to their own families. God chose these men and equipped them to communicate long-neglected biblical principles necessary to point a searching generation back to its Christian roots.

In the process, God pointed us back to the true litmus test of our spiritual temperature: the health, vitality, and godliness of our relationships—God to man, husband to wife, father to children, mother to children, sister to sister and brother to brother—spanning the rocky terrain of race, culture, and denomination.

Among Promise Keepers' staff, it has become almost an inside joke that our own efforts have had little to do with the impact of the ministry. Anyone familiar with the organization would quickly agree. *Only* God could raise up the wellspring of momentum from such a tiny, disorganized beginning and sustain it through subsequent years of constant chaos and human error. But without a mostly anonymous network of faithful, determined supporters and volunteers working behind the scenes, not to mention an incredibly committed and long-suffering national staff, it wouldn't have happened. For my part, prior to heeding God's prompting and coming on as CEO in 1996, I've had a comparatively small role throughout. But like most, to have had *any* role humbles and overwhelms me.

Needless to say, beyond the original vision of seeing men coming together *en masse* to celebrate Christ, I was much like any other man drawn to a Promise Keepers conference. I longed to go deeper spiritually, but was far too busy and distracted by career goals to make the leap. I wanted to do right by my family and cried out for balance, but was caught up in a system that continually told me my self-worth was measured by job performance. It is only on my knees, through many trials and tears, that I have come to realize God's infinite forbearance in using me—the "least of the saints." It wasn't as if I were ready or prepared for any of it. I was just struggling along, doing my best, missing the mark in critical ways, when suddenly I was being used in a move of God that has dwarfed anything coaching ever offered.

People undoubtedly want answers—"Why *you*?"—but I have none. Having done nothing more than posture myself as a child and pray, "Here am I. Send me!" God did! There is no other rational explanation—with all of my public gaffs and hidden warts, I was suddenly gaining recognition as a Christian leader, asked to speak out on a range of topics from abortion to homosexuality.

I was, and remain, a man who loves Jesus. I have been gifted with an ability to lead men. I am not ashamed of His gospel. To the best of my ability, usually under extreme duress, I tried to say yes when God spoke at key points along the path. I trust in the power of prayer. I do not shy away from public scorn when Jesus' name is at stake. End of story. There are many with much richer gifts in each of these areas. There are spiritual gifts I haven't even asked for.

Interestingly, I can see how God lifted me to an unmerited position of national prominence in sports, *first*, in order to provide the public platform to launch Promise Keepers. God's thoughts are not man's thoughts, and His ways are not our ways—and no man could have hatched such a scheme and seen it fly. I've always said, "I am an ordinary man with an extraordinary God." By using me, He chose a man with whom any struggling person can identify, but who also steadfastly believes "I can do everything through him

[Christ] who gives me strength" (Philippians 4:13). But I've only recently come to understand the gravity of the stakes.

Heady Early Days

After that spring day in 1990, when my friend Dave Wardell and I shared our hearts about men's ministry on a long drive to Pueblo, I was caught up in a swirl of anticipation. As we began praying about it and networking among friends, businessmen, and various Christian associates, a picture began to emerge. "What is God up to?" we began to ask excitedly. Before long, seventy-two of us were praying for God's direction for a germinal idea called Promise Keepers. We began working toward a men's conference to be held at the end of July 1991 on the CU campus.

We chose July because it was the only vacation month for CU's football staff. Then I would be back in full swing at work, preparing as our players began reporting for preseason camp. A date was set—July 31. A few weeks before the conference, a carload of us embarked on a statewide road trip to drum up enthusiasm. We stopped at churches across Colorado, dropped off flyers, and spoke to pastors, inviting them to bring their men to Boulder. It was a blast. We could feel the enthusiasm building. We conducted radio interviews along the way and occasionally stood before a gathering to spin our vision, calling men who love Jesus Christ to stand up and be counted.

"The decade of the 90s is going to be a time of revival," I said. "But if things are going to change, it's got to come through husbands and fathers." I can still see the men fidgeting in their chairs. "The church and the home no longer have any influence," I continued, "so an entire generation of young people are getting their advice from their peers. They no longer go home because there's no longer trust—there have been too many broken promises.

"We want to challenge the men of God to provide an alternative," I pressed on. "Almighty God is returning the fathers' hearts to the children and the children's hearts to the fathers. When men come together, there's tremendous power in that. By the year 2000, Christian men across the nation are going to have a booming voice." It was right up my alley—a real grass roots recruiting campaign.

Colorado and surrounding states responded by sending forty-two hundred men to the CU Events Center on July 31, 1991. This first-ever Promise Keepers conference is still remembered affectionately by most everyone who attended. Compared to packed stadiums of between forty and seventy thousand men, that intimate setting seems almost a footnote to what God was about to stir up. Still, it was the modest seed from which Promise Keepers sprang. It was the small beginning. (Frankly, at the time, gathering four thousand men together for any kind of Christian function was huge.)

I still recall the groundbreaking messages by speakers like Gary Smalley, who challenged men to go home and "super honor your wives." Or Gary Oliver, who dismantled the macho myth—"cardboard Goliaths," he called us—vividly detailing the deepening spiritual crisis of the modern male.

That conference laid the groundwork for Promise Keepers' men's small group ministry. An unpolished platform skit demonstrated the basic model still used to graft men into groups for weekly prayer, Bible study, and mutual encouragement within the context of the local church. The idea being that, over time, men will begin to break through walls of isolation that make them easy prey to temptation, and overcome shallowness, to begin holding one another accountable to higher standards of personal purity, integrity, and godliness. The value and success of these groups is uniformly acknowledged, and well-documented, but it continues to be among the most difficult things to get men to actually do. It's just a fact: Men stubbornly resist committing to anything deeper than the usual news, weather, and sports as it relates to other men.

At the end of that 1991 conference, I brought Lyndi, Kristy, and Marc up on the stage to demonstrate something I'd been doing for years: praying God's health, power, and blessing over my family, asking the Lord to draw out the treasure in each of them and to bring my children a godly husband or wife. As I prayed for God's true joy and purpose to bathe Lyndi, the audience was deeply receptive, breaking into sincere applause. It was fascinating to observe. Something that clearly felt so right to so many was a completely foreign concept to the men in that hall. Seven years later, untold tens of thousands of men are quite comfortable praying God's daily blessing over their families.

Chapter 21
The Giant of Racism

THAT FIRST BOULDER CONFERENCE helped identify a disturbing issue that would become a prominent ministry goal of Promise Keepers. Toward the end of that program, as I casually gazed out in amazement on the crowd, my eye caught something. It sent a chill down my spine. The crowd was almost entirely white. I knew the Holy Spirit was prompting me. As we were about to close in prayer, I walked back up on the stage with a simple word of caution, one that would drastically alter my own life. If each man in the arena brought twelve friends the following summer, we said, we'd have fifty thousand men. "Men," I said, "next year at Folsom Stadium we expect a sellout. But I believe that if we fail to gather a fair representation of *all* of God's people, God will not join us."

The elated crowd left on a wave of exhilaration that would only be multiplied in years to come. But my last remarks on the racial issue had clearly hit a raw nerve, igniting a minor firestorm of hate mail and caustic letters, chastising me, saying, "How dare you imply that in a stadium filled with men glorifying Jesus Christ, God won't be there." Others stated angrily, "God did not state in Scriptures, 'Go ye therefore and eradicate racism.' He said, 'Go preach the gospel to all nations.'"

Many quoted the Scripture where Jesus says, "For where two or three come together in my name, there am I with them" (Matthew 18:20) to debunk my exhortation. And I understood their point. But what it really gave me was a first glimpse of the seething *giant* of racism lurking within the fabric of the Christian church.

I never backed off my original statement. As I have since learned, Matthew 18:20 probes deeper into the heart and the character of His church than most want to believe. For I believe that in order for God to bless His people with a true measure of fullness of power and blessing, He requires more than mere proximity, numbers, and verbal assent. God's commands always convict; they expose our true condition. God knows it's easy enough for His people to *say* they agree when they gather in Christ's name. But His gaze is all-discerning. It knows whether or not His children are truly joined in wholehearted purity and oneness of spirit; if we are bonded at heart, in undisturbed harmony, in seamless unity; if we are truly humbled, broken, and contrite.

God knows it when we are authentically "together," or when we're simply paying lip-service. He knows when we are truly of one accord by how easily we defer to one another with servants' hearts and count others as better than ourselves. I venture a guess that when *those* conditions are in proper place, we have full right to expect God to come and dwell amongst us in all His unfathomable abundance and bless the prayers of His chastened saints.

I therefore make no apologies for concluding that, in a huge setting like we see at any Promise Keepers conference, God's heart is for the full complement of His people to be gathered together in His name, represented in all the incalculably rich, heavenly splendor of racial and cultural diversity.

Where could it be more clear than in Colossians 3:11: "Here there is no Greek or Jew, circumcised or uncircumcised, barbarian, Scythian, slave or free, but Christ is all, and is in all."

As His church, we're instructed to know and love all who call upon Jesus' name, and so clothe ourselves with "compassion, kindness, humility, gentleness and patience. Bear with each other and forgive whatever grievances you may have against one another. Forgive as the Lord forgave you. And over all these virtues put on love, which binds them all together in perfect unity" (Colossians 3:12–14).

Please, show me where these principles are being put into practice, and I'll show you a people enjoying God's illustriously sweet, transforming presence.

A Hard Teaching

Shortly after Promise Keepers' first stadium conference of twenty-two thousand men in 1992—again, a mostly white audience—a much heavier burden for this racial issue fell upon me. I had begun to see many of the subtle ways our culture inflicts pain, shame, and lack of opportunity on the minority communities in our midst. And it horrified me to see this dynamic thriving in the church as well.

With the help of Christian broadcaster James Dobson, I began scheduling speaking engagements at churches across the country, delivering a controversial message on racial reconciliation. I'd show up to churches filled with men eager to hear about the marvelous move of God called Promise Keepers—and I'd begin to share. I spoke from my experience as a football coach, recognizing in my players' faces a conditioned resignation toward cultural injustice; I tried to explain how a subtle spirit of white superiority has unwittingly alienated and wounded our brothers and sisters within the church, and how the ten o'clock hour on Sunday morning is the country's most segregated hour of the week.

"My heart is broken for why I am standing here today," I cried out. "The church is standing on the shore while the tide is taking our brothers and sisters of color out to sea. We must get in touch with reality. We have oppressed men and women of color. We will not have revival until we have reconciliation."

Drawing from Scripture I tried to show how God expects the stronger to care for the weaker; how we must shake off the dust of complacency to pursue intentional relationships with our precious brothers and sisters. I even demonstrated biblically where God lifted up an ambassador of reconciliation in King David, who assumed generational responsibility for crimes and injustices committed against the Gibeonites that he did not personally commit (see 2 Samuel 21).

But always when I finished there was no response—nothing. No applause. No smiles. Everyone instead looked crestfallen. In city after city, in church after church, it was the same story—wild enthusiasm while I was being introduced, followed by a morgue-like chill as I stepped away from the microphone. It was as if God had commissioned me to single-handedly burst everyone's bubble. I repeatedly returned to my prayer room shaken and dejected. "Am I hearing You, Lord?" I asked. "Is this really the message You want me to share?" And every time He would impress on me, "Just be faithful. Just be obedient."

As my speaking tour came to a close, I had an engagement at a church in Portland, Oregon. My message ended to the usual wall of silence. Yet before I could leave the podium, a black speaker at the back of the stage stood up. I paused as he began to walk toward me. As he got closer, I could see tears in his eyes. He approached the podium and stood there for what seemed like minutes, trying to gather himself. After a long delay, in a broken voice, he finally said, "I never thought . . . that in my lifetime . . . I'd ever hear a white man say . . . what this man has said." He paused to compose himself. The church was stone silent. In a tone that broke my heart, he concluded: "Maybe there is hope."

Maybe there is hope. Those were the words I'd waited to hear. They validated me, confirming that what I'd been saying was truly from God's heart.

To this day, the racial message remains a highly-charged element of Promise Keepers' ministry. Recent correspondence told us that, of the 1996 conference participants who had a complaint, nearly 40 percent reacted negatively to the reconciliation theme. I personally believe it was a major factor in the significant fall-off in P.K.'s 1997 attendance—it is simply a hard teaching for many. But many in Jesus' day also turned back from His "hard teaching" and followed Him no more (John 6:66). In all actuality, I suspect that much of the criticism leveled at Promise Keepers from within the Christian community—typically cloaked in assorted, usually untested claims that we're an ecumenical movement, or that we preach a gospel palatable to Mormons or fringe cults—has as its true root a deep-seated cultural resistance to the message on reconciliation. It simply tells me we're on the right track. If God be with us, who can be against us.

In the past two years, I have held meetings with ethnic pastors in over sixty U.S. cities. Everywhere I go, pastors of color are profoundly encouraged, eagerly waiting to see good intentions put into action, while some among the white clergy remain aloof. It's such a simple message: We are all one in Christ and should treat one another as such. Even within Promise Keepers there has been pressure to de-emphasize or soften the racial message. But we hold firm. We press on, taking our cue from ethnic brothers and sisters who, for the first time, are expressing hope of seeing these racial walls fall once and for all.

Today, at most any stadium event, whenever we challenge men to confess and repent for prejudicial beliefs and behaviors or to embrace a brother of a different hue, the Holy Spirit's healing touch resonates so sweetly through the stands. The outpouring of emotion, weeping, and joyful release is unlike anything we've ever witnessed. We continue to hear reports of Anglos, Hispanics, African Americans, Asians, and Native Americans approaching one another and finding themselves unexpectedly enriched by new long-lasting friendships. I have new hope that God will continue to stir the hearts and open the eyes of His people to this probable prerequisite to true revival. Every day, I continue to cry out that by the year 2000 racism within the church will have been eradicated.

Chapter 22
Promise Keepers: Memories to Last a Lifetime

SO MANY UNBELIEVABLE MEMORIES, so many highlights. Several books could be filled with the sights, sounds, drama, and mystery of each heartwarming, life-changing story that has unfolded in the past seven years. They just keep coming. I remember the cool July night when, from a single flame, Folsom Stadium was set ablaze with more than fifty thousand candles; it was an unforgettable visual covenant: God had commissioned an army of men to keep their promises to God and family. I recall the sun-drenched Saturday morning when Chuck Swindoll roared into Folsom Stadium on a Harley Davidson motorcycle, accompanied by a squadron of leather-clad Christian bikers; or the conference in Denton, Texas, when a near cyclone ripped through Fouts Field.

I could speak of the realization of a personal dream, when nearly forty thousand pastors from all over the world and from every conceivable ethnic, racial, and cultural group, gathered in Atlanta for the three-day 1996 Men's Clergy Conference. To open that historic event, a contingent of Native American pastors representing over seventy tribes marched 168 miles from Cherokee, North Carolina, to the Georgia Dome to triumphantly declare: "We're proud to be Native Americans by race, but we're more proud to be Christians saved by grace. We are *all* precious in His sight."

The same spirit of forgiveness and reconciliation saw pastors from every denominational affiliation and para-church ministry—mainline, Pentecostal, Southern Baptist, non-denominational, and Catholic, inner city, rural, and suburban—erupting in praise of their mutual Savior and rallying around the event's unapologetic theme of biblical reconciliation. Following a time of corporate repentance for racial and sectarian divisiveness near the program's end, God unleashed His Spirit on the Georgia Dome, assaulting spiritual walls that had for generations divided and neutralized the church. Two years later we're still receiving reports from pastors, some of whom have walked faithfully with the Lord for thirty or forty years, expressing their gratitude, praising God for how the clergy conference revolutionized their ministry or their church.

Oh, what incredible memories. They're etched in my heart; they remind me how small and frail are man's best efforts when matched against God's inexhaustible power. Promise Keepers' unprecedented growth alone serves notice to the fact. In 1993, the movement's third year, more than fifty thousand men sold out Folsom Stadium. In 1994, Promise Keepers expanded to seven cities across the United States, and attendance grew to more than two hundred seventy thousand men; in 1995, thirteen conferences from Los Angeles to Boise to St. Petersburg to Minneapolis attracted more than six hundred thousand men. In 1996 and 1997, Promise Keepers held approximately forty conferences that drew over 1.5 million men.

Growth is wonderful. And we have every reason to believe God is poising us to go all over the globe. But in all frankness, if Promise Keepers had begun and ended with forty-two hundred men in a Boulder basketball arena, that one memory would have lasted me a lifetime. No man deserves to have witnessed, much less be involved in, all that we've seen God do through seven seismic years.

Looking back, I can clearly see that, if nothing else, the Lord raised up Promise Keepers to be a catalytic force to bring people together who have been stiff-necked and hard-hearted toward each other. I've seen it too many times at conferences—the Holy Spirit sovereignly, supernaturally, softens a person's heart, exposes his prejudices, convicts him of sin, frees him of emotional and physical strongholds, and sends him home with a completely different spirit.

The "Man on a Mission"

It almost goes without saying—Promise Keepers has also been a convicting, catalytic force in my own life. Yet through most of its rapid-fire history, I was the same guy I'd always been: the "man on a mission," charging ahead, *all or nothing*, eyes on the prize at breakneck speed. One would think that being around all the high-minded messages and spiritual energy would transform me by osmosis. But much of the time I was too busy and preoccupied to grant God the deep, penetrating access to my heart that He requires.

From the beginning, I'd dive directly from an all-consuming football season straight into Promise Keepers' busy summer schedule, hardly stopping to take a breath. I was loving it. Steering a nationally-ranked football program *and* calling men to godliness through an upstart Christian men's ministry were, to me, incomparably significant, worthwhile callings. Each required total focus, commitment, and dedication. For a time, the sheer energy and excitement of these dueling endeavors camouflaged a thinly-veiled underlying hypocrisy. It may sound unbelievable, but while Promise Keepers was spiritually inspiring to my core, my hard-charging approach to the ministry was distracting me from being, in the truest sense, a promise keeper to my own family.

It came into clear focus for me at a Promise Keepers conference in Dallas Stadium some years back. I sat in the press box with noted Christian speaker and educator Howard Hendricks. On the platform, Dennis Rainey, president of Family Life Today, delivered a heart-wrenching message on marriage. At the end, Rainey asked each man in the stadium to grade his marriage on a scale of one to ten; and then, "Choose the number you think your wife would give your marriage, and write it down."

Rainey went on to say that women instinctively know how to make a good marriage, that they're able to look at another couple's marriage and automatically know if it's a good one. "Whatever your *wife* gives your marriage," he concluded, "that's the more accurate grade."

He instructed everyone to huddle in small groups to discuss their scores. Howard and I stood in a small circle with two other men in the pressbox and shared our grades. Howard went first. Without a second's hesitation he said, "My marriage is a ten, and my wife would also give it a ten." The other two guys gave their scores, but when it came time for me to share, I can only remember feeling humiliated, ashamed. With deep embarrassment I—Promise Keepers *founder*—gave my marriage a seven. My eye's teared up and my voice cracked. I said Lyndi would probably give it a six. Under my breath, I vowed I would put up higher numbers next time.

It was a typical coach's response: Rather than let God minister to the pain I felt, I vowed to put up a better score next time—to *perform* better. I didn't know what that pledge would ultimately involve. It was clear that something had to give. My present approach wasn't working. I didn't want to keep compromising those relationships I kept saying were all-important to me. I longed to be able to say with a clear conscience: "Therefore I do not run like a man running aimlessly; I do not fight like a man beating the air. No, I beat my body and make it my slave so that after I have preached to others, *I myself will not be disqualified for the prize*" (1 Corinthians 9:26–27, emphasis added). I knew that if left unchecked, silent contradictions and mute concessions would potentially cancel a powerful testimony to millions of men.

I might have known God would call me out in a way that would shake our lives. It was time. A violent showdown was long overdue, pitting the oft-repeated intent of my heart against the louder proof, the inarguable consequences, of my actions. I was about to turn a page in life. I would find myself standing on shaky turf, questioning everything I thought I was, or might one day become. There was no turning back. I was entering a realm that would force me to choose between those values I knew were worth fighting for—and the dreams I would have to let go—as I entered the home stretch of my life.

Lyndi: Reflections on Promise Keepers

When Bill wanted to pray over Kristy, Marc, and me at the first PK rally, I was excited! I hustled the kids along so we could arrive very early. Waiting off stage, we took in the excitement of the men present. The singers were on stage, and the arena was filled with the overpowering sound of men worshiping God in song. It's absolutely awesome to hear men singing to the Lord in that way! I teared up at the beautiful sound. As Bill brought us up on stage and seated us, the men seemed to be mesmerized. Bill knelt before our daughter Kristy first, then our son Marc, then me. He prayed love and protection over each of us. I was so caught up in listening to Bill I didn't see anyone else.

When he finished, I felt moved to speak to the men. I walked over, grabbed the microphone, and told them what Bill's act of praying over me and our children meant to me. I explained how his prayers peeled away past hurts and began a healing process in our marriage. I encouraged each of them to pray with and over their wives and children, then to watch what God would do. As I turned to walk away, I realized how impulsive I had been. I felt embarrassed that I'd been so bold as to take the microphone and speak when it wasn't planned. I looked at Bill; his smile and big warm hug as he escorted us from the stage told me that he liked what I had said.

When Promise Keepers was in its early stages, I experienced tremendous hope mixed with relief. I heard my husband saying things like, "Men have abdicated their roles as husbands and fathers for far too long. Women have carried the burden of relationship and family without their support for too long. It's time for men to return to their God, their wives, and their children and accept the call God has on every man's life. It's time men learned how to be true followers of Jesus Christ, faithful husbands and fathers." This was beautiful music to my ears! In my soul, I sighed a big sigh of relief. *Finally!*

My favorite teaching was on the subject of servant-leadership. PK taught, "A leader is a servant who enables those he leads to be all they can be." Oh, joy indescribable! At home, Bill joined in on the family fun and responsibilities more than he ever had before. Our quiet time was spent together, sharing discoveries in God's Word and enjoying the freshness of it all. That's when PK was still small. As it grew, life changed for us.

Spiritually, Bill was again growing in leaps and bounds. He had taken on an authority and strength that I had never seen in him before. His career was at the top. The birth of Promise Keepers brought a new excitement and spiritual dimension to Bill. His time with the Lord was deeper and richer. I loved what Promise Keepers was doing for men across the country; I loved that the Lord was using Bill in His mighty move. But as PK grew, every ounce of Bill's spare time was spent on this additional love in his life. Coaching demanded him to keep a grueling schedule ten months of the year. Then PK took up his two months "off." Something had to give, and all he had to offer was the time he spent with me and our family. Instead of his time just being consumed during football season, it was consumed all year long—in the name of an organization that promotes being a godly husband and father. The irony was too much for me!

I grew to resent PK as just another thief that stole my husband away from me. I still believed in what God was doing through Promise Keepers, I just wanted to see the fruits of it in our relationship too. We had moved into a new home, with a prayer room where I had hoped we would kneel together each morning, but we no longer shared our quiet times together. Alone again! I was back to hoping for the crumbs of my husband's time and attention—after his involvement in PK took another major bite. The hope I had felt so keenly at the start of PK proved fleeting. It was swept away in a flurry of good activities for a worthy cause. And yet, I felt guilty for resenting something that was true and good. I became disillusioned, but this turned out to be good. Bill came to see that the distance between his beliefs and his behavior could not be spanned by mere strength of will and human effort—no matter how sold out he was. Oswald Chambers addresses this issue when he writes:

> Disillusionment means having no more misconceptions, false impressions, and false judgments in life; it means being free from these deceptions. However, though no longer deceived, our experience of disillusionment may actually leave us cynical and overly critical in our judgment of others. But the disillusionment that comes from God brings us to the point where we see people as they really are, yet without any cynicism or any stinging and bitter criticism. Many of the things in life that inflict the greatest injury, grief, or pain, stem from the fact that we suffer from illusions.

He goes on:

> Refusing to be disillusioned is the cause of much of the suffering of human life. And this is how that suffering happens—if we love someone, . . . we demand total perfection and righteousness from that person, and when we do not get it we become cruel and vindictive; yet we are demanding of a human being something which he or she cannot possibly give. There is only one Being who can completely satisfy to the absolute depth of the hurting human heart, and that is the Lord Jesus Christ.[1]

I must confess, I did become cynical, critical, and bitter for a while. But, by the grace of God, I did not stay there. The Lord showed me that it was too much to expect total perfection and righteousness from Bill, even though he was holding up the standard of godly perfection and righteousness for others. The Lord Jesus Christ is the only one who can keep all the seven promises of a Promise Keeper. And He is willing to do so *in and through* any man who realizes and confesses that he can't do it on his own.

This is not to say that Bill's faith was dead because it was without works for a season. His faith in God's standard for godly manhood was right and good. Bill was discovering what the apostle Paul wrestled with himself in Romans chapter 7 when he wrote,

> So then, the law is holy, and the commandment is holy, righteous and good. . . . And if I do what I do not want to do, I agree that the law is good. As it is, it is no longer I myself who do it, but it is sin living in me. I know that nothing good lives in me, that is, in my sinful nature. For I have the desire to do what is good, but I cannot carry it out. . . . What a wretched man I am! Who will rescue me from this body of death? Thanks be to God—through Jesus Christ our Lord!
>
> —Romans 7:12, 16–18, 24–25

If the apostle Paul himself could not live up to the standards of righteousness he knew were right by mere strength of will, why should we expect ourselves or our husbands to do so? Unless it's done in the same way Paul did it—through Jesus Christ our Lord! This realization frees me from my cynicism. As Bill came to this realization his own way, he was able to confess his inability to do the good he desired to do. But, like Paul, he discovered he could do it through Jesus Christ our Lord.

I've heard it said that men who call themselves "promise keepers" are not speaking the truth, because no man keeps all seven promises of a promise keeper all the time. I think this misses the point. The seven promises present God's ideal of what He intends to transform men to become by the power of the Holy Spirit. Just because this transformation may be in its early stages is no reason not to agree with God's ideal. God told Abram to call himself Abraham, which meant "father of many nations." Was this a lie or an act of faith? In reality—at that time—Abram was not a father of many nations. He was an elderly fellow who had a son by his wife's maid. Calling himself Abraham wasn't a lie; it was an affirmation of the promise God had given him of what he *would become* by the work God intended to do in his life. It was an act of faith, agreeing with God even though his life did not *yet* bear out what God promised to do.

Men, go ahead and call yourself a promise keeper, even though you will fall short of that ideal repeatedly. God does intend to transform you into a real promise keeper. When you fall short, call out, "Oh, wretched man that I am!" but don't stop there; ask Jesus to free you from your inability to keep the promises you sincerely desire to keep. That's what Bill does; and the Lord continually answers those prayers.

Women, if your husband attends Promise Keepers events, you may grow cynical if his walk at home doesn't match the PK talk. But don't be too hasty. The fact that he dares to call himself a Promise Keeper is an act of faith that God will honor, even if that means going through disillusionment. It just takes time. Don't worry that one PK conference doesn't do a complete make-over on his character and conduct. My husband was on the stage, speaking at ten PK conferences before he realized how much he needed to change his relationship with his family. It took ten times, but he finally got it! Praise God if your husband goes to Promise Keepers. Just keep sending him until it takes! God works relentlessly toward having him possess in reality what he professes by faith, little by little.

Chapter 23
Quick to Anger

Everyone should be quick to listen, slow to speak and slow to become angry, for man's anger does not bring about the righteous life that God desires.

—JAMES 1:19–20

Journal Entries:

10/21/90—Beat KU 41-10. Victory tarnished because I berated an official who made a bad call. For a while it looked like the call might turn the game around, and I became irate. Lord, forgive me—I regret my behavior and once more some of the joy of the victory is lost.

10/13/91—Beat Mizzou 55-7. When we lost the shutout, I reacted angrily with Hank and sinned against him and You, Lord. I regret my words or the spirit of my words. In fact, the whole game I was tense and explosive—not gentle or loving like You require.

11/19/91—Yesterday we beat KU 30-24. I raged some on the sidelines and at halftime, and sinned against You and Your program. At the half I called the players on the sidelines———for warming themselves instead of watching the game. Lord, have mercy on me—I regret this and apologized after the game. That behavior has stolen the joy of the game and lowered my spirit.

6/9/92—Dear Lord, today marks 10 years at CU. I continue to sin with quick retorts. Lord have mercy and please give me grace to overcome sin in Your blood.

9/13/92—CU 57, Baylor 38. I was mellow the first half and sinning the second half. I need to pray at half-time. I need to pray in the Spirit during the game. "So what!" should be my response to whatever happens.

9/20/92—CU 21, Minnesota 20. Lord, thank You—I lasted almost the whole game and didn't sin. Yet at the very end, I was mean.

10/17/93—Yesterday, at OU, I assaulted the officials with accusations of unfair officiating—today I regret it. It has happened four games in a row.

11/17/93 —Yesterday I sinned by erupting in anger in a meeting—Lord, I am sorry. Have mercy on me, O Lord.

Out of the same mouth come praise and cursing. My brothers, this should not be. Can both fresh water and salt water flow from the same spring? My brothers, can a fig tree bear olives, or a grapevine bear figs? Neither can a salt spring produce fresh water.

—James 3:10–12

Beginning of the End

The work of the Lord is never finished. As soon as He sheds His light on one darkened corner of our lives, He immediately sets it on another. From my first season at CU until the year I resigned, I battled a persistent, often uncontrollable rage on the sideline during games. This flash temper had a quenching effect on my intimacy with God and a devastating impact on my Christian witness. Brothers or sisters in the Lord who watched the Buffs on TV must have cringed those times I blew my stack at an official or player.

In the world of sports, especially in the college and professional ranks, such displays are commonplace, almost expected of coaches. The average fan laughs it off as good entertainment. Throughout my years as an athlete and coach, I had a fiery, combustible temper, and made no apologies for it. Once I became a born-again Christian, however, the Lord began to severely chasten me in this area. As the Buffs continued to rise in the rankings and drew an ever larger national spotlight, I was convicted that I simply couldn't react so explosively when things didn't go my way.

Since I had come to Colorado I had not been shy in proclaiming my love and allegiance to the Lord Jesus Christ. I had made it known far and wide that I served a God of unending love, gentleness, and self-control. When I walked on to the football field, I knew it wasn't just me the fans were seeing—they were watching a disciple of Jesus Christ who had been born again in the power of the Holy Spirit. As a Christian who was also a public figure, I had an even larger responsibility to embody the purity, composure, and peace of my Lord in my sideline comportment. For that reason, it pained me no end to know that in spontaneous fits of wild-eyed fury I was raining shame down on the Prince of Peace who came to wash away the sins of the world.

I knew exactly what was happening, but it didn't seem to matter. When a penalty flag flew or a mental mistake stalled an important drive, my anger would often gush to the surface. It didn't happen every time, but it was as if a little brute spirit lurked beneath a normally calm countenance, feeding on my total disdain for failure and igniting whenever the tide turned against us.

I clearly recall an incident in 1991. The Buffs were playing Missouri in Boulder, the year after our infamous "fifth-down" touchdown in Columbia. That was when an official inadvertently allowed CU an extra down near our goal line with only seconds to play. In the pandemonium, we scored and won the game, but the controversy dogged us through our national championship run. This time, however, we were thrashing MU in Boulder by a score of 55 to 0—a complete rout. The final minutes might have been a time of relaxed celebration, a brief moment to enjoy a satisfying performance against my old alma mater. Instead, at the end of the game, with all of our substitutes on the field, Missouri scored, spoiling the shutout. I was furious. I stalked over to our defensive coordinator and unleashed a verbal barrage you wouldn't believe, chastising him for those unpardonable points. Walking away, I was fuming—with *myself*. How could I have exhibited such unbelievable arrogance? I quickly apologized to my coach. But I was ashamed. It was nothing new. In certain situations I found I could not stop myself.

A pattern, eerily similar to how my drinking manifested itself years earlier, had developed. After such outbursts, I'd instantly recognize that I'd sinned and be filled with sickening anguish. I'd go through the confessing and repenting and apologizing—and then I'd go out and do it again the next game. It was a rare game that I *didn't* lash out at someone. Whether it was an official, an assistant coach, or a player, with my short fuse game days were open season. Even the annoying sight of players huddled around a space heater during a sub-zero blizzard instead of watching the action on the field could trigger my ire. It's one thing to hold folks accountable for bad conduct and mistakes, something I normally handled with an attitude of consistency, discipline, and respect; it's another to belittle, berate, and humiliate. How I hated it. In the heat of the moment, it could get ugly.

From a spiritual vantage, I figured it was some behavioral stronghold over which I had little authority. But the truth is, I had *unlimited* authority in the name of Jesus, the name above all names, the Author of creation, who defeated Satan on the cross. It was me who held the Holy Spirit at bay. God's power was freely available to help me exercise due restraint, but it was like any filthy habit—it was *sin*. And by its nature, sin brings fleeting pleasure or relief. When the pressure was on, it felt good to unleash a good one on an official. Afterwards I felt like scum (also a universal quality of sin), but I still, repeatedly, *chose* to visit that dark place in my heart. It was like picking my own pocket to pay my adversary. It snatched me from God's presence and stripped me of any anointing I might have had to meet the day's challenges.

One time a female CU office assistant told me to my face I was a Jekyll and Hyde. It didn't exactly make my day, but she was right. I can only imagine what my players, my coaching associates, and attentive onlookers must have thought, after one of my barrages, when I'd turn on a dime and be thanking the Lord for our victory, or detailing the incomparable mercy and forgiveness of Jesus Christ. It couldn't continue. I'd been granted unbelievable favor—a highly visible platform—in which to share my Savior. It's scary to think that the only thing many of these people *knew* about Jesus was what they saw in me.

It says in the Word: "Do not be deceived: God cannot be mocked. A man reaps what he sows. The one who sows to please his sinful nature, from that nature will reap destruction; the one who sows to please the Spirit, from the Spirit will reap eternal life" (Galatians 6:7–8).

Once again my actions exposed me. My inability to control my temper when the very reputation of Christ was on the line betrayed that I actually had a deeper gut-level passion to win football games than to win souls for the Lord. It was a bombshell. And as long as this kept rearing its head, my witness for Christ would be neutralized. It was just another telling bit of hypocrisy that ruined my joy and repelled some who might have otherwise been reached.

As years passed with no true closure, I feared that as long as I coached I would be a stumbling block for others. I worried that as long as I coached, just the intensity and pressure of the game would always make this an area of vulnerability. I was right. The Word says to "flee from idolatry" (1 Corinthians 10:14). Had my career become an idol I must actually flee? I knew I couldn't continue losing my cool in public and expect God to keep using me. From time to time I suppressed this urge to unleash my anger with a sense of great relief. But it always flared up again. It gave me a nagging suspicion that, somewhere down the road, God had something for me besides coaching.

Chapter 24
The Dream Is Not All that It Seems

IT'S AN ODD THING—in hindsight, everything is crystal clear. I see now that my incessant climb up the career ladder was fueled by the assumption that one day I would find surpassing joy and fulfillment in achieving lofty goals. And there were certainly many wonderful, satisfying moments along the way. My obvious goals had been met. By 1992 the Buffs had won a national championship—every coach's dream come true. Our family was financially secure. And I was now immersed in a wonderful move of God called Promise Keepers that had begun to redefine the popular notion of masculinity—calling men back to God and family. By any stretch of the imagination, these were exhilarating, gratifying endeavors.

Less public goals, however, remained. A host of personal issues stared me in the face like angry inquisitors. It was time to face facts: who I appeared to be in public, who I *said* I was, and who I remained *behind* the scenes—in God's sight and my family's—were different people. Jesus said to be *doers*, not just hearers, of the Word. He said only those who obey His commands truly love Him. All the rest are lukewarm and will be barred from His presence. There were still grave areas of disobedience in my life. But, oh, how I hungered for the Lord. I wanted to know Him and love Him the way He set forth—through *obedience*.

My youngest son Marc, to this day my biggest fan, once told me that when I prowled the sidelines during a game, I could look straight at him and not recognize him—as if he weren't even there. When I heard that, it deeply disturbed me. That kind of focus is hypnotic, sinister. It meant I wasn't really in charge. At the same time, I readily acknowledge that there is no more fitting picture of how I approached my career. Focused. Single-minded. Blind to distractions. Stand aside!—even if you are my own family.

I don't deny it. Coaching can be a rich challenge. At the Division 1 level it is lucrative. You are well compensated for your efforts, widely recognized, and, if you happen to excel, applauded at every turn. As our culture measures such things, coaching elite athletes, building their characters, instilling values and discipline, is a noble endeavor. To have the rare opportunity to speak truth to high-spirited, ambitious young men, to have the chance to impart principles that will follow them through life—oh my, it's an awesome, gripping responsibility. You've heard the saying, "It gets in your blood." Well, it's true, it does. It's *intoxicating*.

Great men, living *legends*, go to their graves still gripped by its spell, still fixated by the challenge and ego and adrenaline of it all. For all that they do, for their commitment to the nation's youth, for the sacrifices they make, they are celebrated and revered, saluted and enshrined. Their lives stand out; they stand for something *good*—good for youth, good for society. In each of these respects, I'd made my own mark. Even those who held my spiritual beliefs in contempt applauded my work with athletes, teaching them discipline and a good work ethic. By appearances, I'd "made it."

Not long ago I read a Dilbert comic strip in the newspaper. It's the satirical cartoon that pokes fun at corporate America. In it, a female employee complains to the company's director of human resources that the firm's new "family friendly" benefits package really wasn't all that friendly to working families. The evil H.R.

director stared at her for a moment, then said, "Friendly, yes, but you act like you *love* your family."

It made me chuckle—until I realized with revulsion that *this* truly is the system most of us serve one way or another. We live in America; the economy's on the move, the stock market's up, people are spending, homes are selling. Life is *good*. But the dark underbelly to all this is insidious, satanic—it wars viciously against the things of God. For in an upwardly mobile, materialistic culture like ours, deeper questions, troubling questions, are just sort of left dangling out of view. Ticklish personal issues get lost amid the busyness and chaos. Failure in one's marriage, failure in the home, is often met with a resigned shrug that says with a trace of indifference, "It's a shame, but to excel at anything, there's a price to be paid." More so in a sports-obsessed culture—our heroes are forgiven all manner of personal turmoil and public indiscretion. If the MVP gets busted for drugs or cheats on his wife, all is forgotten the moment he reels in that fingertip grab in the end zone. The sense of the sacred has faded into the background. If the coach, in carrying out his demanding mission, happens to lose sight of his family, or perhaps forfeits his marriage, or his health—well, that's a shame. The larger question is: *Will it affect his performance?—or ruin his concentration?*

To win that gold ring, whether it be the national championship, the fat contract, or the handsome estate, we're quick to avert our eyes when a relationship goes sour. It's too bad if the CEO's kid gets in trouble, but a conscientious executive must first worry about the bottom line. Family intimacy, rich bonding time, living out the gospel of Jesus Christ in the warm company of one's loved ones, are, if acknowledged as virtues at all, deemed expendable icing on the cake of career achievement.

Career tunnel vision like I had can be very lucrative, very heady. So what if coach hasn't spent a quality hour with his own daughter in months. So what if that heart-to-heart talk with his wife never happens. It's OK—"Dad's got an important job. He's going for the gold ring." And if the smile has vanished off his wife's face, or if she has lost that bounce in her step or the gleam in her eye, well. . . . Or if she were ever to grouse about waiting at home night after night. *Shame* on her. Coach is out there fighting the battle, doing good, building into young men's lives, chasing that trophy. The family learns to roll with the punches. They keep it to themselves.

Chapter 25
Idolatry: The System

IN A CULTURE INUNDATED with all manner and forms of idols—idols of wealth, celebrity, vanity, privilege—the most pervasive still revolve around those that directly affect our lives; like our jobs. The rewards available to those who excel on the job, the energy and focus required to perform one's job—the very stigma attached to certain types of jobs—have created a culture of success that cause many to drift into a subtle worship of their professions, if not in spirit then at least in terms of time and energy invested.

Remember the definition of idolatry? It's placing a value on anything in excess of the value we place on God. And remember, actions speak louder than words. The Christian illustration of idolatry is found in the Bible in Jesus' encounter with the rich young ruler in Luke 18. The young baron, inwardly convinced of his own righteousness before God, nonetheless asks Jesus for the key to eternal life. Jesus immediately sees through his conceit and instructs the aristocrat to give away his wealth so that he "will have treasure in heaven. Then come, follow me" (v. 22).

Christ's short admonition reveals the true cost of being a Christian. The young man sadly turned and walked away. His longing for eternal life gave way to his idolatry of title and wealth. His quest for truth was superficial at best. If it meant sacrificing what made him comfortable and important in the world's eyes, He did not really want to walk alongside the Savior. Like the average Christian in the church, he blatantly disobeyed a direct word from God. "Come, follow Me!"

It has stood the test of time, this spirit of idolatry and disobedience. And it's alive and well in the Church today. For most of my life, it was thriving in me, even though I would have said differently. With our heads we know the truth, talk highly of Jesus, understand the requirements of obedience. But in our hearts and—most importantly—in our actions, the average Christian walks sadly away, far too comfortable and complacent to follow Jesus.

Jesus says, "If anyone loves me, he will obey my teaching" (John 14:23); and God says we must seek our identity in His Son alone—not in jobs, not in material lack or abundance. In *Him alone!* He tells us not to worry about tomorrow; He says seek first the kingdom of God . . . and all these things will be added to you (see Matthew 6:33). Look around. Even many self-proclaimed "on fire" Christians look first to their *jobs*—not God—as their primary source of security. But the Word of God says, "The LORD sends poverty and wealth; he humbles and he exalts" (1 Samuel 2:7). Do we believe this? Is the Word of God true? Then why are Christians looking to the *world* for affirmation and identity, when God is the one who knit us together in the womb and has the map of our lives laid for His unsearchable purposes?

It is because we are products of our culture—and because we have been lulled to sleep. I did it for many years. I gave up almost everything to excel at my career. Dallas Willard, author of *The Spirit of the Disciplines*, cautions: "Let's be clear about one thing. Whoever cannot have riches without worshiping them above God should get rid of them, if that will enable him or her to trust and serve God rightly."[1] Today I know my real value was not in coaching; it is in how much I'm willing to give of myself to *know* God.

No teaching is harder for today's Christian to receive. Much like the rich young ruler, we're eager to embrace the Truth and we desire God's blessing, yet we beat a fast retreat from God's command to open our arms in total trust and surrender. Rather than trusting God to show me how to achieve His proper balance throughout my coaching years, I placed an inordinate amount of trust in my ability to succeed in a career. Failing to embrace Him as my sole source of identity, I became locked into a system that convinced me my value as a human was in my ability to meet challenges in the work place.

In the world's eyes, mine was a noble pursuit. I was successful on its terms. But to succeed on the level the world required took too much. As I poured out my youthful strength and vigor to feed this voracious idol, I was slow in realizing these were God-given gifts that rightfully belonged to Him, and to my family. As God tenderly, insistently opened my eyes to this truth, it spelled the beginning of the end of coaching for me.

Chapter 26
A Marriage Built on Sand

LYNDI WAS WASTING AWAY before my eyes. Over the past twelve months she had lost eighty pounds. From all indications, she'd simply stopped eating. She had begun to isolate herself in her room. She had stopped communicating; she had stopped taking phone calls; she had stopped seeing friends. She accepted no visitors. She had cut ties and closed the walls of despondency around her.

It was the spring of 1993. Lyndi had suddenly and unexpectedly come to the end of her rope. Life had become too disappointing, too draining. Having invested her all in our marriage and family for thirty years, she'd come to a horrifying conclusion. Weighed in hindsight, the evidence demanded a guilty verdict. In her mind, our lives together had been a waste. She had weathered raging storms of discouragement and was now sinking in the undertow. A series of events had led her to this point. She was weary.

Suffice it to say, Lyndi's depression was the toxic fallout from a vast legacy of my chronic insensitivity and neglect toward her. Like a sudden illness, it came without warning. Her emotional defenses had been beaten down through years of wanting, of waiting. Now her disappointment flared up with a gravity and dimension she found unbearable. Proverbs 13:12 says, "Hope deferred makes the heart sick, but a longing fulfilled is a tree of life." Lyndi's hopes for a husband who counted her as a teammate, who was as sold out to her as he was to his job and his ministry, had been deferred almost since our wedding day. Our habitual lack of emotional intimacy had pushed her past the breaking point. God's Word is true: Unmet longings had given her a sick heart.

Awash in solitary anguish, she believed all of the love she'd invested, all of the grace she'd extended, all of the unseen tears she had shed—all of her prayers that, one day, all of this would be worth it—had been little more than a cruel joke. And the joke was on her. She perceived that our relationship was a shifting illusion; she sensed she'd been in terminal denial, kidding herself that I was going to change. The great love she once had for me had turned to ashes in her hands.

I didn't know what to do, what to say, how to act. My efforts to comfort her were not well received. When she tried to smile, it was forced. When she spoke, there was an icy distance. She went into a mode of just trying to cope. She closed herself in her room and over the summer read more than a hundred self-help books on spiritual and emotional healing. Emptiness ate away at her daily. It broke my heart to have caused such pain, such despair, in the woman I loved. Ralph Waldo Emerson said, "there is no way out, but *through*." And he was right. There *is* no way out of it. No way around it. It was pure torture—taking in the daily sight of someone so ravaged, so damaged, and knowing it's your lack of character that caused it.

I knew, as the summer proceeded, that if Lyndi had simply done what she wanted, she would probably have left me. Her hopelessness was that complete. There was nothing I could say to mitigate the tremendous pain she was in; my actions had for too long shown indifference. She told me later that the only thing that kept her in the marriage during this dark night of the soul was her commitment to her marriage vows. She had made a covenant with me in God's presence, and, for now, she would have to stand on it alone.

There was a sad resignation to her weathered resolve, because by this point it certainly wasn't love that kept her hanging on.

After several weeks of this, I was beside myself. I had done everything I knew to excuse myself of responsibility and talk her out of her oppression. It left me feeling broken and foolish. All my rationalizations had blown up in my face. Confronted by her spine chilling torment, I soon realized that all of the excuses in the world rang hollow. I finally decided to face the evidence: I had caused this. I had opened this yawning wound in my wife's soul. It was time to stop making excuses. "No more self defense," I said to myself. "Whatever my lot is as a result of this, I'll go through it without complaining. If she stays with me, I vow to make the next thirty-plus years different than the first thirty." In hindsight, I had no idea how ill-equipped I was to honor that vow. In the best of scenarios, we were left with two options: Give up, or start over.

The Slow Healing

Ultimately, Lyndi emerged from her isolation resigned to try and make the best of a difficult situation. Her time crying out to God and hiding in His presence had steadied her. It had rekindled a flicker of desire to give it another try. Re-emerging from her seclusion was Lyndi's way of saying she was prepared to start over. And she, much more than I, knew it would be a long, bitter road. We would have to pick up the broken shards and try to fit them together as best we could.

We both agreed that marriage counseling was a start. That summer we began seeing a Christian professional whose name had come highly recommended. He immediately impressed me as a very discerning fellow; right away he seemed to identify with Lyndi's pain. Somehow he understood what she'd been going through. I still wince recalling our first ego-bruising sessions. He sat forward and listened to us both patiently. Lyndi shared, then I shared from my heart. I gave a somewhat defensive accounting of what I thought our biggest problems were. While I was still in mid-sentence, he abruptly halted the session. He laid down his glasses, carefully placed his pencil on his desk, took a deep breath, and stared me in the eye.

"If I decide to take this case," he began, "I want you to understand something." He knew who I was. He knew all about Promise Keepers, that it was now expanding across the nation, going full throttle. He wasn't impressed. Fixing his gaze on me, he said, "If I get involved, you must understand that this is going to be a war. Not a battle—a *war!*" A war?

It took me a few minutes to catch his drift. In no uncertain terms, he was telling me that, from what I'd said, I was out to sea—I didn't have a clue. He was saying that in spite of my genuine remorse and all of my good intentions, my heart was out to lunch when it came to Lyndi. He was telling me that, yes, it was possible to be an outspoken, on fire, sold out Christian leader and still have a blind spot—or blind spots—toward one's own family. It was painful, but instructive, to hear. And though Lyndi had never told me some of the things she told our marriage counselor in my presence, he confirmed that I was grossly out of touch with what she needed from me. The sharp edges of my personality had inadvertantly inflicted heavy damage. Once more he asked me if I was prepared for a protracted war against pride, selfishness, and insensitivity. I had already determined that I would do whatever I had to do to save our marriage. If it was going to be a war, so be it. The counselor took our case. Lyndi and I embarked on the most difficult, yet revealing, period of our lives.

It almost goes without saying that marital counseling was an exercise in ineptitude for me. It taught me a number of very disheartening things about myself, things that I'd long suspected were probably true but which I'd conveniently glossed over in the crush of endless coaching and ministry distractions. I learned, for one, that I am not a good listener. In our sessions it came out that, rather than allowing others to fully express their opinions, I'm always quick to give mine. It comes from arrogance, and an ability to overpower people. (To this day, I still find it difficult to maintain focus on what others are saying, and, more than I care to admit, I'm usually ready with an aggressive counterpoint to any dissenting opinion.)

For Lyndi, this had exacted an enormous toll. Day after day, year after year, it caused her to feel that I was never really hearing her, that she had little or no meaningful access into my life. What a blow, realizing that you're a stranger to your mate. And, try as I might to disguise it, she was right. You can't hide something like that from your wife. Today, I'm still not a great listener, though Lyndi tells me I'm making progress. In the ugly final analysis, in most situations I think about *myself* first: my comfort, my reputation, my rights. My, my, my . . . And when I am confronted or criticized, I have a strong propensity to defend myself. By defending my actions to Lyndi, I was subtly imposing my will on her. And the truth is, I have always found it difficult to accept criticism.

As harmful as these disturbing character traits had been to my marriage, it was as devastating to grasp how I had unwittingly dishonored Christ's selfless sacrifice in saving me. I had been bold to proclaim Jesus as the perfect model of godly manhood to stadiums full of men. But had I forgotten that Jesus never saw the need to defend Himself, even in the face of vicious lies meant to destroy Him? He was a sinless Man. His trust was in God alone. Jesus came to serve and not be served. He came to die so that I might not perish. To cleanse me of my depravity, Jesus joyously allowed Himself to be poured out like water. "Let us fix our eyes on Jesus, the author and perfecter of our faith, who for the joy set before him endured the cross, scorning its shame, and sat down at the right hand of the throne of God" (Hebrews 12:2). So that I might be reconciled to a holy God, Jesus shed His glory and clothed Himself in mortal flesh.

Jesus said the *meek* will inherit the earth; He said blessed are the poor in spirit, that those who mourn will be comforted. He said those who are merciful will be shown mercy. I *knew* the correct responses to the matter of a man's character. Countless times I had told *others* to leave any defending that might be necessary—even against direct attacks on one's character and reputation—in God's hands.

I wanted to be like Jesus more than I wanted to live. I had made what I thought were tremendous sacrifices in order to proclaim His beautiful Name and run the race in such a way that, having preached, I wouldn't be disqualified. I *wanted* to be a meek man, wanted to show mercy to others. But a meek man has no rights to defend. He is a man who has died to himself and his personal needs; he has forfeited his agenda and found his sole identity in Jesus Christ. The meek joyfully endure persecution for the sake of righteousness. The meek do not have to defend themselves. A meek man is dead to himself—and a *dead man* is *free*. In the face of fierce criticism, he knows that, if the truth were known, it's really a lot worse than anyone suspects. Such a man is a paradox to the world, but he is exactly who Jesus Christ calls His people to be—a royal priesthood, dead to themselves but alive in Christ, set aside for good works.

This is the kind of man my wife and children needed, the man who my brothers and sisters in the Lord needed. For in the final analysis, who really needs an overpowering Bill McCartney? Who needs a husband who storms ahead, thinking he's always right? Who needs a friend who intimidates others to see things his way? Who needs a brother who makes excuses for his actions . . . always defending himself? I knew all these things, but I hadn't allowed God to give them expression in the marrow of my soul, in the depths of my heart. I, chief of sinners, knew as few others that Jesus' path is the path of mercy, of true victory. But I had stubbornly kept one foot planted firmly in the world, where one is always compelled to defend his actions against constant second guessing; where one must do whatever one can to ward off demeaning critcism; where one must make feeble excuses for his sick marriage. But Jesus said, "Whoever wants to become great among you must be your servant, and whoever wants to be first must be your slave—just as the Son of Man did not come to be served, but to serve, and to give his life as a ransom for many" (Matthew 20:26–28).

It was a necessary exercise, seeing myself in this unfamiliar, disturbing light. And it gave Lyndi reason to hope. There was some genuine communication, some genuine sharing between us. I arrived at a point of speechless surrender. Counseling got my attention; it slowed me down enough to simply sit and listen. And as Lyndi talked, recounting the hurtful ways I had unwittingly dissmissed her over thirty years, I didn't resist. I simply listened, and as I listened, I began to feel her pain. My heart began to chafe, then ache, and then, finally, my heart broke. Oh, it hurt. It broke for missed opportunities, for wasted years, for needless pain. In each instance I would tell her I was sorry; I would ask her forgiveness and try to assure her that I would try never to repeat it. After a time, a miracle occurred. These simple acts brought healing to Lyndi. She was finally being heard. I was finally taking responsibility. One incident at a time, we began to clear the slate. High, thorny walls were being scaled. We were on the road to a breakthrough.

And then the 1994 football season landed smack in our laps. I lost momentum. As the pre-season got underway, I squandered opportunities to bring about greater healing. My earnest assurances faded yet again. While the progress we made was real, I put our healing on hold. I put Lyndi on hold, again. It soon became obvious to her that, while I was indeed on a path of self-discovery, my progress was going to be agonizingly slow. She didn't want to be put on hold. I am a slow learner. Lyndi's expectations were dampened; she was disappointed. Understandably, her mind harkened back to all of my shortcomings and past mistakes. She didn't see me continuing the transformation to becoming a more attentive, nurturing partner. All the ways in which I didn't measure up became magnified in her mind.

I was naïvely satisfied, however, thinking we'd dealt with the crisis. We'd gone to counseling; we'd had many probing discussions;

there had been obvious healing. Now, from habit and necessity, my time—my mind—became riveted on getting the Buffs back to the Orange Bowl. I knew we had as talented a returning team as I'd ever fielded. Maybe this was our year to repeat as national champions. I scarcely realized that the healing process in our marriage had only begun. It was a fragile *beginning* that needed to be protected, tended to. But I was back out on the race course, feeling freed up and ready to move on. Lyndi lapsed back into a sullen season of resignation and futility.

In an act of emotional self defense, she began a slow, back-pedaling retreat. In her secret heart, I can now see that she would have much preferred to simply back out, slip away, and disappear. Only her faithfulness to our marriage saved us. Only the immense love and sustaining mercy of the living Christ worked to counterbalance my dull insensibility. It wasn't over. The real crisis lay ahead.

Chapter 27
A Question of Integrity

Integrity: the quality or state of being complete; unbroken condition; wholeness; entirety; the quality of being of sound moral principle, uprightness, honesty and sincerity.

—WEBSTER'S DICTIONARY[1]

WAS I REALLY A MAN OF INTEGRITY? Because it came at a critical crossroads in my coaching career, our marital crisis in the spring of 1993 pushed the question to the forefront of my thinking. Now that I had seen the full extent of Lyndi's torment, I had to seriously ask myself: Would I finally be able to balance career and marriage?

The CU football program, still basking somewhat in the afterglow of our 1990 national championship, was back at the grindstone. In the intervening years CU had either won or shared in consecutive Big 8 titles, followed by frustrating bowl losses to Alabama and Syracuse. We were now trying to perfect a troublesome new passing offense implemented in the 1991 Blockbuster Bowl and intended to secure the Buffs among the nation's elite. CU's power running attack, used so effectively to resurrect the program and beat Notre Dame in the 1990 Orange Bowl, had worked well against like-minded Big 8 opponents. But the consensus among our coaches was that to compete with the Miamis and Florida States of the world we'd need a pro-style passing game and the talent to match.

After years of *no* expectations for CU, Colorado fans now expected the Buffs to be a perennial, nationally-ranked contender.

No one had higher expectations than our players and staff. Our workload that spring reflected it.

Looming in the background of these heavy-handed preparations were plans for Promise Keepers' third annual conference in late July. It was an event that would see fifty thousand men jam Folsom Stadium and formally launch the movement headlong into the national consciousness.

By this stage, Promise Keepers had appropriated the phrase "Men of Integrity" to describe its ideal participant—a man who agreed with our statement of faith, adhered to the principles contained in our seven promises, and was generally committed to being, well . . . a promise keeper. Men of Integrity was an expression used often and proudly in our promotional videos and newsletters. It had been boldly emblazoned on thousands of hats, T-shirts, and sweaters worn by men who supported the ministry.

It was a fitting epigraph if only because it gave those convicted enough to wear it a standard to shoot for. It also worked as a subtle reminder to conduct oneself accordingly in the company of any who might be taking notes. But the fact is (and statistics bear this out), in the emotional wake of a conference, after the white-knuckle excitement and adrenaline wore off, many who sported PK T-shirts, made vows of purity, and lifted hands in worship returned home to resume their carnal, less-than-promise-keeping lifestyles. It was to be expected. God is never pushy when taking hold of a man's heart. And no one ever kidded himself by thinking that attending a conference, wearing a shirt, or drinking from a Men of Integrity coffee mug made one a bona fide promise keeper. The Word says, "Man looks at the outward appearance, but the LORD looks at the heart" (1 Samuel 16:7).

In much the same way, being founder of a fast-growing Christian men's movement didn't automatically make *me* a true man of integrity. The truth is, I'd been feeling tension with the term for some time—or at least with its underlying implication. For while it's true that integrity means being of sound moral principle, whole, unbroken, and sincere, it also speaks more softly to the honest, harmonious *integration* of a person's public and private lives.

By this definition, a man of integrity is someone whose public persona is squarely reconciled to, and in full agreement with, his private reality. Therein lay the problem. Therein had *always* been the problem—the undeniable contradictions between who I *wanted* to be and who I *was*. The tightrope I was walking in the spring of 1993, juggling a frantic coaching load while serving as Promise Keepers vocal, visible front man, drove a wedge further still between my private and public selves. Circumstances seemingly out of my control accentuated gaping discrepancies between who I was *portrayed* to be and who I was in private. By the latter definition, I wasn't a man of integrity.

I *said* God was number one, but did my life bear that out? I regularly told thousands of men I was sold out to my wife and family, but . . . had I *ever* been? The tension this stirred in my heart had created a very thorny dilemma. There were those who, because of what I appeared to be, had me pegged as something of a saint. My standing in Christian circles had become somewhat aggrandized. I knew this and wanted—no, *intended*—to do something about the incongruity. But what?

What's Fundamental?

Some time ago a friend shared with me a comment that Vince Lombardi, legendary coach of the Green Bay Packers, supposedly made when Chrysler chairman Lee Iacocca asked, "What's the secret of your success?" Now, everyone knows Lombardi was one of the greatest coaches of all time, *period!* He led the Packers to their first two Super Bowl wins by setting standards for discipline, instilling a passion for excellence, and inspiring uncommon unity among his players. When someone quotes Lombardi, I'm paying attention. Without pausing, Lombardi purportedly replied, "Master the fundamentals, instill discipline, and do everything in love."

It is a straightforward formula. *Master the fundamentals . . . instill discipline . . . do everything in love*. All are good solid principles. But it seemed simple—*too* simple. Anyone who has ever coached, or who has had to forge a tight-knit team from a high-strung, raw-boned collection of self-reliant athletes, knows the true secret to success is *execution.*

In Lombardi's case, simply knowing sound principles didn't cut it. It was his skill and determination to put principles into action that made him a great coach. As a coach, I, too, always emphasized fundamentals; I was a strict disciplinarian and did my best to instill a sense of unselfish teamwork and mutual respect among my players. Without the benefit of Lombardi's counsel, I had managed, through experience, to put these principles into action in sports.

Yet the longer I thought about Lombardi's quote, it sounded like something Jesus might have said to His disciples. *Master the fundamentals, instill discipline, and do everything in love*. What, I wondered, is fundamental to a Christian? What fundamentals had I neglected in my spiritual walk? In my marriage? These were the two areas where I struggled to strike a reasonable balance. The balance was always tipped heavily toward career. So no matter how God had blessed me since accepting Jesus, or in spite of how He was using me with Promise Keepers, or regardless of my growing hunger to be a man of integrity, I always found myself back at square one. Career *idolatry*. *Success*. It feeds on itself. My hard work and steely focus had, indeed, bred success; which bred more success, which led to a more intense obsession with success, until I was completely bogged down with the unending responsibilities of maintaining a certain level of success. It was a type of spiritual and professional gridlock that robbed me of the fundamentals I needed to lead a decent, well-balanced life.

I was driven. I had sacrificed much to climb the ladder of my profession. I loved my job. I was energized by competition, inspired by the rewards of accomplishment. I had been awarded what amounted to a lifetime contract at CU, ensuring my family's comfort and security for the remainder of our lives. Several walls in our new home housed the trophies of my coaching career. My focus was hard and narrow when it came to success. I would travel great distances to charm a prized recruit. Most of my waking hours were spent assessing our team, evaluating last week's mistakes, and pouring over next week's game plan. I had trained my mind to detect the smallest chink in the enemy's armor. Most days I was up and out of the house before anybody else was awake. Most nights I came home long after everyone else had gone to bed.

And while I remained a paradox to most, I was no one-dimensional jock. I was fully impassioned on a separate track. Anybody who knew me would say I was a devoted Christian, a man unashamed of the gospel and, if anything, *over*-energized and outspoken about God. In football stadiums, before many thousands of men, I was a zealous defender of the faith, quick to exalt the name of Jesus Christ, and first in line to sing the virtues of godly manhood and everything that implied. I faithfully attended church, supported my pastor, and, by all appearances, seemed like the real deal—a sincere believer, on fire for Jesus Christ, a humble servant of God.

But man looks at the outward appearance; God sees the heart. Let's take a closer look. If anyone had trailed me from daybreak to midnight on a typical day at CU, he would have witnessed something quite perplexing. He would have seen me arriving at my office early to pray over every chair and fixture, anointing everything in the precious blood of the Savior and invoking God's blessings and purposes over every item of business to be conducted there that day. He would have seen me on my noon-hour walk praising God and asking His mercy and protection over every player and staff member. He would have seen a man who was quick to close the door of his office in order to kneel in private prayer with a brother, a man who brought Jesus into most conversations, a man who credited God for his successes and tried to strike a humble posture.

But by the end of that twelve-hour period, the same eyewitness would have seen a troubling disparity. For while I said I was excited about my relationship with *God*, he would have noticed that most of my prayers sought wisdom to lead the football team to its next victory. While I said I was excited by my marriage, he would have likely noted that I had hardly seen or *spoken* with Lyndi that day. He might have seen me praying over my sons or daughter before I left for work. But he wouldn't have beheld a man who often took time to listen to their hearts or ask them about their hopes and dreams, their fears or concerns for the day. He would have beheld a man who had a list of coaching tasks two feet long and wouldn't rest or take a breath, or smell a rose—wouldn't even notice whether it was sunny or cloudy outside—until that interminable list was completed. And then he would have seen a man incessantly brooding over tasks left undone—or not done to perfection—a man whose mind kept churning and turning and wrestling over some new football challenge or predicament.

By day's end, probably still holed up with me in my office overlooking Folsom Stadium, the beleaguered onlooker would have had no choice but to conclude: "Coach *says* he's excited about God, but his actions tell me he's really excited about football. He *says* he's excited about his marriage and family, but . . . I *really* think he's excited about football." He would have been left with one insurmountable impression: "Coaching takes so much of this man's time and energy that it's really no contest: Coaching, not God, comes first in his life." I'm ashamed to say he would have been right.

In previous years, I had had a month or so of vacation time in which God and my family got considerably more of my time and attention. But now, with Promise Keepers shifting into high gear during the summer, even that small window began to shrink. The rest of the year I was in an all-out sprint, expending my energy and youth on a treadmill called coaching. I knew what was required to win football games—*everything!*

Yet I was still under God's tender custody. He was not permitting me to be lost totally to the system. I think it says much about God's unfathomable ways and His sovereign timetable that it was not until I was neck deep in Promise Keepers that

He began to reveal how little I actually knew about loving Him—or my wife.

Sure, I knew the fundamentals of hand-picking players to fit into a proven system, then training them in the skills, conditioning, and attitudes they needed to be a consistent winner. But what fundamentals were required to truly be a man after God's own heart? How could a compulsive football coach craving a few extra minutes with God master the fundamentals of a vital spiritual walk? How could a man who couldn't free his mind from football for thirty minutes during dinner at home discipline himself to attend to the deeper needs of his wife and kids? What fundamentals had I missed? Which ones would I now have to revisit?

Loving God: It's Fundamental

Few would argue that God's first commandment to "love the LORD your God with all your heart and with all your soul and with all your strength" (Deuteronomy 6:5) is fundamental. It is, in fact, the fundamental, number one cornerstone command of the Christian faith. It forces anyone professing to love Jesus Christ and enjoy His offer of salvation to take a hard look in the mirror. It did me. Jesus affirmed this command several times in His earthly ministry. *Love God with all of your heart, mind, and strength . . .* then *love your neighbor as yourself*. It's not a suggestion. It's an ultimatum. But the practical details seem to escape us. How are we, in this culture of constant chaos, carnality, distraction, temptation, and busyness able to make God such a focal point in our lives that we actually come to love Him to that extent? It's a fundamental question that the Bible addresses repeatedly. We must be in relationship, for how is it possible to love *anyone*—to *any* extent—short of a deep personal relationship? Anyone who has been in a lasting relationship knows—and as I eventually learned—true love involves a constant striving and learning; it is an unconditional investment requiring both partners to place top priority on the union. True love requires two people to work tirelessly through difficulties, communicate effectively and constantly, and bear with one another at all times. Does the Creator of life deserve less of an effort?

I ask the question because even a distracted coach like me, whose focus was never far from staff meetings, recruiting trips, film sessions, or Saturday games, instinctively knew that to really love God like I said I did, God must be the top priority of my life. But the cares of the world, if given the slightest rein, quickly crowd out even one's most paramount objectives.

The Bible says whatever a man treasures, that's where you'll find his heart (see Matthew 6:21). Well, from the time I was a small child, I treasured God. But at pressure-filled points along a feverish career path, I got sucked in and either forgot, or never really understood, the true value of that treasure.

A Taste of Freedom

My earlier attempts as a rookie head coach to give our coaches Sundays off to be with their families didn't work out. Good intentions weighed against a formidable workload, and the daunting expectations of a losing program didn't allow it. Now, however, we'd turned the corner at CU. While the pressure hadn't gone away, it had *changed* somewhat. We weren't exactly having to prove ourselves to an entire state now—it was more a matter of not digressing. I was emboldened to take another stab at being a man of integrity.

In a slightly less disruptive move, I drew the line on how late our coaching staff would stay at work certain nights. It seemed like a small step, but it was really a step of faith. It was definitely a significant concession during a game week. Nonetheless, though some were dubious, I told our coaching staff we simply wouldn't meet on certain nights. And it freed us up once or twice a week to be bona fide husbands and fathers. It didn't noticeably detract from our work week, but it occasionally allowed us to get to bed at a decent hour.

The first fruits were quickly seen on the home front. Now, for a couple of nights a week during the season, I could sit down with my family and have dinner, talk, and enjoy some relaxed time together. With the extra rest, I found I could rise earlier the next morning. It enabled me to do something *fundamental* for my faith that I hadn't had time or energy for in years.

By 4:30 or 5 A.M., I would be up and in my prayer room, attempting to wrap my mind around the number one fundamental: pursuing God with all of my heart, mind, and strength. Oh, what an exhilarating experience it was. In fleeting moments stolen away from a fast-encroaching work schedule, I rediscovered the incomparably sweet, tantalizing taste of God's presence that I had been craving. I longed for more. I *needed* more.

And those infrequent evenings at home with Lyndi simply alerted me to how much I'd missed out on while chasing my dreams. God took that tiny investment of time and showed me how much *more* there was, how indescribably rich were those untapped treasures of intimate fellowship I had forsaken. A simple decision to take an occasional night off began to dismantle my world view, producing an almost helpless sense of desperation. I began to pray, "What do I do, Lord? How do I love You and my family the way You *expect* me to *and* keep winning football games? How do I master this fundamental principle of my faith?"

From almost that very moment, a brutal tension arose. It was clearly going to be a war between my desire for God and family, and what I'd have to sacrifice to get it. It had to start with work, I knew, because when the Big 8 title was on the line, my track record didn't lie. I became obsessed and maniacal in my drive to win the trophy. And because nothing else in the way of discipline, structure, or organization said "God comes first, family comes second," I was forced to admit: I *didn't* love God first. If my seasonal obsession to win football games continued unabated, my public and private lives would never match up. I'd *never* know God fully. I'd *always* be praying on the run. I'd *always* be waving to my family as I flew out the door to the next practice or coaches' meeting, or, yes, the next Promise Keepers conference. I had to choose.

After wrestling with this maddening tension for years, I made a silent decision to myself: Loving God would be my top priority. And I *would* be a promise keeper to my family. I'd now made a small inroad at work, but it wasn't enough. The question lingered for some time as I kept praying, "How, Lord, in a high-pressure, win-or-else profession, do I do it?"

Chapter 28
Sunday Morning Warrior

> Journal Entry 9/11/90—I am enslaved because I am focused on myself and not others. Lord, help me to see the need in others and respond to it instead of my particular needs dominating me. . . . I deserve death and have received life.

SINCE I STARTED COACHING at the college level, Sunday mornings at the McCartney home were a challenge. In truth, it would be difficult to imagine a so-called *Sabbath* day of rest being more harried or chaotic. It would have almost been comical, in fact, if it weren't so stressful. Especially considering this was the one day the whole family could spend a little time together at church.

I know it's not uncommon for families to occasionally find themselves at odds (or at each other's throats) as they try to get out the door to church. But a coach's family has an altogether different set of challenges—namely, the *coach*. Sundays, you recall, are the unofficial first day of the week for a coach, a critical time to get a head start on preparations for the next game. When the kids were still living at home, by the time we piled in the car for church I'd already put in a quarter-day's work—with more to come.

Typically, the morning after a game I'd rise early. If I had the energy, I'd spend some quiet time studying the Word or in prayer. Either way, I'd be out of the house by 6:00 A.M., rushing to the office to break down Saturday's game film, shutting myself in the projection room for a good two hours or more. It never failed to be a gut-wrenching experience, isolating and analyzing each mistake in minute detail.

Mornings after a loss were especially rough. By the time I got to my office in the Dal Ward Center, I'd already replayed the defeat in my mind at *least* a hundred times. But reenacting it on film was another story; it was pure torture; watching the flickering news-reel highlight each technical imperfection and coaching error was a drill in suffering that would soon have my head pounding, my pulse racing. Mornings after a victory were better. An enjoyable buzz of satisfaction usually lingered, granting fleeting vindication for having earned my keep another week. But even then, rolling the film to grade the team's performance brought on pangs of anguish.

Biblical scholars say that without Jesus Christ's standing between God and man as a purifying Mediator, the purest, most humble prayer ever uttered by the greatest saint contains enough sin to condemn him to hell. I realize the stakes in football don't warrant comparison, but I'm here to tell you that there are enough aggravating mistakes in the most well-executed play to give any coach an ulcer. Sitting there every Sunday morning in the film room, my blood pressure would slowly rise. Any recollection of victory would soon be muted by the indicting evidence of poor execution. Within minutes, anxiety would set in and everything would be refocused on the encroaching menace of next week's opponent. Serenity would be replaced by crashing waves of doubt—*Are we good enough, or are we just pretenders?* The battle mentality would click in, every nerve ending and synapse teaming up to solve the malevolent threat of the next imminent rivalry. After an hour or so of this, it would be time to pick the family up and go worship the Lord.

It sounds ridiculous. I know it may come as a surprise to many, but the only time most coaches ever really enjoy the *moment* of a big win—I mean really get to sit back and bask in the thrill of it—are the hours immediately after a game. That's when the hard work seems worth it. The locker room is electrified and the post-game press conference is buoyant, even playful. While some coaches take the family out for a nice dinner, with all the smiles, handshakes, and back slaps, I'd go straight home and turn on whatever game was on TV. I'd watch the day's scores and unwind in the privacy of my home. And then it was basically over. A fog of exhaustion could hit me so hard and fast that I could barely make it to bed. I'd usually be snoring before Lyndi brushed her teeth.

Sunday morning, the celebrating's over. Time to crank up the engine and do it all again. Rick Pitino, former basketball coach at the University of Kentucky, gave his heart and soul trying to resurrect that sanction-plagued program. When he finally led the Wildcats to the 1996 NCAA basketball championship over Syracuse, it was an eloquent tribute to his unyielding tenacity. But do you think he was ready to relax, or rest on his laurels? What about the morning after the championship celebration? Did Pitino stay in bed to try and make up for all the sleep he lost rebuilding that program? Was he out on the golf course blowing off steam? Was he packing for a Carribean cruise with his wife? Not even close. I read that Pitino and his coaches were up even before *dawn* the next morning embroiled in an intense five-hour meeting. They were trying to come up with a strategy to ward off, as he said, the curse of *complacency*. "If it ain't broke," he said, "*break* it."

I know the feeling. In my entire career I rarely allowed myself the luxury of fully relishing a victory. Even after our January 1, 1991, Orange Bowl win sealed Colorado's first-ever national championship, I was back at it hard the next morning. So were all our coaches. We knew we couldn't afford to miss a single day on the recruiting trail. There was another season to prepare for, another class of recruits to sign—another formidable set of challenges to confront aggressively.

Again, it's all part of the bargain, exactly what most college coaches have worked for all of their lives. We know the rules—win, or start packing. That's how I'd been trained. You just could not afford to let your guard down or relax, even if you had achieved your lifetime dream. Once you had lost your edge, there were a dozen or so up-and-comers ready to knock you off the hill.

Interestingly enough, the rigidly-structured, pressure-packed roller-coaster lifestyle complemented my personality. It fed an insatiable desire to establish myself as a top coach. From high school on through the college ranks, my aspirations had grown proportionately. By the time I was hired at CU, nothing would have satisfied me but one day to be counted among the best in my profession. It had been a reckless obsession, and I never felt I'd *arrived,* so to speak. Still, I embraced the job and all its trappings. I never stopped to consider if there might be a reasonable alternative.

Would I ever allow myself to slow down, even for a moment? As long as I coached, no. I *couldn't.* To do so would be, in effect, conceding defeat. It would be risking everything. *What about genuine professional enjoyment? . . . or reveling in the moment? . . . or taking a few days off to regroup spiritually or to simply reflect on one's achievements?* Those thoughts didn't enter in. I was always off feverishly preparing for another game.

Preparing for the start of the 1994 season, however, I found myself getting tired. I was not a young man anymore. The full-throttle schedule and the crazy, busy Sundays after a game had long ago begun to feel like a cop-out, like hypocrisy. Was this gridiron chaos on the Sabbath the kind of radical devotion to the local church I'd called others to through Promise Keepers? Turning on the adrenaline switch week after week, always gearing up for another week of battle, working to keep that edge, was wearing on me. For some time now, in my private thoughts, I wondered how much longer I wanted to do this.

The Look in Lyndi's Eyes

It was early fall 1994, another in an endless string of hectic Sunday mornings. CU was in the final push of its fall campaign. We were undefeated heading into the climax of our schedule. Lyndi and I were now empty nesters. Mike was a scout for the Chicago Bears; Tom was head football coach at Fairview High School in Boulder; Kristy was busy raising two young sons; and Marc was close to a degree at Baylor University. Waking up in an empty home didn't affect my routine, but it made for a more relaxed Sunday morning for Lyndi. She could now get ready at her leisure while I wrapped up my pre-dawn film review. This morning I drove home, picked Lyndi up, and arrived at church determined that I would stay focused through the entire service.

Few would have suspected it—I certainly didn't advertise it—but I didn't easily enter into a spirit of worship once the music started in church. Try as I might to stay focused during the sermon, I was often distracted. My mind was always drifting back to Saturday's game. I'd start ticking off details for the upcoming week, or imagining ways to stop so-and-so's All-American fullback who'd just crushed whoever's defensive line. It was frustrating. My attention would flip-flop; it would return to the present—back to the sermon—and I'd repent and try to tune back in to the preaching. Then I'd flash right back to football. I'd find myself on the sideline watching Nebraska's Tommy Frazier break another point-blank tackle for a first down. It was maddening. One thing's for certain, if the sermon didn't grab me in the first couple of minutes, my concentration was out the door.

It'd been this way for years. I rarely left church feeling deeply ministered to or satisfied that I'd received the full benefit of God's Word. Others would be drying their eyes or hugging neighbors, but the minute church let out, I was up and out of my seat, hustling the family off to breakfast so I could return to the office to watch some more film and map out Monday's practice schedule. My mind was always in two places.

So it was, weighed down with the usual emotional entanglements and assorted bits of mental baggage, that I took my seat next to Lyndi in the sanctuary. My curiosity was already piqued. I knew we had a guest pastor, Jack Taylor, from Florida, who would be stepping in for our own gifted preacher, James Ryle. Knowing that Pastor Ryle didn't lightly turn over his pulpit, I had a feeling we were about to hear a strong word from the Lord. As Pastor Taylor rose to stand before our congregation, I was at full attention. He began his sermon with a simple yet unsettling question: "Do you want to know about a man? Do you *really* want to know about a man's character?" The whole church was silent. I was perched on the edge of my seat.

He continued: "If you want to know about a man's character, then look into the face of his wife. Whatever he has invested in or withheld from her will be reflected in her countenance." Those words made me squirm. Pastor Taylor then began to teach from Scripture. He demonstrated in book after book of the Bible how God has *mandated* that every man bring his wife to full splendor and radiance. By the time he was through, the point had been hammered home. It was an inarguable position: It's the man's role to nurture and affirm his wife, so she can blossom and flourish in all of her rich womanhood and God-given gifting.

I turned and looked squarely into Lyndi's face. My heart sank. What I saw stunned me. Her face. It was sad and empty. Her eyes, once so bright and effervescent, had lost their sparkle. They were dull, downcast, and discouraged. I didn't understand. She was riddled through with disappointment. Instead of radiant splendor, I saw pain; instead of rich contentment, I saw slow decay, emotional torment. Rather than reflecting the joy and vibrant glow of a healthy, satisfying life with the husband of her youth, Lyndi appeared drained, depleted, and unfulfilled. A shiver of panic gripped me.

What had I done? How had this happened? Was it too late? I didn't know what to think, what to say. I muttered to myself; my mind was reeling. Hadn't we taken care of things? Hadn't she noticed that I'd been trying harder at home? I thought our marriage counseling brought needed healing. We weren't there, I knew that—but not *this!* I hadn't noticed the look in her eyes. It was serious. All of a sudden, with no warning, all I could see was Lyndi's face. It was magnified—a battle-weary monument to my neglect. The house of cards I'd pretended were built on rock came crashing down. In one arresting moment, the scales fell off my eyes. In all her years following me down my private path, Lyndi had lost her way. All her years waiting at home, praying for a few hours of my undistracted attention, hoping for a day when I'd be secure enough in my job that I could put *her* first, had left my wife crestfallen, ashen-faced. The depression I saw months earlier was back. How had I missed it? How could I have looked the other way?

Fortune 500 or Bankrupt?

On the surface, Bill McCartney's credentials were daunting. A Christian resume might have read: *Devoted, godly man; unashamed, energized,and outspoken about the gospel of Jesus Christ. Visionary founder of one of the fastest-growing Christian groups in the country; prayer warrior; leader of men; fiery proponent of family values; outspoken advocate for women and healthy marriages; robust witness to the ideal that a "man's man is a godly man."*

It was a Fortune 500 resumé. But the man behind the coat of arms was spinning toward bankruptcy. What I saw in Lyndi's eyes that day exposed me as a fraud. I had bought into the world's view of what success looks like. And it had eaten a sink-hole in the foundation of our marriage. I'd tried to mesh the world's view with God's view, and now, in Lyndi's wilted smile, I saw with agonizing clarity that those views were wholly incompatible. It was as if, for the first time, I saw all the things Lyndi had been trying for years to help me understand.

Here I was, back in the Big 8 hunt, back in the top five nationally, back to seeing Lyndi between practices or at the end of long, exhausting days. My efforts to pray with her each day, to tell her I love her, to kiss her good-bye as I headed off to war weren't enough. Her hollow gaze told me she had needed me to *be* there, to linger away entire afternoons just listening to her and hearing her heart. She had been begging for it in subtle ways for years, and she had waited. But I hadn't responded. I had resisted, thinking that everybody understood and accepted how busy I was. The tension had been building. Lyndi had grown weary of waiting. Now it appeared as if she had given in to despair while I marched forward, always forward, convincing myself all was well.

That morning, God told me all I needed to know: Lyndi was in crisis. Our marriage was terminal. Pastor Taylor's words rang in my ears: *Do you really want to know about a man?* I couldn't deny it any longer. My time, my very *best*, belonged to CU football. As long as I coached, it always would. Lyndi had every right to expect a *relationship* with the man she'd invested her life in. But she had given up on the notion. It made my blood run cold.

It should come as no surprise that, contrary to the evidence staring me in the face, I tried to defend my position to myself. For the next couple of weeks I argued hard with God, trying to convince Him and myself that it wasn't as bad as it seemed, that perhaps Lyndi was just going through a temporary depression. Once the season was over, I'd really focus in on the marriage. I was kidding myself.

That morning it struck me how meaningless my dedication to my career would seem if it turned out I had lost Lyndi in the process. It took thirty years to sink in: God doesn't appraise my worth by my won-lost record. Victory in His eyes is the happy bounce in Lyndi's step. Integrity in His eyes is the self-assured, contented smile on her face. God measures my character in the secure, affirmed countenances of my children—and of my children's children. God weighs my righteousness not in the hours spent at work, but on the scales of my daily fellowship with Him.

There it was, laid open for all of heaven to see. I saw the truth, and it did not set me free. It pierced me like an arrow. The dull glaze in Lyndi's eyes was a spotlight God used to expose my double-minded heart. I had honestly not seen it before—proof of my inattentiveness, proof of my eagerness to put a band-aid on our problems and move on. But now there was a dizzying finality to it. The final piece of the puzzle had dropped into place. Was it . . . ? Could it be . . . ? Was this the end? The fire in my belly toward coaching suddenly went cold. The ravenous, driving impulse that had pushed me on and kept me fighting for more than thirty years had shut down like an overheated generator whose cord had been cut. And the Buffs were *undefeated* at the time. Yes . . . this felt like the end.

I lowered my eyes and lifted my prayer to the Lord in full surrender. *Oh, Lord, please forgive me. By whatever means necessary, make me the man my wife needs; make me the man You created me to be. I will do whatever You say.* With those words, something else deep inside loosed its grip. It felt like peace: unsettling, unfamiliar peace. I knew then. Escorting my wounded wife out to the church parking lot, I began to pray about the timing of my resignation from the University of Colorado.

Lyndi: Reflections on Marriage

When we were first married I felt like Bill's "Trophy Wife." But my top-shelf status quickly turned to bottom-shelf existence as he put one interest after another above me. He always *said* he loved me. I'm sure he did love me. But he thought it was enough to just tell me he loved me and trust that I perceived it that way. I measured his love, in part, by how much time he gave me. Meanwhile, he gave himself and his time to his work, his dreams, his friends, and football. When these all took precedence over me, his actions said I was worth less than his array of other interests. Therefore, I grew to feel worthless.

I was begging for his attention, but couldn't get it. So I did what many women do: I allowed my children to fill the love gap. I put them first and foremost in my affection. That certainly kept me busy and distracted me from my unfulfilled longing for a relationship with Bill. But kids grow up, and unfulfilled longings grow deeper.

When we moved to Colorado, I understood the increased pressures Bill faced, and wanted to help him. I'd always been the enthusiastic, number one loyal fan of Bill and his team. Throughout the university community I was seen as the pop-up wife, always there at my Bill's side, smiling as I helped with countless events that revolved around CU football. Our kids were supportive too. Our lives whirled around him and football—always.

We had all willingly climbed with him to get to this pinnacle in his career. Our lives were built on that mountain. We enjoyed it, each one of us. I was a coach's wife, through and through. When we finally made it to CU, I wanted to be as supportive as ever. But life had changed; I had changed. In the past, I'd been able to balance the load of home and family alone. But as Bill's burdens exploded at CU, so did mine. Our kids were in their teens, and they were not handling the move well. I could see their struggles, but Bill didn't have time to notice. They needed a mom *and a dad*. I tried, but I couldn't be both anymore. Everyone needed me too much, and I needed Bill more than ever, but he wasn't available.

We came to CU in 1982, and I certainly wasn't miserable during our first years. I was as happy as ever—90 percent of the time. I was still extremely proud of Bill as a coach, a mentor to young men, a leader, a Christian, and a caring person in his community. In all his public duties, he was as wonderful as ever. It's just that I needed him as a husband and father. That was the part of him that I longed for. The pressing needs at home brought that longing to the forefront. I tried to *tell* Bill, but he couldn't hear what I was saying. I'd always managed before; he figured I could manage now. He didn't realize I had reached overload. It was not until I could no longer give him the support he needed to do what he wanted, that he realized everything was not all right at home.

Bill was about to reach his dream, nearing the peak he'd been aiming for his whole life. With his gaze set on reaching the summit, he didn't see the rest of our family dangling on the ropes behind him, unable to get a foothold on *our* dreams. It seemed everywhere we went, someone was saying, "Oh, your husband is so wonderful!" Honestly, it was enough to gag a rhinoceros. That's when I dubbed Bill "Mr. Wonderful." But when I saw Mr. Wonderful on TV or in the newspapers I cried, desperately wishing that Mr. Wonderful could just be Mr. Available to me and our kids.

When he didn't get the message that he was *needed* at home, I turned up the volume of my complaints. "You do everything for everyone else!" I told him, "What about us?" Finally, he became so exasperated he asked me, "Do you want a divorce?" Coming from my Christian husband, to whom divorce was not an option, this question hurt deeply. I took it as a threat that he'd get rid of me if I didn't behave. He says he never wanted a divorce; he wanted reassurance of my love. I didn't want a divorce; I wanted a marriage!

We went through nine more years, nine more football seasons, before God got Bill's attention with regard to our marriage and family life. It was 1991, when he began to catch the vision for Promise Keepers. You might think Bill an unlikely candidate to receive such a vision. I thank God that he captured Bill's heart with the *desire* to be what he knew God called him to become: a devoted husband and father. He sincerely prayed and sought God to help him live these ideals. He just had no idea how far he had to go to reach them. I think it is encouraging to see that God went after the heart of a man who was so utterly consumed by his career and brought about a series of events to challenge and change him.

These events in 1993 brought our marriage to a crisis. They were like shouts that set off an avalanche in the glacier of past hurts that had been frozen in time while Bill was too busy to attend to them. The pain of the past came hurtling down on us. This took Bill completely by surprise. He said this came "suddenly and unexpectedly." While my downfall was sudden, it would not have been unexpected if Bill had noticed it building up for decades. We had been looking at the same marital landscape all those years. To his quick glance, our marriage held no impending danger; while I had long studied the mounting weight of pain and feared that one day all that I had put into emotional deep-freeze would come crashing down on us—and so it did. And when it did, the love I had so desperately held onto for all those years seemed to be crushed and swept away under the cold weight of all that pent-up pain that had been suddenly shaken loose.

In my weakened state, it seemed there were too many problems unresolved, unattended to, and not made right throughout our marriage. I could no longer cope or function. I went into self-imposed isolation and considered taking my own life. That's when Bill noticed I was wasting away before his eyes. He wrote, "from all indications, Lyndi had simply stopped eating." That is a sad commentary on how separate our lives had become. He didn't *know* what was happening with me; he had to go by "indications." He didn't know that although I was eating, I vomited every day for more than seven months. I was so upset, I couldn't keep anything on my stomach, but he didn't know. How could he? He wasn't around. I should have told him, but by then I had completely cut myself off. I had tried *telling* him, but he didn't hear. It was not until I became nonfunctional that Bill could *see* there was a problem. (Oh my! This realization is worth ten counseling sessions!) Bill could only see or hear my pain when I stopped supporting him.

When Bill realized there was a problem, his willingness to go to counseling and the counseling itself helped. Then football season started up and other commitments, including Promise Keepers, took him away from me again. My hope, that had just begun to rise, fell flat. It was harder to come down than if I had remained down as I was before. After that, I figured it was over. That's when I began building emotional siege walls. Was I leaving? No! I remained committed to my marriage vows. Although I wanted to run away from him, our marriage, and life itself, my commitment got in the way. Regardless of what Bill did or didn't do, I saw my vows as my responsibility.

God was continually and patiently working. While God was convincing Bill that things *needed* to change in our marriage, God was convincing me things *could* change. I withdrew *from* Bill, but I retreated *to* the Lord. I prayed, "He's yours, Lord. You fix him anyway you want, in your time frame." Meanwhile God was directing my attention away from Bill, back toward seeing how desperately *I* needed to be fixed. The lady who once could balance two platters full of life while waxing floors and talking on the phone, could now barely hold on to a demitasse saucer with two hands. I started out praying for God to fix Bill, and ended up praying for God to fix me.

Through counseling, reading books, prayer, and worship, I slowly began to see how greatly Jesus valued me. This offset my view that Bill's disinterest had devalued me. As I focused on God's love for me, the accumulated hurt and bitterness changed into hope. It wasn't hope that Bill would change, or hope in our marriage, but hope in God.

God showed me many things: that Bill was hurting too, and God wanted to heal us both; that neither of us could fix or change, or do for the other, what God alone can do. I saw that God wanted my attention as much as I wanted Bill's. God wanted me to stop reacting to Bill, and start responding to Him instead.

The Lord led me to stop focusing on Bill's shortcomings and start trying to understand my own. I wrestled with this. I had always tried to be a good wife. I did all the right things; but I came to see that I had been doing them from the wrong source. I was relying on me rather than God. I was living according to His principles, without consulting Him. I had been trying to do it all in my own strength, until I ran out of me. That was when God was able to take over and help.

Blaming Bill had become a stronghold of the enemy in my life, which God broke down. When I stopped blaming Bill, that freed him. Whereas before he could not bear to hear my hurt and pain; now he could listen without being so defensive. As he listened and acknowledged his responsibility for how he had hurt me, I was freed even more.

For his part, Bill determined he would become a promise keeper to his family. But God had to show him that he could not accomplish this in his own strength. He had tried to solve our marriage problems, and they had gotten worse. Now Jesus was knocking on the door to this area of his life. Bill finally agreed to open the door to let Jesus come in and show him what to do. He had to admit that he could not be a promise keeper on his own, even though that was his heart's desire. Again he had to die to himself, so that it was not Bill McCartney who lived, but Christ living in him, empowering him to keep his promises.

That's when our marriage started getting better. I vowed to take him "for better or for worse." I didn't know it would take over thirty years for it to start getting better. Our marriage is better now than ever. And it will get better still, because God isn't finished.

What about you? Have you given up on your marriage? I had. But Jesus hadn't. I know our story sounds discouraging because it took so long. I pray it doesn't take thirty years for you. Maybe you can learn from our mistakes and speed up the process. Men, do you really know how your wife is doing? How she is feeling? Are there problems she has tried to tell you about that you have dodged or been too busy or too defensive to hear? Women, are you sulking, burying yourself in self-pity and blaming your husband instead of being the kind of wife God calls you to be by relying on God's strength. Are each of you accepting full responsibility for your side of the marriage?

When Bill saw how ravaged I was, he wondered if it was too

late. It wasn't too late for us. God didn't give up on us, and He will not give up on you. If you are still asking, "Is it too late for us?" then take heart! It's not too late.

Chapter 29
The Unmistakable Sign

THE BIBLE SAYS WHATEVER a man treasures, that's where you'll find his heart. Scripture teaches that God is a jealous God (see Deuteronomy 4:24), jealous for our love, time, and attention. He *expects* to be number one in our lives. And only when we have installed Him in that rightful position, through our time, thoughts, and actions, do we begin to taste the full measure of sweetness of His tender love and abundant blessing. "Come near to God and he will come near to you" (James 4:8). God has lofty expectations for how we represent Him to the world. And He holds us accountable for lavishing the unconditional love He extends toward us on those around us. Left to ourselves, we are helpless, hopeless. Our hearts are carnal; without the Lord living His life through us, we will fail every time. We need the Lord to teach us how to surrender to His Spirit and to teach us how to love others like He loves us. We need the Holy Spirit to continually fill us so that we might have the power to consider others better than ourselves and to think of another's needs and desires first, rather than always thinking first of ourselves.

Such principles are only spiritually discerned. Nothing in man's nature ever ponders such ideals. They are holy aspirations held only by those who have the Spirit of God dwelling within; they are attained only by those who cry out to Jesus with all of their hearts. And then it takes time. God works His nature into our lives slowly, as we grant Him greater access through acts of deliberate surrender.

The Holy Spirit's influence in our lives is like pouring a pitcher of clean, sparkling water into a glass brimming with foul, rancid water. It would seem that to make the water drinkable again, the dirty water must be completely poured out then the glass thoroughly washed and refilled with clean water. It isn't so. Try it yourself—by slowly pouring the purified pitcher of water into the filthy drinking glass, the sludge is slowly displaced, until the contents are once again pristine. Likewise, as we allow the Spirit access to our lives through our obedience and surrender to His Word, Jesus will fill us, purify us, and make us clean vessels useful for service. And He will purify us precisely where we are most foul.

Only Jesus can redeem the time we squander stumbling about in blindness; only the Lord can soften a heart hardened through years of neglect. Only the Savior is patient; He doesn't cast us off because we are too dull to ascertain the truth. He won't let us remain in our slumbering stupor. It may take time; He may have to strip us of our pride, and all the things that matter most to us. But He ultimately gives us eyes to see and ears to hear what matters most to Him. Having revealed His perfect plan, He leaves it to us to respond according to our free will.

It had taken time, but God finally snapped me awake. Jack Taylor's message in church that day was like a thunderbolt; it jolted me to attention and showed me how long I'd been in denial, how thoroughly I'd been blinded by allegiance to a system that had me serving the idol of career. I was giving my love, time, and attention to a profession. I was carefully attending to a career like a skillful gardener tends his crop, while the garden of my marriage lay fallow and choked with weeds. Yes, it took the Lord a long time with this hard-charging achiever. But He had my attention now. I may be slow to hear, but when I do, I am less hesitant to comply. The fog was lifting. The path He had laid out for me was becoming clearer.

Seeing what the years had done to Lyndi's countenance drove me to my knees. "Lord, what would You have me do?" I prayed. I had tried to draw a line at work, but my efforts to scale back had failed. I was left with a choice. If I was really going to demonstrate that I treasured God and my family, long overdue changes had to occur—*now!* I had explored every option I knew to sustain CU's success and move the program to the next level. None of them accommodated spending *less* time at work so I could spend *more* time with my family. No scenario I could envision at Colorado ever would.

By early November, I'd made my decision to resign at Colorado. It was a frightening choice that cut against the grain of everything I'd worked for. But in what seemed like a radical choice, I felt the peace of God that transcends understanding. There were other factors at work. Contractually, it was good timing. I had a five-year escape clause in my fifteen-year contract with CU that would allow me to continue as the Buffs' coach well into the twenty-first century, or step down free and clear at the end of the 1994 season. But . . . *quit my job*? The job I'd groomed myself for, sweated and labored over? Colorado had given me my big chance. I had built my reputation in Boulder.

It wasn't the first time I'd thought of quitting. Even beyond trying to re-seed the scorched earth of my marriage, I couldn't see coaching another ten years in Boulder. It had been a hard road—for both my family and me. There had been deep wounds inflicted alongside the countless blessings. All other things being equal, I could have convinced myself to keep going and finish out my career at Colorado. But the way things stood, my heart wasn't in it. Coming to terms with the sacrifices I'd made at home only seemed to cement the sense of burnout I felt.

Because of the success we'd experienced, it was going to be a round-the-clock challenge simply to maintain our position. Case in point: We finished out our 1994 season with a 10-1 record and overpowered Notre Dame in the Fiesta Bowl. CU would finish number three in the nation. Yet the success of our season, indeed the legitimacy of our entire program, always seemed to hinge on beating Nebraska. With the good fortune we'd had in the past, if CU lost to Nebraska during the regular season, nothing we did afterward really seemed to matter. It was as if we played every game pointing to that one winner-take-all contest. That takes a toll. After thirteen years, I guess I was ready to step aside and see what else the Lord might have in store.

Other opportunities had presented themselves. Michigan State had made an inquiry about my interest. It was a tempting scenario. I asked the Lord, *Am I supposed to return to my home state to finish out my career?* It was a tantalizing thought. Going home to Michigan would have been, in many respects, a dream come true. Growing up around both the University of Michigan and Michigan State had given me an incredible sense of intrigue toward their programs. Maybe, I thought, *this* was God's will. Maybe we just needed a change of scenery. Perhaps it would give Lyndi a new outlook to go back home. I certainly wouldn't have to travel as much, or as far, to recruit.

I think in some respects I still harbored a suspicion—or perhaps it was an *illusion*—that Colorado itself was a part of the problem, that trying to maintain an elite program effectively isolated from the country's major high school football hotbeds imposed unique stresses on a marriage. Recruiting blue chip players to CU had always been a travel-intensive, costly proposition. A coach has to almost *stay* out on the road to have a chance to compete for the best players in Texas, California, Ohio, and Illinois, athletes to whom other universities have year-round access. Perhaps at Michigan State that burden would be lifted somewhat and I could function effectively as both an attentive husband *and* a successful coach. I'd forgotten that I hadn't had much time for anything besides football since my first assistant coaching job in high school.

But that's the way my mind was operating at the time. Even with the answer staring me in the face every night at home, it's hard to let go. "Lord," I prayed, "make Your will clear."

One thing was clear: I would not coach another year at CU. Now I had to decide how to tell the team. Our last road game of the season was against a tough Kansas team. We flew to Lawrence on a Friday. That night and Saturday morning before the game, I spent extra time going around to each player and taking them aside. I looked each of them in the eye and personally thanked them for their contribution to CU. I'd decided I would wait to announce my decision until after the regular season. So no one knew this would be my last road trip with Colorado.

It was very emotional. I kept having to gather myself and steady my voice. It was heart-wrenching. I'd recruited every one of these young men. We'd battled it out in the trenches together. I knew their hearts. We shared the same competitive spirit. Going through the entire traveling roster, shaking each player's hand, saying something personal to each one, I lost my composure. At one point I was standing in the middle of the visitor's locker room, weeping. I'm sure the team was puzzled. They didn't know I was saying goodbye. We went out and beat Kansas, then returned to Boulder. I started to prepare myself for the end.

The Friday preceding our final regular season game against Iowa State, I was in my office overlooking Folsom Stadium. I was thumbing through the game plan like I'd done a thousand times before. Only this time my mind was far away. I was still entertaining thoughts of coaching elsewhere. I'd begun to distance myself emotionally from the normal frantic pressure. I wasn't relaxed, but I wasn't on pins and needles either.

Randy Phillips, a long-time friend and, at the time, the president of Promise Keepers, had called to see me that morning. I was curious to hear what he had to say, figuring it had to do with Promise Keepers. He arrived a short time later. The first thing he did when he walked in the door was take off his shoes. He was standing in the middle of my office in his stocking feet, an uneasy look on his face. Now I was extremely curious. I sat waiting for him to begin. Finally, he said, "Mac, first of all, I'm coming to you as a brother in Christ. I'm not here on my own accord. What I'm going to share with you, I truly believe is from the Lord."

I sensed he was confident, but I hadn't expected what he said next. "Mac," he continued, "I feel the Lord wants you to quit coaching." He stopped. I just stared at him. Then he added, "I'm not saying you should quit coaching at Colorado. I believe the Lord would have me tell you that you're not supposed to coach *anywhere* next year."

I sat there stunned, trying to absorb what I'd heard. Had I heard him right? I was set to resign at Colorado. But I still thought a chance remained I might coach elsewhere. Now, however, Randy Phillips was standing before me, telling me I was to quit coaching *altogether*. My heart was pounding. I'd always counseled others to make sure that, when they pray, they're ready for God's answer. I'm not in the habit of categorically accepting, carte blanche, whatever someone says is a word from the Lord. But sometimes you *know*, and this was one of those times. Randy's unsolicited remarks were God's way of issuing a spiritual veto, canceling any thoughts I might still have entertained of keeping my coaching prospects alive even after He had made it clear my marriage was at stake.

I had prayed for God's *specific* guidance. And, in hindsight, even though I hadn't acknowledged it, several factors had pointed in this direction for some time. God had been leading me down a path, getting me used to it one idea at a time. Now He was speaking plainly, sternly, asking me to step out in faith. Asking me to trust Him. I knew it was God, but I still wasn't prepared for it.

It was a moment of truth. I didn't balk. To waffle now would invite grave consequences. I could tell Randy had heard from the Lord and had tested it long in prayer. It was new territory for me. I leaned back and took a deep breath. I closed my eyes for a moment and sensed the Holy Spirit's soft, calming confirmation. Then I looked Randy square in the eye. "Phillips, I'm accepting what you've told me on faith. I receive it as a word from the Lord." His shoulders dropped. He seemed relieved. I added: "I will not coach *anywhere* next year."

That was it. It was settled. From that moment on, I had no doubt. I was going to step down at CU. No matter what opportunities presented themselves, I wouldn't coach in the coming year. All the fears and tension melted away. I was at peace. I still had no idea what I was going to do, but I knew God did. And to get me there, He had to pry me away from coaching. Unsearchable peace came in simply knowing God was in total control. The next day I stood in front of the State of Colorado and announced my resignation.

Chapter 30
What Excites You?

MOST CHRISTIANS ARE FAMILIAR with the Scripture verse, "Let him who boasts boast in the Lord" (1 Corinthians 1:31). What does that verse mean to you? As I have meditated on it over the years, I've come to understand more fully what God is saying. He's saying, "If any man should get excited about *anything*, he should first get excited that he knows Me."

In a world of provacative distractions, alluring enticements, and pressing material concerns, the lists of potential causes for excitement defy calculation. Scripture puts it in perspective. God tells all mankind, Christian and non-believer alike, exactly what He expects: Before we get excited about all the things we're constantly told will bring us happiness and fulfillment, we should be *first* excited that we know and worship the living God.

Statistics tell an interesting story about our society. They report that most people believe in God; they say a vast majority consider themselves "Christians." So what do we make of this? What's the criteria? What is it that really excites all these God-believing folks? In my opinion, the surveys should be rewritten to ask: "What *really* excites you?" It would tell us more about who the real Christians are. How many who have made a lifetime commitment to follow

Jesus Christ, who trust in Him alone for their salvation, and who make an earnest effort to emulate Jesus according to His Word are truly *excited* about God.

Be honest—*What excites you?* Would you say, "Walking eighteen holes with Tiger Woods would get me really excited," or "I'd be pretty excited if someone gave me ringside tickets to the Evander Holyfield-Mike Tyson rematch," or "Winning the lottery," or "A new Mercedes?" Trust me, you'd have lots of company. It's the world we live in. Next to nothing in our culture points us to God or fans our excitement about Jesus. How many Bible-believing Christians today would say, "My relationship with God is the most exciting thing in my life!" and then be able to prove it by their actions? Who among us is so red hot about Jesus Christ that the first thing from his or her lips in a conversation is, "Oh, I am so excited about Jesus. You cannot believe what the Lord has done in my life"?

Let's not kid ourselves. These are not the words of a fanatic. In God's eyes, that's not even *radical.* It's the way it *should* be. What's normal for God is radical to us. Jesus said in Luke 10:20: "Do not rejoice that the spirits submit to you, but rejoice that your names are written in heaven." This was directed in part at well-intentioned Christians deluded into thinking successful service for God replaces intimate *relationship* with God. Think of it: *Rejoice that your names are written in heaven!* Oh, that everyone on the planet would be able to make that statement. What would this planet look like if everybody understood that this is the central truth of our existense? What would this world look like if all God-fearing Christians lived in a single-minded quest for intimate, eternal fellowship with their Creator?

The sobering truth is, a nuclear holocaust wiping out life as we know it does not begin to compare with the epic calamity of millions of people going through life, out of touch or indifferent to the Savior sent to save their souls. If we haven't grasped this, we can't go any further—life itself is meaningless. God says that *nothing*—none of the things that commonly cause our hearts to race—

should *ever* compete with our affection for Him. There shouldn't even be a debate. Bottom line: If *anything* gets us excited, it should be *God.*

So if you said, "I'd rather watch Michael Jordan in the fourth quarter when the Bulls are down by ten points," or if you would rather read the newspaper or financial page than study the Word or pray or talk about God, then admit it!—You're not hot after God. In fact, your flame barely flickers.

I had to admit it. Some things are clear only in hindsight. If I've learned anything since quitting coaching, it's that the time and focus I gave my career was unhealthy. God was merciful; He used it for the good. But the intensity with which I pursued coaching crossed the line. With others it may be TV, recreation, entertainment, or simply the sum total of their busy lives—the apparent good things of life that grievously blind them to the *best* things of God. I bought into a *system,* a prevalent culture of success, that in my case revolved around coaching and lured me repeatedly away from my most important teams—God, my wife, and my family.

This is no homespun anecdote constructed from personal experience. It's laid out graphically in the Word of God. Look, for instance, at the life of David, Israel's greatest king, widely recognized as a man after God's own heart. David was the ultimate success story of his day. He was the slayer of Goliath, a courageous warrior, undefeated in battle, a leader among leaders, a prophet, a musician, and a brilliant psalmist. David was revered for his love of God, and for his righteousness. He was a seed to the royal bloodline that brought the world its Savior.

Because of his tender, trusting heart toward God, God bestowed upon David unequaled favor; God entrusted him with a kingdom. So how did David end up? His life ended in loneliness and failure. He was father to a nation, but not to his own children. He was the root of the Messianic line, but an adulterer in marriage. David's children did not really know him. They spent their formative years in aimless, self-centered pursuits while David's legend and power grew. David's son Absolom was so estranged and envious that he led a violent uprising against his father's throne. In his folly he died violently and broke his father's heart.

So we see, David had an incomparably successful "career" as king of Israel and Judah. Yet success at work did not translate into success at home. He died a stranger to those who should have been his greatest strength and joy in old age. No question, David's heart for God was unmatched. I'd love to have half of his faith and passion for God. But I don't want to end up like David. Do you?

We've seen that what a man treasures is where you'll find his heart. Scripture teaches that God is a jealous God—jealous for our love, time, and attention. I loved God; I loved my family. But once football season rolled around, I gave my time and attention to a career. Only as I gazed upon Lyndi's desolate face in church did I see the brazen hypocrisy at work in my words and ways. Once God finally got my attention, the correct path stretched out before me. I had to draw a line. If I was really going to demonstrate that I treasured God and my family, changes had to occur. If I really was a man who "boasts in the Lord," it was time to prove it.

God's ways are not our ways; His thoughts are not our thoughts. What we expect of ourselves rarely has much to do with what God expects of us. Seek first the kingdom of God; love the Lord your God with all of your heart; let he who boasts, boast in the Lord. "Who may ascend the hill of the LORD? Who may stand in his holy place? He who has clean hands and a pure heart, who does not lift up his soul to an idol or swear by what is false. He will receive blessing from the LORD and vindication from God his Savior" (Psalm 24:3–5).

Obeying God's commands seldom includes the path of least resistance. There are those who will not like what I'm about to say. But I'm convinced the demands placed on those in any number of occupations or professions make it almost impossible to maintain a proper balance. The *system*, with all of the expectations, nonstop pressures, and promised rewards, practically *requires* some to compromise what God expects of them. It compels many to neglect their wives and families and to allow their prized friendships to stagnate.

My case is not unique. Success is a harsh taskmaster. Wherever people are made to feel that their job performance is all that matters, that's where lives are tilting violently out of balance. Don't misunderstand: Great challenges, normal pressure, and ambition are not evil in themselves. Properly reined in and managed, hard work and noble goals bring out the best in us. But many, through a numbing combination of cultural conditioning and worldly incentives, have their priorities corrupted.

Whole generations have been blinded to reality by the *system*. For what greater challenge could there possibly be than pursuing God with all of one's heart? What greater reward? What conceivable blessing could outshine the diligent act of breathing life and wholeness into one's family as a yielded vessel of the Holy Spirit? What greater need could there be in a world gone crazy than to aggressively reclaim, fortify, and stabilize these cardinal relationships as God intended?

I've stood before hundreds of thousands of men telling them that their *character* is what's important. I thought I had character. My football teams thought I had character. Then I looked at Lyndi. Her face told me I *didn't* have character. I see guys every day who think they have character, but whose careers or past-times have taken on a form of god-ship. They've bought into the sinister notion that jobs, self-centered goals—even having *fun*—are more important than their marriages, their children, and particularly their eternal standing with God. It's sickness—a form of insanity. It's *idolatry*.

Some may argue, "My job won't *allow* me quality time with God and family." My response is simple but blunt. I speak from experience: If the demands of one's job are such that a person won't *ever* realistically be able to give God or their family quality time and attention, then it's time to reexamine priorities. God gave us jobs for provision and, occasionally, for purpose. But I won't mince words: If a job or any other activity dominates or determines our precious relationships—especially our relationship with God—that's idolatry. It's attributing worth to something in excess of what we give to God. God says to flee idolatry. Plain and simple. Please do not interpret this to say, "Do as I have done." But whatever you do, find the Father's heart for your life first!

Do you want to guage your spiritual temperature? Do you want to determine, once and for all, if you're really excited about God? Then listen to the prophet Isaiah: "Surely God is my salvation; I will trust and not be afraid" (Isaiah 12:2). Ask yourself a question: "Have I been born again by the Holy Spirit?" If the answer is yes, then according to God's Word we must *trust* in Him by whose name we are saved. No one can please God, or pretend to boast in the Lord, unless he trusts totally in Him.

Can we honestly say that we trust in God? Does He excite our hearts above all else? Do our lives back it up? When I was faced with the real likelihood that I would leave coaching, I found myself wrestling with all the pros and cons. It forced me to ask myself, "Is it really God that I trust? Or is it my won-lost record? Do I trust in God's eternal promises to provide richly and abundantly more than I could ever think or ask, or is it my paycheck and my job security that I trust? Do I trust what other people think or say about me, or do I draw my identity from Christ alone? Once I had resolved these questions in my mind, obeying God was a huge relief.

As Randy Phillips walked into my office that day and challenged me with a stern word from the Lord, I stand before you today. What stands between you and unreserved passion for God? Do you *want* to be excited about God? Then what are you prepared to do to afford God the time He needs to capture your affections? Remember, God is jealous for our time, love, and attention because He *loves* us, He wants to be *with* us—wants to *bless* us—more than we can imagine. To turn our backs on His offer, or regard it with passive indifference, is sheer lunacy.

Am I saying that you should quit your job in order to restore your marriages, mentor your children, and pursue deeper intimacy with the Lord? No! Not everyone has the same difficulty preserving balance that I did. I repeat, I am *not* saying you should quit your job to find another, less demanding livelihood if you find your life's priorities out of balance. What I *am* saying is that the time has come to take stock. Every person will one day answer the tough questions God's Word poses. Are you on God's path or your own? God's path leads to glory and life; our path leads to decay and destruction.

If a man can't honestly say, "I will not fear," believing that God causes all things to work together for good even when it doesn't *feel* good, then there is hypocrisy in that heart. It's not a heart that trusts in God; it's not a heart that is *hot* for God. I loved my profession with its financial rewards and perks and all the awesome challenges it presented. But when I was forced to choose God's path or my own, it was no contest. Because when I stand before God, I do not think my first report will be a detailed account of how successful I was as a coach, or even how many athletes' lives I touched. It will be a thorough accounting of how fervently I pursued Him, how radiantly I nurtured my wife, and how attentively I raised my children. Faced with this unsettling reality, it was only by saying, "Lord, I'll step out in faith and trust You for the next chapter of our lives" that I was able to finally look at Lyndi and say I was sold out to our marriage. Only by saying, "Lord, I'll even give up coaching, but I must have You" did I find strength to set parameters that proved God was my deepest longing and highest priority.

Chapter 31
Saying Goodbye to CU

The Announcement

I stood before a CU locker room packed with media and football players. The day was November 19, 1994. CU president Judith Albino was there, as was athletic director Bill Marolt. Assorted friends and family were gathered around. Most were curious about why I'd called a press conference. Rather than keep them all waiting, I just blurted it out: "I'm resigning effective this year. I'll stay and see us through the bowl game."

The stunned reaction told me it was the last thing anyone expected to hear. We'd just beaten Iowa State in our last regular season game, and CU tailback Rashaan Salaam had surpassed the 2,000-yard rushing mark, sealing his bid for the Heisman Trophy. Lyndi was by my side, arm around my waist. In front of us were a sea of dumbstruck expressions. Members of the team struggled to contain their emotions. All I could see was a room filled with faces etched in disbelief. Some wept. Reporters demanded to know why. Some tried to get me to say I was Michigan-bound.

Rumors floated that I was disenchanted at CU. It wasn't the case. Though I was being pursued at the time by two great universities, coaching elsewhere wasn't an option. I'd already resolved that I would not coach at least through the 1995–96 season. Though I hedged a bit on a possible return, the announcement had a ring of finality to it. In my own heart, I felt it was over. I was intentionally vague, saying simply, "After thirteen years as the head football coach of Colorado, it's time. This chapter has ended."

Earlier in the day, both Albino and Marolt had tried to talk me out of it. Albino asked that I delay my announcement or, short of that, take a sabbatical and think it over. I thanked them both for their support. But I was at peace. I truly believed God was calling me out of coaching. I told our coaching staff I'd lobby hard for the administration to replace me with someone from our own staff, which it did. The announcement led all the local newscasts and crowned front pages. Initially, reports were glowing. Stories chronicled Colorado's rise from the cellar, praised the program's integrity, and quoted former players. There was a sense that a majority appreciated what we'd accomplished and genuinely felt a loss at my departure.

The Un-American Eccentric

"You're going to *what?*" It still surprises me how few truly understand. To this day, die-hard Buffs' fans approach me and ask why I resigned. Others chide me and try to get me to divulge when I'm going to return to coaching. It was not the most peaceful parting. Only those who knew Lyndi and me well met my resignation with an understanding smile or offered their unwavering support. Nearly everyone else had to pick their jaws off the floor. Their faces would turn pale; their eyes would narrow, and they'd nod irritably. Then they might offer a grudging farewell. Others, we are told, simply shook their heads in disgust, chocking it off as another loony chapter in the fanatical life of an overwrought Christian. I'm sure many thought I was going over the deep end.

As expected, the pleasant afterglow following the announcement quickly faded. Within days, I was being criticized for everything from poor timing to grand standing, from intentionally detracting from Salaam's record day to dragging the spotlight off of our 10-1 season. Some were convinced I was just trying to focus attention on myself. My departure emboldened some to suggest that my "unfortunate preoccupation" with Christian causes had always been a conflict, and while they appreciated my contribution, they were, at heart, glad to see me move on.

As for the timing of my announcement, as anyone within the program understood and appreciated, it was intended solely to help the university get on with the business of hiring a new coach and signing waiting recruits. But I knew that was beside the point. I never believed timing was the issue that grated on people. It was something else, something unspoken—perhaps even undefined—that sparked the backlash. My resigning simply struck some as an ungrateful rebuff of mainstream values—definitely *not* "politically correct." What sane man would do such a thing? An article in *Sports Illustrated*, published the week of our Fiesta Bowl victory over Notre Dame, voiced an opinion likely shared by many: "What man walks out on a $350,000-per-year contract with 10 years remaining? So that he can spend time with his wife and his God? There is a word for this behavior. '*Un-American.*'"[1]

Un-American. Some clearly felt I was bailing out of a system I'd freely exploited. Others, aghast that I'd decline a lifetime contract of lucrative proportions, decided I was doing none other than spitting at the American Dream. The same *Sports Illustrated* article laid out some deeply flawed assumptions about my resignation. It mocked my reasons for leaving CU, proposing that only an idiot would leave a great job to save his family, or draw closer to God. It trained its sights on my family members and went to great lengths to portray me as a hand-wringing, Bible-thumping eccentric.[2] And I'm sure that to those writers and many *SI* readers I am. In hindsight, I was naïve to allow a secular publication to cross-examine my motives. God makes it clear in His word that "the message of the cross [of Jesus Christ] is foolishness to those who are perishing" (1 Corinthians 1:18). And, frankly, the thought of quitting a high-powered career to save my family was a relatively novel one even to me.

I have long since learned not to take public attacks against me to heart. I understand why it happens. I once was blinded to my own need for a personal relationship with Jesus Christ. I, too, was unfamiliar with the wondrous, if seemingly illogical, ways that God can steer our lives if we are open to Him. Things I now speak of with steely assurance were once "foolishness" to me. So I have no place to judge. In fact, I have tried over time to adopt the mindset of the apostle Paul, who said, "For Christ's sake, I delight in weaknesses, in insults, in hardship, in persecutions, in difficulties. For when I am weak, then I am strong" (2 Corinthians 12:10). It's a grand mystery—how Christ's power is perfected through our weakness. And I've never felt weaker than those times my family suffers because of me.

The Bible says in John 15:19 that *God* chooses those to whom He will reveal His salvation. I believe part of the reason God called me out of coaching is to pray for and speak to the spiritual blindness weighing on our country. My constant prayer is that the Holy Spirit gives sight to all whose hearts have been hardened to the gospel of Jesus Christ.

In this light, when directed at me, personal attacks from the media are like spitwads bouncing off an aircraft carrier. Not so with my family. They hurt deep down when I take a blind-side shot. And it kills me when any member of my family comes under unwanted scrutiny. Ultimately my family has little recourse but to weather the storm and lean on one another.

Only a trusted circle of friends saw behind the headlines, articles, radio-talk speculation, and armchair editorials. These close friends knew there were besetting contradictions, grave imbalances, and pressing issues in my marriage that needed to be addressed out of public view. The initial shockwaves ended soon enough, and Lyndi and I were able with relative calm to settle down and enjoy those final days leading up to the Fiesta Bowl.

In the game's immediate aftermath, however, the *Sports Illustrated* article triggered a media ambush of reporters clamoring for a response. They would have to wait. *Hawaii, here we come!* We couldn't wait. It felt like heaven to escape the spotlight for a few weeks.

A Haunting Legacy

The ocean breeze outside our window was cool and peaceful. But I couldn't sleep. My mind was racing, and my dreams were restless. Normally, soothing sounds of surf lapping on the beach would make me sleep like a log. Instead, a fast-motion newsreel was spinning in my head, dialing up the pressure and tension of a lifetime of football seasons. Images and emotions collided. Scenes of bowl games, plane trips, staff meetings, game plans, Hail Mary touchdowns, penalty flags, botched calls, and coaching errors flashed by. Isolated in our tropical retreat, I could do nothing but lay there, tossing and turning.

Where was the healing, the rest and relaxation? These were, after all, why Lyndi and I had come to Kauai. We were now both in our fifties; we needed rest and rejuvenation. We were looking to start over.

Nine days earlier I'd coached my last game for the University of Colorado. I was officially retired. And my, what a satisfying way to go out. It had all the ingredients of a perfect bon voyage: a wily old rival in Lou Holtz; a worthy nemesis in the Fighting Irish, my favorite childhood team and CU's high profile adversary in our quest for a national title; a New Year's Day bowl game with a top five ranking on the line. Is there any doubt why I loved college football? Leading Notre Dame at halftime 31-3 and finally outscoring them 41-24, my last team sent me off with a dominating performance. In fact, in my thirteen years at Colorado, I couldn't recall such an overpowering win against so worthy an opponent. I received the victory and all its trappings as a parting gift from God.

Now we were in Hawaii, trying to unwind from a thirty-year whirlwind. It was going to take time and patience. Even though it forecast dramatic changes in our lives, Lyndi and I were both at peace with my decision to resign. Rather, I should say we were as peaceful as we could be after surrendering a high-paying job with nothing definite to replace it. I trusted God, but there were real concerns. I hadn't decided what I'd be doing, and we did have a mortgage to pay.

Other issues were *crystal* clear. Three decades of hard-charging intensity had caught up with me. It wasn't something I'd have thought possible even a couple of years back. I'd always *thrived* on pressure, operated on adrenaline. There was no mistaking it: For the first time in memory I was feeling burned out, deep-down dog tired. It had been a long, crazy ride. Thirty-three years chasing a dream had taken a toll. It felt good to finally have even the remote prospect of a little rest. I knew that for what lay ahead for Lyndi and me, I'd need all the energy I could summon. The biggest challenge of my life stared me in the face. Our marriage was sick and needed immediate attention.

Resting in the Lord

Our Hawaiian getaway was just the beginning of what I figured would be a long healing process. Immediately after the Fiesta Bowl we hopped on a plane for Kauai. I was entering a season of firsts. The Fiesta Bowl victory was the *first* time in my career I was able to sit back, really take my time, and simply enjoy the scene. It was a beautiful, festive day. The team was executing our game plan beautifully, like I knew they could. And there were no recruiting trips staring me in the face immediately after the final buzzer. It felt wonderful.

Lyndi and I were high-spirited, eager, and expectant. Before we left Sun Devil stadium, I'd warned the media, "None of you will be able to find us." I wasn't kidding. Tucked away in our isolated bungalow, I could sense God's brooding presence settling us down, retraining our focus, reconnecting our hearts. We wasted no time unwinding. The first few days we spent lounging on the beach or relaxing in our hotel room. We had no particular agenda—another unprecedented first for me. We rose early for coffee, read the Bible together, wrote in our journals, and did whatever whimsical things came to mind. We spent an inordinate amount of time, together and alone, in prayer. The days floated by like a lazy dream.

It was a personal revelation. I discovered something wonderful in the process. Psalm 62:1 states, "My soul finds rest in God alone." I never really knew what that meant, witnessed by all the times we'd gone on "restful" vacations and arrived home more exhausted than when we left. Those trips would be filled with bustle and commotion. I'd be off at the crack of dawn, playing golf or talking shop with friends or coaching associates; Lyndi would be off at the beach, sightseeing, or shopping with her friends. But God's Word says true rest is found in God alone. Lyndi and I brought books and spiritual materials to read and meditate on, things we could discuss and share over breakfast or before we retired for the evening. It was calming in a way that ministered deeply to my heart. I found what it really means to *rest*. With the Lord dominating our thoughts from dawn to dusk, our days were healing and restoring in the purest sense.

The Night Watches

The watches of the night were a different story. Since the day we arrived in Kauai, sleep had turned into an exercise in agitation and unrest. My dreams were almost delirious, and fiercely intense—like an action adventure movie reel of my gridiron exploits. My subconscious was stirring up exaggerated recollections of the just-completed football season. I had no idea I was so tied in knots. Something deep within me had begun to agonize over past mistakes. Fears surfaced from nowhere: *Why am I retiring at the peak of a career?* A skeptical inner voice hounded me: *Did you really hear from God on this one?* It was tough to argue. We were forfeiting a substantial package. The CU job had become one of the nation's top coaching positions.

I'd never really dealt with insomnia before. Not like this. The act of leaving coaching tripped open a trunk full of stressful memories. Even in blissful Kauai, seemingly a million miles from Colorado, I may as well have been neck deep in recruiting season, racing to make a red-eye flight. Fitful sleep found me chasing hot prospects all over Texas and California, rehearsing my sales pitch on "Why you should play for the Buffs." Random thoughts flickered in and out: *Uh-oh, I'm losing an All-American cornerback to Nebraska; oh, no, the NCAA has refused our freshman's transcripts; how will we replace our graduating seniors; injuries are taking their toll; assistant coaches are leaving for jobs at other schools; we need to be preparing harder, better, longer.*

I should have seen it coming. What did I *expect?* Coaching, football, *sports*, had dominated my life since before high school. It had consumed me and distorted reality. The lure of the game was enveloping, like a swollen river overrunning its banks into places it had no business going. For more than thirty years it had permeated my thinking. Even today, thoughts of the *career* can still trigger galloping anxiety. It retains power to frustrate, haunt, and stir up pangs of inadequacy, pride, fear, elation, and rejection. Time has healed and brought perspective, and over time its stranglehold on my identity has loosened. Yet in those first weeks of self-imposed exile in Hawaii, its lingering influence was just rearing its ugly head. Over and over the cycle repeated itself: I would bolt awake in the middle of the night, barking orders from the sideline, berating refs for another unfair call, and feeling my blood pressure soar and my pulse start to race.

Things from Above

The dreams, the sleeplessness, simply confirmed the timing of my retirement. On Kauai, greeting each morning with Lyndi by my side, both of us eager to see what God might have in store, was a joy I hadn't experienced before. Our lives had always revolved around my breakneck routine. Only in recent months had I begun to see Lyndi and me as a *team* and her as my *teammate*. She was the one God placed in my life way back when we jumped headlong into this roller-coaster adventure. She was the one who had gritted it out and stood by my side as I poured heart and soul into coaching. God had been whispering for a long time: *It's time to be sold out to Lyndi*. My senses were now wide open. How I wished I'd seen it before now. How much easier it might have been if I'd only included my wife. God had changed my heart. All I wanted now was for Lyndi and me to team up in the coming years, while we both still had our health. I was intrigued to see how God might use us as a couple. With almost every breath, I prayed it wasn't too late.

Make no mistake, it would take time to adjust. I would miss the challenge, the excitement, the players, the game day energy, the team camaraderie. And our family had certainly benefited greatly from the comforts and opportunities coaching afforded us. But trappings of success—ample income, career growth, rich professional challenges—had for too long clouded the underlying issues of neglect tainting our lives. Our marriage couldn't withstand any more denial. A change was long overdue. Recuperating together in Hawaii, getting reacquainted, our future stretching out before us, Lyndi and I both knew we were exactly where we needed to be.

The dreams kept stubbornly returning those first weeks. I was eager to put football behind me, out of my mind. "Lord," I prayed, "release my mind from the past." By the end of our Hawaii escape, I would lay in bed watching Lyndi, envying her peaceful sleep. I'd listen to the waves and watch the moonlight dance off the walls. Snapshots of cheering crowds, of former players, of violent collisions, would click off in my mind. The mental images heaped up over thirty years were deep waters indeed. They wouldn't be quickly or easily erased. I wondered, "Lord, why are you allowing me to endure this? Haven't I been obedient to Your prompting? Haven't I done what You asked in quitting my job?"

It wasn't clear until later. On the eve of a new adventure, embarking on this new pilgrimage with Lyndi, I came to understand that God desired that I drink deeply of the utter futility which I had so completely given my mind to all those years. It would be a valuable reference point when twinges of self-doubt stirred. I would be quickly reminded to set my heart on things above, where Christ is seated at the right hand of God (Colossians 3:2). Then I would take a deep breath and fix my eyes on the delicate serenity slowly returning to Lyndi's face.

Lyndi: Walking His Talk

Bill had *said* God was number one. He had stood before thousands of men and *said* he was sold out to his wife and family. But there came a time when Bill had to ask himself if he had ever truly been sold out to those things God wanted him to be. That question was at the heart of Bill's decision to resign from CU and from coaching.

I certainly didn't raise the issue! God did. I had stopped competing against football long before. I never would have dared to give him the ultimatum of choosing me or his career in football. Since I knew I couldn't win against the competition, I had made friends with it. I'd made football my best friend. I grew to be as nuts about football as Bill was. It directed and filled our lives. Everyone we associated with lived and loved football.

Besides, I appreciated what a privilege it was for Bill to be able to make his living doing what he loved. My dad had aspired to be a screen writer for the movie industry in Hollywood. I remember how happy Dad was while pursuing his dream. But he couldn't make enough money at it to support a family of six, so he gave up the work he loved. That's when I saw lights go out in my dad's eyes. I didn't want the lights to go out in my husband's eyes.

Over the years, people sometimes suggested that Bill should leave CU, or that he should leave coaching to go into the ministry, or that he should change careers because football's time commitment didn't allow for family togetherness. My reaction was always emphatic. No! No! No! Bill *is* a football coach! Bill *is* Colorado football! No other school, no other career, was even a possibility in my mind. Regardless of the cost to me or our family, I *never* would have asked Bill to give up coaching. I was proud of him. We built our lives around his career. We benefited financially, and in numerous other ways because of it. In short, it was impossible for me to envision him in any other profession.

When Bill's concern grew because of my depression, I realized he was considering giving up coaching on my account. I was horrified. My greatest fear was, *If he gives up coaching for me, he'll grow to hate and resent me for the rest of our days*. I thought giving up the career he loved would be the beginning of the end of our family and our marriage. I did *not* want Bill to retire on my account.

When Bill called me from his office and told me he had decided to retire, he made it clear that God had led him to the decision. I knew it was for my sake, but this was between Bill and God. It was the step he had to take to be able to walk his talk. The peace I heard in his voice as he said it put my fears to rest.

The media was incredulous that a man would "leave a $350,000-per-year contract with ten years remaining so he could spend time with me and with God." The questions raised at the press conference after he announced his resignation sounded like a desperate scramble of thoughts to try and understand. It just didn't make sense to the ever-observing eye of the press that a man at the pinnacle of success would step down for any reason, especially family and being obedient to the call of God. Try as they might, they couldn't extract any negative reasons from Bill or any other explanation, so their inquiries ended. I must admit I had my own reservations. I sort of emotionally held my breath for months until I could see if there was some catch. But there wasn't.

Bill's retirement has been quite a transition for both of us. I've had to give Bill lessons on how to go to the beach and simply relax. He's getting better at it, but it's still not easy for him. Besides, he didn't resign to just sit on the beach or stay around the house and commune with me. His work with Promise Keepers is ongoing, but now we have time together. Most days he is home by four o'clock, and we're learning to share a life. We are working together and enjoying each other again as we used to when we were first dating.

As for me, I am learning to enjoy my privileged position as Bill's wife. Previously I told you how I had stopped calling him Mac and began calling him Bill because I had lost affection for him. Well, I still don't call him Mac, but it's not for lack of affection. To me, Mac is the name for the coach and the friend to all the guys. When I used to run with the pack and compete for my husband's attention, I called him Mac. His resignation helped me realize that I'm not just one of the crowd competing for his attention anymore. That's why today, I don't call him Mac. He's just Bill, a better Bill than he used to be, but he's *my* Bill.

About a year after he resigned, we went out to dinner with another couple. The woman asked me, "Lyndi, don't you feel guilty that Bill gave up such a good job for you?" Without hesitation I answered, "No. I gave up my life for him. In turn, he gave up his life for me. What's there to feel guilty about?" I think of it this way: Bill always said he valued and loved me. When he actually gave up that which he valued most, for my sake, he demonstrated what he had said all along. He showed that he was a man of his word—not just to say it but to live it. Now our marriage demonstrates the kind of love God wants us to have, where we really lay down our lives for each other.

When Bill resigned his position he didn't stop being sold out. He simply started pursuing excellence in his marriage and family life with as much vigor as he used to pursue excellence in football. It took all his energy and brilliance to turn around the football program at CU; now he's giving his best to turn around our marriage. It's going to take devotion, hard work, and perseverance. It's going to take training, a review of the fundamentals, and teamwork. But we're both committed, and so is our coach—God.

You know what we've discovered? This is not easy! I think of how Bill used to review films of past performances after every game. That was a gut-wrenching process of carefully examining aggravating mistakes, imperfections, and missed opportunities then learning from those mistakes, correcting them, strengthening the weak spots, and coming up with new strategies. That's what it took so the team could go on to victory. The process we're going through in our marriage is somewhat like that. We know we will have some wins and some losses to deal with; but we are committed to making the most of each one. God is with us to review the film, and He's determined to keep working on us until He takes us on to victory! We will trust Jesus Christ to give us His strength and guidance. We will remain sold out to our marriage and to God until we enjoy as much success on the home field as Bill has already enjoyed on the football field. Who can blame a guy for wanting success in his most important relationships as well as in his career? I can't!

God wants every Christian man to walk his talk. For those who are husbands and fathers, that means being *godly and devoted* husbands and fathers. This doesn't mean God wants all men to quit their job to have more time at home. For some men, being a godly husband and father will mean that they go out and get a job! Each man needs to consider his wife's needs and seek God in prayer about what He is calling *him* to do. He needs to take some time to be quiet before the Lord and allow the Holy Spirit to review some of the film of his life. Then he can consider where his walk doesn't match his Christian talk, and take whatever steps the Lord directs him to take, in God's strength.

Bill said part of the reason God called him out of coaching was so he could pray for and speak to the spiritual blindness sweeping the country. I see God doing this in astounding ways. I also believe God chose Bill because he is a product of our American culture and therefore can be an example of common mistakes men in our culture make with regard to their wives and children.

The press dared to call Bill's resignation "un-American." I pray our country has not slipped so far that devotion to family is worth less than a big salary and an exciting job. We seem to be struggling to find a common understanding of what the *American Dream* means to us today. To some it means being able to own a home, provide for one's family, and enjoy freedom. But to others, it's become primarily materialistic. It took Bill thirty years to see that losing his wife and children—whether emotionally or some other way—would have made his career, his big salary, his achievements, and his possessions meaningless. What does it profit any of us to own a beautiful home, if we do not have loving relationships with those who share that home? I think we all—men and women alike—need to prayerfully consider the lives we lead, and what really matters in the long run. Then we need to adjust our lives so that the way we spend our time, the causes for which we expend our energy, and that to which we are sold out will be that which truly matters most.

Chapter 32
Training for Holiness

I HAVE NEVER LACKED ZEAL to draw closer to God. Even before I entered into a personal relationship with Jesus Christ, and later, as my life and ministry suffered from various unsettling contradictions, my zeal to know and please God never varied. *Zeal* has remained constant even as my actions fluctuated. The consuming nature of this lifelong pursuit has led me repeatedly into different types of disciplines aimed at training my mind and body to stay fixed on God. Working in concert with God's unsearchable power, I believe this willingness to discipline myself for godliness helped to open my eyes and soften my heart. It ultimately enabled me to better discern and obey God's superior plan for my life, marriage, and ministry.

Dallas Willard, author of *Spirit of the Disciplines*, observes that at some point the Christian church simply neglected, or plain forgot, how to teach the disciplined lifestyle that characterized Jesus' earthly ministry. The insurmountable evidence, he says, is seen in the general futility, mediocrity, and powerlessness that typifies the average Christian. "So we do not have the strength we should have," he writes, "and Jesus' commandments become overwhelmingly burdensome to us. In fact, many Christians cannot even believe He actually intended for us to carry them out. So what is the result? His teachings are treated as a mere ideal, one that we may better ourselves by aiming for but know we are bound to fall glaringly short of."[1]

Citing the modern Church as the source of these shortcomings, Willard continues: "If the steady, longtime faithful devotees to our ministries are not transformed in the substance of their lives to the full range of Christlikeness, they are being failed by what we are teaching them."[2]

Christ's commands were intended to be more than ideals; they were intended to be hard and fast behaviors that set His people apart—*high* above the norm—and which testify to the authenticity of our faith. Not surprisingly, the gap between the two is a function of lifestyle and commitment. Adds Willard: "The general human failing is to *want* what is right and important, but at the same time not to commit to the kind of life that will produce the action we know to be right and the condition we want to enjoy."[3] He contends that sincere followers of Jesus will only find themselves transformed, tapped into the life of transcendent power and purpose Jesus *intended* for His church, as they steadfastly embrace the types of *activities* Jesus practiced.[4]

Disciplines like prayer, solitude, silence, fasting, simplicity, service, and intense study and meditation upon the Word of God not only polish our character and grant us wisdom, but usher us into the reality of godly obedience and hoped for intimacy with Jesus. Disciplining ourselves spiritually, Willard adds, involves "arranging our whole lives around the activities Jesus himself practiced in order to remain constantly at home in the fellowship of His Father. The practice that prepares us for righteous living includes not only putting our body through the motions of actions directly commanded by our Lord. It also involves engaging in whatever other activities may prepare us to carry out His commands—and not just carry them out but carry them out with strength, effectiveness, and joy."[5]

Without a disciplined lifestyle, Christians will always find Jesus' teachings impossible to obey. We will remain stunted in our growth, frustrated by our weakness, and thwarted from becoming what He has ordained that we become. How, for instance, will we ever be able to truly rejoice in the face of persecution, or cleanse our hearts of lust, bitterness, worldliness, and envy, unless we *practice* disciplines that purify our hearts and motives? How, trapped in carnal, fleshly bodies, will we ever manifest the purity and holiness of Jesus unless we start putting into practice what Jesus tells us to do?

We are told to "be imitators of God, therefore, as dearly loved children and live a life of love, just as Christ loved us and gave himself up for us as a fragrant offering and sacrifice to God" (Ephesians 5:1–2).

Jesus told all who aspire to be disciples: "Blessed are those who hear the word of God and *obey* it" (Luke 11:28, emphasis added). He said, "If you love me, you will *obey* what I command" (John 14:15, emphasis added); and "Whoever has my commands and *obeys* them, he is the one who loves me" (John 14:21, emphasis added).

Noted Christian pastor and teacher A.W. Tozer says, "Remember, we are compared with what we *could* be, not just what we *should* be. God being who He is, and Jesus Christ being His risen and all-powerful Son, anything we ought to be we can be. Anything that God has declared that we should be we can be."[6]

There nevertheless seems to be a prevailing, albeit unspoken, attitude within the church that Christ's call to unconditional obedience is optional. This is fatal, satanic thinking. The truth is, we may say we love and follow Jesus all we want, but unless we obey *all* He tells us, Jesus Himself says we will ever remain strangers. There is a decision to make and a steep price to pay if we intend to be disciples of Christ. If we want genuine relationship with our Lord, we must discipline ourselves for obedience. Do not confuse this with a "*works* versus *faith*" theology—for one is dead without the other—but look to Jesus as our model. No one was ever more disciplined than He in cultivating a relationship with His Father and subsequently carrying out His purpose on earth in the Father's full power and authority. Therefore, no one should be found more disciplined than the Christian in working out his or her salvation.

Obeying Jesus' commands to be holy requires a methodical submission of our bodies and minds to the pursuit of holiness. We submit our tongues to righteousness by *making* it bless those that curse us, when the tongue's natural tendency is to curse back. We submit our minds to holiness by praying for those who persecute us, even when our natural response is to retaliate. We submit our bodies to purity by closing ourselves in a room and meditating on the Word of God, when our natural inclination is to collapse on the couch and turn on the TV. We submit our arms and legs to righteousness when we engage them in physical labor in service to others; we submit our whole bodies to righteousness when we do good deeds without letting them be known, even though everything in us wants to cry out about what good things we are doing. We love our wives and families as Christ loves His Church when we demonstrate consistent, measurable *acts* of love rather than just uttering empty words.

These are the kinds of disciplines that train us for righteousness. And frankly, if we're unwilling to embrace the lifestyle of rigorous discipline needed to appropriate His nature and accurately represent Him to a beleaguered world, then let's admit it: Our faith is a hoax and our salvation is cheap. Even if we did manage to convert a few souls to Christ, we would only be converting them to the same powerless, lukewarm Christianity *we* practice. Are we really excited about Christ? Then since Jesus was a great Master of the spiritual life, our lives must be just as deeply characterized by His practices. We should be training ourselves for holiness, disciplining ourselves for maximum effectiveness. Oswald Chambers speaks of a Christian's spiritual growth in terms of an athlete's physical conditioning. Nothing happens, as the Nike ad suggests, unless we *just do it!*

"The question of forming habits on the basis of the grace of

God is a very vital one," observes Chambers in *The Psychology of Redemption.* "If we refuse to practice, it is not God's grace that fails when a crisis comes, but our own nature. When the crisis comes, we ask God to help us, but He cannot if we have not made our nature our ally. The practicing is ours, not God's. God regenerates us and puts us in contact with all His divine resources, but He cannot make us walk according to His will."[7]

A Fasting Lifestyle

Since retiring from coaching and coming on board fulltime with Promise Keepers in June 1995, I've been moved to undertake different types of fasts, some as long as forty days. Jesus fasted for forty days as a time of preparation for His ministry. "Out of such preparation," Dallas Willard writes, "Jesus was able to lead a public life of service through teaching and healing. He was able to love His closest companions to the end—even though they often disappointed Him greatly and seemed incapable of entering into His faith and works. And then He was able to die a death unsurpassed for its intrinsic beauty and historical effect."[8]

Can there be any doubt about Jesus' disciplined lifestyle? For a man, however, to undertake such a fast requires absolute certainty that God has called him into it. (I advise reading *God's Chosen Fast* by Arthur Wallis before considering it.)[9] In the winter of 1996, I felt such a call from God. It occurred in the days leading up to Promise Keepers' Men's Clergy Conference in Atlanta. With nearly forty thousand pastors from all over the country expected to attend for a time of renewal and reconciliation, I felt God's prompting to fast forty days and pray that God's purposes would be fulfilled through the gathering. Even so, one needs to understand that *nobody* fasts for forty days unless he is desperate to get closer to the Lord. *That* was my primary objective.

Over the next forty days my weight dropped from 206 to 184 pounds. It's the kind of weight loss that attracts attention. Quickly losing twenty pounds makes people wonder what's going on—some thought I had an incurable disease. It taught me what it's like to be socially unacceptable in certain settings. Try sitting down to a sumptuous banquet on a crowded dinner cruise off the coast of San Diego and having to politely decline each course while everyone else is chowing down. People ask why. You tell them, "I'm fasting for the Lord." Yet instead of treating you with deference or respect, it sparks revulsion. They recoil from you as if you were a lunatic.

Our culture simply doesn't understand the concept of fasting, much less sacrificing something as basic as food, to draw closer to God. Still, I gladly endured being a social outcast for a season, because I wanted more of God.

It was a struggle. I never felt like I fully understood God's heart for what He had called me into. And then, on the thirty-ninth day of the fast, God revealed Himself. He told me specifically why He had called me to such an extensive fast. Reading John 4:34, in which Jesus says, "My food is to do the will of him who sent me," I suddenly knew. *That's it!* That's God's pure motive for all of us. In my spiritual hunger, He awoke me to the fact that *my* food, my sustenance, literally, is to do His will. That's where the power lies in a Christian's life. *Do* His will.

Other Fasts

I've tried other types of fasts. I recently completed a forty-day fast in which I ate only vegetables and fruits. It had health benefits to match the spiritual discipline of avoiding rich foods. I've pursued prolonged seasons of fasting from reading the newspaper; driving in my car, I rarely listen to the radio, but I put in a Bible cassette tape and work on scripture memorization. In each case, time I would have wasted lost in the sports page I spent instead with Lyndi or with our family. Or meditating on and studying the Word. Suddenly, time normally spent in mindless, insipid activities that catered strictly to the flesh was redeemed, transformed into rich seasons of fellowship that brought depth, intimacy, and variety to my relationships.

Negativity Fast

The most impacting discipline I've ever undertaken, however, is what is known as a "negativity fast." It's a spiritual fast in the purest sense and stems from the biblical principle: "The heart is deceitful above all things and beyond cure. Who can understand it?" (Jeremiah 17:9). I have labored for years with a hard heart—the chronic tendency to harbor animosity, level criticism, and find fault with others. It can be triggered by almost anything, even silly things. I have been known to get upset if someone talks too long or wanders aimlessly in conversation, or if they constantly qualify themselves before making their point. Something as petty as a phone left ringing too long by someone standing nearby can destroy my serenity.

For years, I would get privately unnerved at meals if a companion took too long to eat after I was finished. This quirky mannerism speaks shamefully to the hardness of an impatient and irritable spirit. I'm a fast eater—always have been. I just take big bites and gobble my meal down. When others naturally take their time to just relax and enjoy their meal, I can get moody and distracted; I might even drop a few hints for them to hurry up. It's not that I have anywhere special to go in such a hurry—that's the tragedy of it—I'm just *impatient*. I'm in a hurry. It's a symptom of my uptight resistance to simply *be* in the moment, to really enjoy the person I'm with. Worse, it communicates that I don't really value the person's company, or that they're not important enough to merit my full attention for more than a few minutes. It's a sign of a hard heart. It exposes me; in those moments I do not have a heart that's sensitive to how the Lord would have me treat others.

Jesus said, "You judge by human standards; I pass judgment on no one" (John 8:15). If anyone ever had a right to judge another, it was Jesus. He did not pass judgment, even when He was being falsely accused and crucified. He left the defending, the judging, to Another. Jesus always deferred to His Father. Jesus desires that we stop passing judgment on one another. He wants us to leave the judging to Almighty God, the final Source of justice. The Holy Spirit reveals another's faults to us precisely so we can pray for them—so *God* can heal them—not so we can build a case against our brother or sister. My offenses in this realm must be contemptible in God's sight.

We've already seen how a critical, hard heart caused me to rage on the sidelines as a coach. Today it sometimes manifests itself in other strange ways. Lyndi loves to entertain, and we often have guests over to our home. She's a wonderful cook and has the genuine gift of hospitality. She makes everyone feel totally at home. After dinner we'll often sit down to play a game of some sort. Everyone's sitting around, laughing and having fun. Yet, in my mind, I want to *win* the game. Instead of enjoying myself and celebrating when others do well, I'm out to *compete*. If someone beats me, I'm privately plotting to win the next game.

It sounds humorous, and it is. I know I'm not alone in this. But while this behavior seems innocent enough, it is not of God. It is completely *un*-Christlike. Jesus said blessed are the meek, blessed are the merciful, blessed are the pure in heart, and blessed are the poor in spirit (see Matthew 5:3–7). He did not say blessed are those who always win and who are impatient and critical and hyper-competitive. Just as often, and with even more brutality, this hard heart of mine can turn back on *me*, sparking within me indescribable feelings of guilt, inadequacy, unworthiness, and downright filthiness. These thoughts are not of God—they are lies. But when my heart is not sufficiently softened, nor my ears tuned to hear what *God* has to say about me under such circumstances, demonic impressions linger and make me miserable. I can't let go of them.

Oswald Chambers wrote that the goal of a Christian's life is to be so closely identified with Christ that our senses are perpetually tuned to His voice alone. "If I am united with Jesus Christ," he says, "I hear God all the time through the devotion of hearing. What hinders me from hearing is my attention to other things. It is not that I don't want to hear God, but I am not devoted in the right areas of my life."[10]

I was introduced to the concept of the negativity fast by a wonderful Christian couple, Bill and Jeanne Dohner of Denver. It's exactly what it says—a fast from negative thinking. Jeanne shared how God revealed the process in the midst of exposing in her a critical nature she hadn't been aware of. As a discipline, it's based on 2 Corinthians 10:5, in which we are instructed to "take captive every thought to make it obedient to Christ." It requires one to carefully, continually guard one's heart, mind, and tongue, letting no negative, critical, or judgmental opinions to form without immediately taking them captive to the obedience of Christ.

To do it, one must develop a kind of mental switch that clicks on whenever a sinful or critical thought drifts in, and edit it out before it begins to snowball. In my case, having pledged for forty days to take every thought captive to Christ, I asked the Holy Spirit to prompt me each time an unclean or critical thought entered my mind. It allowed me to immediately halt the thought, confess the sin, and repent. Then I would confess Jesus Christ as my Savior, acknowledge that He purchased me for a price, and proclaim that I no longer belong to myself. Often I would ask, "Why did I have that thought?" Each time God clearly revealed an underlying root of pride, fear, doubt, anger, or insecurity. It allowed me to confess the root sin and praise God for His conviction. Instantly, I'd receive His forgiveness and love; I'd be able to move on, freed from the deadly chain reaction of thoughts that ruin my peace and distance me from my Savior.

By the second day of the fast I discovered, to my horror, that scarcely a minute passed that I wouldn't have some critical attitude about something or someone. I found myself spending literally whole days confessing, repenting, declaring Jesus, then praising

God and gaining release. It was a devastating glimpse into the darkened caverns of a carnal heart. For perhaps the first time I saw from God's perspective how instinctively impure my motives are. It showed me how filled with pride and selfishness I am. I began to see that my sinfulness is ingrained, willful, and mean-spirited, that my fleeting, seemingly trivial thoughts about others (and myself) assault the purity of God. My recurring sins wound God's heart, who sent His Son to die for all those I harbored criticism against.

That was just the beginning. God probed deeply to reveal how desperately fearful I am on a regular basis. He showed me that I am afraid of the unknown, of what the future holds. I saw how lingering doubts still haunted me: Was I right to leave coaching? Will I measure up in the ministry? Will I look bad? Will our finances hold up? Will we lose our house? I had no idea how subtly this parade of subliminal fears impacted my moment-by-moment peace. I wasn't nearly as free in Christ as I'd thought. It unmasked a dishonest streak, such as when I prayed, "Surely God is my salvation; I will trust and not be afraid. The LORD, the LORD, is my strength and my song; he has become my salvation" (Isaiah 12:2). Irrational, repetitive fear told me I *didn't* trust God as fully as I once thought.

Finally, it helped me to see how I would literally bombard *myself* with condemning thoughts. For no apparent reason, I would make superficial judgments about myself around others. Someone could walk into the room—it might be *anyone*, a total stranger—and I'd find myself thinking they didn't like me. Now, that was *my* problem, not theirs. It was purely the enemy whispering my name, yet it caused me to harbor irrational ill will toward the person. When I finally began to identify and deal with this deep-seated insecurity, it was like a piano lifting off my shoulders.

In days to come, as these paranoid fears crept up, I began to confess: "My trust is in the Lord, and I will not be afraid." Whenever a fretful impulse arose, I would repeat: "The LORD is my rock, my fortress and my deliverer; my God is my rock, in whom I take refuge" (Psalm 18:2). And if fear about finances sparked a caustic twinge, I immediately took it captive, repeating the verse: "And my God will meet all your needs according to his glorious riches in Christ Jesus" (Philippians 4:19). When I would feel insecure around others, I would silently pray the verses in Colossians 3:3–4: "For you died, and your life is now hidden with Christ in God. When Christ, who is your life, appears, then you also will appear with Him in glory."

By the end of forty days, the fears that were hardening my heart, blocking my faith and stagnating my growth had begun to dissolve. The battle continued, but I'd learned a priceless lesson. I'd learned how to wage an effective counter-offensive. This discipline spawned a radical change in the way I pursue God. It freed me to trust in God and enabled me to approach God with a pure heart. Only by learning to take every thought captive to Christ can we tell the difference between the conviction of the Holy Spirit and the condemnation of the enemy. When every thought is harnessed and filtered through God's Spirit, we find power to "demolish arguments and every pretension that sets itself up against the knowledge of God" (2 Corinthians 10:5). The negativity fast helped deliver me from the fear and insecurity that made me critical of others. It encouraged and equipped me to "be strong and courageous," to have *radical* faith, and to not be afraid or discouraged, knowing that the Lord my God is with me (Joshua 1:9).

For you it may include an altogether different set of issues. Still, disciplining ourselves according to Christ's commands is the only way we can hope to aspire to His perpetual mindset and share in His nature. Ask God to reveal to you what your issues are. Perhaps it's lack of quality time in the Word; perhaps a struggle with prayer. Perhaps there is persistent sin or carnality. Maybe you are hard-hearted toward a neighbor or family member. Consult a trusted friend or your spouse to help you identify areas of hardness or disobedience. Do it not on the defensive but with a heart hungering for purity and power and deeper intimacy with Christ.

Then move purposefully into a lifestyle of disciplining yourself for godliness. Time is short. The time has come for the people of God to truly become the "a chosen people, a royal priesthood, a holy nation, a people belonging to God" (1 Peter 2:9). Aligned with and empowered by the Holy Spirit in a determined and disciplined effort to obey Christ's commands is the only way He has provided for us to demonstrate our love for Him. Disciplining ourselves to be like Him and cooperating fully with God as He nurtures in us qualities of love, joy, peace, patience, kindness, goodness, faithfulness, gentleness, and self-control is how we will become the church Jesus wants to send forth into a searching, darkened, broken-hearted world.

Chapter 33
Prayer: Realizing His Presence

Journal Entry 3/27/96—*The highlight of my day—praying to the Father in Jesus' Name, in the power of the Holy Spirit. Nothing compares; it's a twenty-four-hour running highlight. Oh, Father, it is a privilege, a royal honor, to approach You in Jesus' Name. It is a wonderful time to worship You—all day long—even through the night. I ask to be courted by You, Holy Spirit, prodded, prompted, directed, subtly, but if necessary, on a billboard. Please, Lord, lead me into intimacy with You. I don't want to start the day in the Spirit and finish it in the flesh.*

IN MY THIRTY-PLUS YEARS coaching football, I had the privilege of knowing and learning from some world-class competitors. Some are still coaching and competing at the highest levels of college and professional sports. Others parlayed their competitive instincts into notable careers or business ventures. The field of athletics breeds fiery competitors.

Yet to this day, the greatest competitors I've *ever* known have been God's anointed men and women of prayer—God's *prayer warriors*. Waging war in the heavenlies, contending for souls against principalities and spirits, they know as few others what it takes to really compete. Prayer is their weapon and they wield it with steely confidence.

The prayer warriors I know have made heavy sacrifices to exercise their gift unhindered by material distractions. They've arranged their lives to maximize the freedom and flexibility needed to ply this most potent artillery for God's Kingdom. It is the work they were born for; it is their ministry, their gifting, their burden. They give it the first, the best of their time, energy, and resources. The act of praying has a way of humbling those called into its service. Most men and women of prayer are a broken, gentle lot. Their calling has stripped them of all selfish conceit or ulterior motives. All they want is to dwell in God's presence and search out His heart.

In Scripture we read that the effectual, fervent prayer of a righteous man avails much (see James 5:16). But I suspect few see the gift of prayer as man's greatest labor on earth. Prayer can be easy as breathing, but it is work nonetheless. It can be gentle and sweet, filling us with inexorable peace and joy and inspiring in us heavenly vision. But it's more often strenuous, taxing deliberation. It is concentrating and travailing. Done well, it is ceaseless. Prayer is wrestling in the Spirit, reading God's Word to find God's will, and then praying God's will back to Him. The most effective prayer is red hot, fiery, and intense. It is *competitive*. Jesus Himself "offered up prayers and petitions with loud cries and tears to the one who could save him from death, and he was heard because of his reverent submission" (Hebrews 5:7).

Nurturing the Spirit of Prayer

We've seen that a disciplined lifestyle is a critical component of our spiritual growth. It aids us in drawing near to God. What must be clearly understood, however, is that *everything* begins with prayer. It is the number one discipline which gives rise to other disciplines. Bypassing superficial pleasures and comforts to spend time with the Lord is possible only by ardent daily prayer. And prayer itself happens only by making prayer a high priority. It involves a willingness to turn off the TV, perhaps to get less sleep; it is a gift born of a tenacious heart, one that will fight and scratch to carve out time with the Lord. Prayer is the springboard to the deeper life with God and, as such, is among the most hard-won disciplines. Without fortifying oneself in prayer, none would be inclined to make a deliberate, disciplined move toward God.

The spirit of prayer is knowing God's voice so well, from having spent such intimate time with Him, that even the softest whisper from His lips cannot be mistaken. The spirit of prayer is waiting on Him for as long as necessary, pressing in and staying with it, until the answer comes. Prayer can't be rushed; there are no shortcuts. It is a challenge unlike any other. Those willing to stay before the Lord with songs of praise and humble petitions will reap supernatural rewards. That person will know what it is to live life to the fullest.

Prayer is the pillar of our Christian faith. Without it we are unable to communicate with our Father. Without it we cannot grow in intimacy with our Lord and we certainly cannot mature spiritually. As it says in Philippians 4:6–7, "Do not be anxious about anything, but in everything, by prayer and petition, with thanksgiving, present your requests to God. And the peace of God, which transcends all understanding, will guard your hearts and your minds in Christ Jesus." Prayer is not just communication, it's *communion* with God. As a spiritual discipline, prayer has no equal. It takes you directly into His throne room.

Finding Time to Pray

Throughout much of my life, my time and my activities revolved around sixteen-hour work days. The round-the-clock regimen had a frustrating effect on my prayer life. It turned me into a guy who too often prayed on the run. There were positive side benefits—this same frustration turned me into a man who *craved* more time with God, into a man who was willing to fight for more time in prayer. It convinced me to restrict the frequency of late nights at work. It seemed a minor concession, but it was one that freed me up to go home to the family, get a good night's rest, and rise early to attend to my highest priority.

Even if it only happened once or twice a week, these early morning times communing with the Lord were too sweet, too empowering, to ever consider turning back. A single unhurried session with God only amplified my hunger for regular, daily time with Him; time that was not compromised by outside intrusions or rigid time constraints. I knew I needed time to read God's Word and to meditate on its relevance to my life. I knew God needed time to break my heart and put me in proper alignment with His Spirit. I knew I must patiently *wait* on the Lord. If I was in a hurry, it wouldn't happen—and it seemed I was *always* in a hurry. Season after football season, as I was always grappling, always clawing to get that consistent, placid time with God, I often wondered: "Is God really ordering my steps? Am I hearing God? Or is my job ordering my steps?" A breakthrough came in simply declaring to God that I would not let football continue to control so many hours of my day. I couldn't have known then that it would set me on a path toward coaching retirement. Yet it took time. The sheer demands of my job made me eat my words more than once.

Meeting with God

I've always loved the Bible passage that says, "very early in the morning, while it was still dark, Jesus got up, left the house and went off to a solitary place, where He prayed" (Mark 1:35). But another verse spoke more directly to my situation: "Be clear minded and self-controlled so that you can pray" (1 Peter 4:7). *Clear minded? Self-controlled?* The implication was clear: Whether I was coaching or not, if I was ever going to make time for a rich prayer life, I needed an organized, systematic approach. I needed to organize my life. I needed to be clear minded and self-controlled *so I could pray*.

I began to discipline myself to rise each morning before dawn, before anyone else was stirring. When others were catching a final hour or two of sleep before a demanding day, I was keeping the most pressing appointment of my day. I was meeting with God when I was fully alert, unhurried, and totally engaged. There was no push to rush off to a coaches' meeting or a business function. I had more important business to attend to. I needed uninterrupted time to complete it without having to check the clock every five minutes.

Oh, what beautiful, indescribable joy. From day one, it was so freeing. For the first time, I wasn't concerned with distracting details; I wasn't trying to rush through my devotions. It was God and me *alone*. It immediately became the best time of my day. I was refreshed and able to linger in His presence as long as I needed—until we were *through*. In a short time, I made an impacting discovery: *Sleep is over-rated!*

Believe me, I know how tiring life can be. I'm not proposing that we deny ourselves adequate rest. Far from it. But spending uninterrupted time alone with God is the most revitalizing thing we can do for ourselves. "To this end I labor, struggling with all his energy, which so powerfully works in me" (Colossians 1:29). It takes practice at first; it takes discipline. It must become a priority; we must know it's worth it—equally as important as rising for work—or we simply won't do it.

The day I stopped letting the clock dictate how much time I would spend in prayer is the day I tapped into the awesome privilege of starting each day in God's presence. "In the morning, O LORD, you hear my voice; in the morning I lay my requests before you and wait in expectation" (Psalm 5:3). Instantaneously, I moved to a level of intimacy with the Lord I hadn't imagined. This new closeness with God showed itself in my marriage, and in my daily demeanor.

Soon, I couldn't wait to go to bed, knowing I'd soon be up with God. Nothing else, no football victory, no coaching award, no public recognition—not even sleep—had ever come close to comparing with spending time with God. In years past, rushing about and grabbing prayer time when I could find it, my spiritual growth had been painstakingly slow; now there were new breakthroughs almost daily. Even when I was tired, or when time pressures encroached, I saw how foolish it would be to sacrifice my time with God in order to grab a few minutes more of sleep. And it never failed that when I chose God, I was always left doubly energized, fortified and properly centered for the day ahead. I have never missed lost sleep.

Once I left coaching and settled into my full-time role with Promise Keepers, this morning fellowship became even more fruitful. I still traveled as much, but I was able to arrange my calendar differently. Each day I now budgeted to give the Lord and my wife top priority. It led to sweeter and sweeter harmony with God *and* Lyndi. Today, when I go to my knees, I am filled with almost childlike anticipation. I can hardly believe God has granted me the gift of approaching Him in His throne room. When He shows up in the morning, I am filled with an inexpressible joy—the kind that tells me I'm exactly where I'm supposed to be, exactly where I was *created* to be. I'm talking to God and basking in His resplendent love. Nothing my mind can conjure approaches the sheer delight of calling His name and hearing His soft reply.

Learning to Listen

The psalmist said, "I rise before dawn and cry for help; I have put my hope in your word. My eyes stay open through the watches of the night, that I may meditate on your promises" (Psalm 119:147–48). It had taken me many years to finally begin experiencing David's vow on a personal level. Yet meeting with God is not always sweetness and joy. The Father sometimes brings stern correction. I rise some mornings to pray and cannot feel God's presence at all—only a chilling sense of isolation. Contrasted with

His invigorating presence, these times bring grave concern, if not outright panic. They are unnerving evidence of broken fellowship.

Recently I spoke at a large arena. As a keynote speaker, I badly wanted to deliver an impacting message. It seemed to go smoothly; the crowd seemed responsive. The moment I stepped off the stage, I began asking friends and associates how I'd done. There were high fives, back slaps, encouraging compliments to the effect that I'd "hit a home run." I went back to the hotel quite pleased with myself.

The next morning, early, I went to my knees. God wasn't to be found. I was alone. I was shaken. I asked, "Lord, where are You? I don't understand. I rose early to meet with you. I spoke of Your wonder and glory last night. I praised You with all of my heart. I thought You would be pleased. What have I done? Where are You?" In that very instant, I sensed God was asking me a direct question: "Last night, when you finished your message, why didn't you ask *Me* how you did? You came to Me for anointing to speak, but you went to your friends seeking their opinions. Why did you not seek *Mine* first? What am I to think? Our relationship is not as deep as I thought."

It was a stinging, bitter pill. It broke my heart to hear it. But it was true. I'd spent weeks seeking God's heart for that message. And it *was* a home run; the power of the Holy Spirit fell upon that arena—not because of anything I said, but because *God* showed up. And yet I didn't seek *God's* affirmation first. I sought the approval of men. I confessed my sin and repented. Immediately God's sweetness returned. It shocked me into seeing that the only One I've ever needed to please is God. The only One who can give me true affirmation and significance is the Lord. God told me in no uncertain terms that I can no longer feed upon the praises of men. Feeling God's pleasure is enough.

It was a humbling experience, but one that also greatly encouraged me. It showed me that, even though I stumbled, I *was* hearing His voice. The morning after, I knew clearly what I'd done. That's what intimate prayer time had fostered—the fine-tuning of my ear to God's voice. My senses were awakened to the Holy Spirit's soft whisper. As I went deeper in prayer, I knew that whenever I would sin, or feel irritable, or entertain the slightest bit of pride, the Spirit was there to instantly remind me, "What are you doing? Be careful! Don't harden your heart."

I have begun to feel such depth and beauty in this relationship. Like the psalmist, I would rather spend one day in God's courts than a thousand elsewhere (Psalm 84:10). Why, you may ask, is it so sweet? Because it's what we were *created* for. To have tasted God's overshadowing *goodness* is to be irreversibly transformed. It is to become hopelessly dependent on His touch; it is to know deep down the burning desire of David's heart in Psalm 27: "One thing I ask of the LORD, this is what I seek: that I may dwell in the house of the LORD all the days of my life, to gaze upon the beauty of the LORD . . ." (v.4). *To dwell in the house of the Lord all the days of my life. To gaze upon His beauty.* Wondrous, unending fellowship with Christ is what heaven promises. Prayer delivers it here on earth.

Hello, Mr. President?

God's Word makes it clear that the primary reason we were created is to be in personal relationship with Him. Seek *first* the kingdom of God; love the Lord with *all* of your heart; God so loved the world that He gave His only begotten Son. Knowledge of this truth carries certain responsibilities. Can we jointly imagine how it must grieve God's heart when His children, aware of His all-consuming love, treat Him with lukewarm indifference, or reject altogether His generous invitation to prayer? God is never cool or aloof. He puts His heart out there for all to see. He *loves* us, and beckons us every minute of every day. He wants to talk to us, to hear our concerns. He wants to pour out upon us blessings of wisdom, joy, and healing.

Let's put it in perspective. Suppose you're sitting at home

watching TV. The phone rings. It's the White House. By some stroke of fate, the president of the United States has drawn your name and wants to meet you. He wants to get to know you; he's willing to fly to your hometown and pick you up in a limousine so the two of you can talk, have dinner, get acquainted. Would you make time in your busy schedule to meet with the president? Of course you would.

Now let's talk *reality*. You and I both know you're more likely to win the lottery than to get a call from the president, or from any of the heralded celebrities or sports stars we so eagerly celebrate. The notion is so bizarre, in fact, that it's not even worth considering.

But Jesus Christ, our Savior, says, "Here I am! I stand at the door and knock." Almighty God, the Creator, wants to come in to our lives and get to know us *personally*. The One who installs presidents in office, the Author of life, the Founder of nations, He who knits together heads of state in their mothers' wombs—the God of Abraham and Moses and Elijah—wants to spend time with *you*. Not only that, He wants to spend every minute of every day with you. Yet countless millions flatly reject His offer every day.

It is beyond incredulous. Satan has truly darkened the eyes of man. For what could possibly compare with spending time with the God of the Bible? What could be more exciting and affirming? Someone explain it to me: Why do we struggle so to spend time with God? Or why, when we do scrape together a few moments, is it typically with our last ounce of energy at the end of a draining day? We pour out our lives to jobs, entertainment, recreation—to a thousand marginal preoccupations and pursuits—while the One and only God, Father of lights, who laid the earth's foundation, breathed life into everything, and loves us with an everlasting love, waits quietly by, longing for a few minutes of our time. Something is horribly wrong here.

Having done absolutely nothing to merit it, we've been granted instant access to the King of kings. Through prayer, God has given us His personal invitation to get to know Him. By disciplining ourselves to pray, we enter His holy presence. And once a man has spent time there, I guarantee it, he'll never want to leave. He's hooked.

Be Fruitful, Then Multiply

People have asked me, "Should I get up at dawn to pray or stay up late at night?" or "How long should I pray?" Rising early is what works for me. It has deepened my faith and caused me to fall deeper and deeper in love with God. For others, there are times that may work better. The bottom line is, *find that time*. Whenever it is. As for how long to pray, a rule of thumb is found in Genesis. When God told Adam to be fruitful and multiply, he was establishing the proper order for the propagation of mankind. I believe it's a timeless principle for spiritual growth as well. Particularly as it relates to prayer.

Whatever time you are initially able to carve out of your busy schedule for God, be certain it's fruitful. *Then* multiply. Whether you get up at 5 A.M. or wait until bedtime, that time with God should be rich, rewarding, and refreshing. If you can only steal a minute or two to say "Hello, God," make sure your heart's fully engaged. Relish the moment. Focus on God alone. Block out all distractions. You will find that your desire to commune with God will grow and grow. It will be a fruitful time that soon multiplies. You'll hunger for more and more time with God. You'll find your prayers giving rise to greater discipline. Spending time with the Lord will steadily become your greatest delight.

Intercessory Prayer

Over time, I've developed a prayer list of several hundred names. These include my wife and family members, friends, prayer partners, and rosters of Promise Keepers employees. I drive in my car and call out their names; I take the list with me when I travel, lifting up each name on the plane or before I fall asleep in the hotel room. Not a day goes by that I don't go through the entire list. It is a conviction born out of my firsthand knowledge that God answers prayer. Often I'll spend an entire hour while walking or riding my bike saturating one person in prayer. I've learned the greatest gift I can give someone is to call out his or her name before the throne of grace.

Everyday I'm praying God's protection over them, praying God's salvation over them and praying God's blessings over them. It's an incomparable act of love that each of us can give our brothers and sisters. Prayer connects us to the ones for whom we pray. God put individuals in our lives, and we must take responsibility for them by praying for them ceaselessly. It is a joy and delight surpassing any worldly reward. It is not a sacrifice; it is not work or drudgery. It is an incomparable privilege God has given us to dwell in His presence, searching out His will for His church, His people, our lives, and our ministry.

Friends, I repeat, disciplining ourselves to know God is *not* a sacrifice. It *is* a discipline—the highest privilege known to man. Jesus promised us that in God's presence our cups of joy will overflow. Don't go through life missing out on what it means to be "filled with an inexpressible and glorious joy" (1 Peter 1:8). Charles Spurgeon said, "Prayer is a high and wondrous privilege. You and I, the people of God, have permission to come before the throne of heaven at any time we will, and we are encouraged to come there with great boldness."[1] God alone knows what blessings are in store for those willing to pay the price to know Him. Today, I challenge you with my whole heart: Discover for yourself this pearl of great value called prayer! It is your passport into the courts of God.

Chapter 34
The Lukewarm Generation

Journal Entries::

12/21/96 — *Last night, I didn't turn on the TV. I wanted to—I was restless. Instead I asked T.C. if he wanted to play cards. He was eager. He had great fun. I retired early. It was not an easy transition. I wanted to be entertained by the tube. I resisted relationships; it's not pretty.*

12/26/96 — *How could I display a proud heart? Jesus, You never modeled pride. You showed me humility. The Father is holy, pure and full of loving kindness. This is an ABSOLUTE! The problem is me! Why do I not mourn and grieve the woeful condition of my heart? Why do I not tremble at Your Word, Lord? Why do I not hunger and thirst for righteousness? Because I am dull. Oh, Lord, please don't leave me like this—apathetic, indifferent, prideful, performance oriented, accusing, comparing, judging, irritable, impatient, lacking deep joy. Please don't leave me dull. Oh, please, Holy Spirit—may Jesus' heart be in me. May my heart be crucified.*

1/25/97—*If You were not accessible, Lord, I would be utterly lost. If the Holy Spirit inside me did not constantly guide and direct me, I would be lost for words. But I truly do talk to You through the power of Your Holy Spirit. Because this time is so rewarding, fulfilling, and sustaining, I want it to last longer and longer, so I get up earlier and earlier—Lord, please draw me closer and closer to You. Lord, I cannot exist without You. Now that I have tasted Your love, I want to stay in the middle of it; I hunger and thirst for fellowship with You. It encourages me to know that You don't change—that with a broken and contrite heart I can always approach Your throne.*

What Will Our Legacy Be?

It was a beautiful funeral, one of the biggest I'd ever attended. Several hundred people were on hand to pay tribute to the deceased, a man well known in the community for his work with youth. He was a jovial, likeable fellow who'd been like a surrogate father to many. We had been friends. Sitting in my seat, listening as one person after another praised him, I was suddenly struck by something in the nature and tone of their comments. Everyone spoke highly, even passionately of his wonderful qualities, his kind-hearted ways, and his expressive personality. They extolled his love for his work and his encouraging manner. People were genuinely sad; there were many tears.

Yet I was becoming very disturbed by what *wasn't* being said. Something was missing. No one mentioned his spirituality. No one stood and praised his faith in the Lord. None of the friends, family, co-workers, or young protegés who knew him best could testify that this distinguished man had ever helped them get to know God better, or had prayed with them in a time of need. The funeral ended and the crowd dispersed, weeping, and grieving.

I left feeling empty. I understood why he was loved. He was a gentleman, always a willing and eager friend. He had incredible talents and fine qualities to be emulated. But none of it compensated for what he tragically *lacked*. I fear he died without ever knowing the inexpressible delight of a personal relationship with Jesus. Even such admirable qualities couldn't compensate for the fact that he had missed the mark. What made it worse for me is that the hundreds of people who gathered to celebrate his life seemed oblivious to the notion that something was horribly wrong with the picture.

Yes, they missed him. He was a good man. By worldly standards he'd lived a good life: He loved kids and definitely enjoyed a satisfying marriage. But he didn't know Jesus, the only name by which we are saved. He didn't know the only One who can take away our sins and reconcile us to a holy God. And now he was dead. It was a sobering thought. It caused me to think of the legacy each of us will one day leave. Will our own friends and family salute us in spite of our indifference to Christ, or will they be able to stand and boldly proclaim how deeply we loved God and how we helped them draw closer to the Lord?

Avoiding the Subject

Recently I attended a Colorado Rockies game in Denver with my grandson. As we searched for our seats, I bumped into a friend who keeps in contact with some of my former players. He's a Christian and a long-time supporter who gave me a wonderful Bible as a going-away gift when I retired from coaching. As so often happens, our conversation drifted immediately to sports. "Did you see the fight?" "Have you got the coaching itch yet?" "The Rockies could sure use some pitching." It would have continued on, but I finally stopped the conversation. I asked about a former player of mine he knew—I'll call him *Ron*—who I'd heard had recently given his life to the Lord. "How's Ron doing? How's his walk with the Lord?"

My friend looked surprised. His face went slack. "Hmmm," he said. "You know, I should know that." He rubbed his chin and finally shrugged his shoulders. "Mac, I'm embarrassed to say it, but

I just don't know." The question clearly made him uncomfortable. I couldn't understand why. He knew I was now in full-time Christian work; *he's* a Christian. It should have been the most natural thing in the world for two Christians to discuss the Lord in normal conversation. But it wasn't. The line of dialogue was unpalatable. We shook hands and went back to our seats. It seemed sad to me that two friends who hadn't seen each other in months couldn't talk about the one thing that *should* be our mutual, cherished delight—not sports, not the Rockies—but our joy in the Lord. We'd wasted precious time.

I keep trying to bring Jesus into my conversations. Yet I continually marvel that so many God-fearing Christians are eager to take random conversation anywhere but to Jesus. Whenever Jesus is mentioned, people clam up. The Book of Malachi says that "those who feared the LORD talked with each other, and the LORD listened and heard. A scroll of remembrance was written in his presence concerning those who feared the LORD and honored his name" (Malachi 3:16). Oh, if we only knew—God *loves* it when we talk lovingly about Him with one another. He tells us to greet one another with a holy kiss; He instructs us to teach and admonish one another in the Lord; to sing psalms, hymns, and spiritual songs to each other with gratitude in our hearts to God; and to always give thanks for what God is doing in our lives (see Colossians 3:16–17). When two brothers in the Lord see one another, they should *run* to one another, saying, "There's my brother in Christ. Tell me, please, what has the Lord been doing in Your life." Instead, we mechanically steer the conversation to sports, news headlines, or the weather. How that must grieve God.

Everything's Not OK!

Some months back, I attended an outdoor function with some friends, Christian men I'd known since I first came to Colorado. We've enjoyed each other's company on dozens of occasions. But our conversations rarely go beneath the surface. This day, as usual, talk strayed to business, the Broncos, the latest on the CU Buffs. Each time I tried to direct the conversation to the Lord, they'd stiffen up. There were things I wanted to share, eternal things I wanted to discuss and get their opinions about.

Lyndi and I had been reciting our wedding vows to one another each morning as a reminder of our marital covenant with the Lord. I badly wanted to share it with these Christian brothers. Gathering them around, I said, "Here, let me show you guys how to cover your wives in prayer every day." I knelt down, recited a few vows, then explained what I'd learned about nurturing and affirming Lyndi. But I looked up and realized I may as well have been talking quantum physics. No response. All I saw were glazed eyes. My overture led nowhere; in fact, they seemed embarrassed I'd even brought it up. The conversation veered quickly back to sports.

Later, I casually asked one of them if he was going to attend an upcoming Promise Keepers conference. "Oh, I try to get to one every couple of years," he said chuckling. "That seems to be enough." I looked at him and asked bluntly, "Would you go if you knew Jesus was going to be there?" He perked up and he said, "You bet I would." I just smiled. "He's going to *be* there. Don't you understand? Jesus shows up *every time*." I wanted to see his reaction, but the conversation went flat. He laughed it off and changed the subject.

Understand, these are some of my best friends. They profess Jesus; they go to church. But I'm worried about them, just as I'm worried about the condition of the church. A.W. Tozer, in *Rut, Rot or Revival*, says, "It is perfectly possible for a good, faithful, loyal church member to be spiritually asleep—being in a spiritual state that parallels natural sleep. What is the present condition of the evangelical church? The bulk of Christians are asleep."[1] I would add that the bulk of Christians are verging dangerously close to being lukewarm. Lukewarm is the state of being neither hot nor cold. It's a state of passive indifference; it's what happens when people try to partition their spiritual lives away from their material lives. They put job, family, and recreation in one category and persistently segment their walk with God to Sunday mornings.

There are some who even make time for an early morning devotion. They dutifully read a scripture verse, perhaps say a short prayer, and then they go about their day, neglecting to have another conversation with the Lord. Their next conversation with God comes next morning, same time, same place. What kind of relationship is that? I contend that you can't compartmentalize God into a ten-minute devotion. What a senseless waste to limit yourself to one conversation with the Lord per day. The apostle Paul says, "Be joyful *always*; pray *continually*; give thanks in *all* circumstances" (I Thessalonians 5:16–18, emphasis added). And "pray in the Spirit on *all* occasions with *all* kinds of prayers and requests" (Ephesians 6:18, emphasis added). Isolated into a little corner of our lives, God has little room to bless or convict or transform. He has no access to our everyday experience.

Lukewarm is what happens when we try to mix the world's system with God's system. You can't juggle both. The Bible says that a double-minded man is like a ship tossed in the waves; he is unstable in everything he does (see James 1:6–8). God says there is no fellowship between light and darkness (see 2 Corinthians 6:14)—but that's exactly what people do when they try to mix the world's system with God's system. It renders a person inconsistent, unstable, and lukewarm. Ironically, the lukewarm tend to be among the most self-assured that everything's OK. Everything is *not* OK. The Lord has harsh words for the lukewarm. He says He would *rather* we were hot or cold, but "because you are lukewarm—neither hot nor cold—I am about to spit you out of my mouth" (Revelation 3:16). He labels as hypocrites those who "honor me with their lips, but their hearts are far from me. They worship me in vain" (Matthew 15:8–9).

Don't think me harsh or judgmental. It's not my place, but Jesus' alone, to judge. Still, my heart breaks; it is a millstone around my neck. I'm afraid for the people of God. There are literally scores and scores of Christians—thousands of guys who've attended Promise

Keepers conferences—who cannot look each other in the eye and carry on the most half-hearted conversation about God. They say they love the Lord; they say they're saved. But the evidence of their love is a lukewarm heart.

Lukewarm is when we don't greet one another in the name of the Lord; lukewarm is when our conversation centers around all the mundane details of everything *but* Jesus; lukewarm is when, at the *end* of the night, the discussion finally works its way around to the Lord. Lukewarm is when we share no burning desire to rejoice with one another in our salvation. The psalmist says, "I trust in Your unfailing love and my heart *rejoices* in Your salvation" (Psalm 13:5, emphasis added). Do we not feel like *rejoicing* with one another in our salvation? Yes, I'm fearful. I worry that many in the church who think they're strong in faith are going to be spit out when Jesus returns.

Where Does It Say to Be Discreet?

Over the years, a few Christians and non-Christians alike have strongly urged me to cool my heels about my love for Jesus. They say I'm going overboard, that my zeal is an embarrassment—even to those in the *church*. Some say my gusto for the gospel will hurt my children, exposing them to ridicule. I don't think so. I've never read in the Bible where it says to hold back or be discreet about one's faith. I've never read where God tells us to keep a low profile about His Son. In fact, I read just the opposite.

I read in Deuteronomy where God tells His people to "fix these words of mine in your hearts and minds; tie them as symbols on your hands and bind them on your foreheads. Teach them to your children, talking about them when you sit at home and when you walk along the road, when you lie down and when you get up. Write them on the doorframes of your houses and on your gates, so that your days and the days of your children may be many in the land the LORD swore to give your forefathers, as many as the days that the heavens are above the earth" (11:18–21). And "impress them on your children. Talk about them when you sit at home and when you walk along the road, when you lie down and when you get up" (6:7).

The name of Jesus is supposed to be constantly on our lips. He should dominate our conversations. Our thoughts and our actions are to be saturated with Jesus—night and day; we are to constantly teach one another and encourage one another to be more like Jesus. Our whole lives are to revolve around Jesus. The lukewarm stubbornly resist this all-out pursuit of Christ, even though they know it's right. The lukewarm persist in compromising the gospel by willfully disobeying Christ's commands. The lukewarm are those who have become so comfortable with the trappings of this world that they conveniently stop their ears when Christ says, "I have chosen you out of the world" (John 15:19).

If God's Spirit is in a man, would that man not yield willingly to the Holy Spirit in every instance? If the Holy Spirit had total access to our lives, wouldn't we be *hot* for Christ? Wouldn't we want to talk about Jesus all the time, with *everyone?* Yet if sin has a foothold in our lives, the Spirit is quenched. If our minds have been so twisted by the sin we continue to flirt with, it's no surprise that we are lulled easily into thinking that everything *else* is important but the most *important* thing. Only the purity of Jesus' heart blazing as one with our own yielded hearts keeps us from being lukewarm.

Early "Fanatics"

Have you ever wondered where the word "Christian" originated? In the Book of Acts, we read that "the disciples were called Christians first at Antioch" (11:26). It was initially held up as a derogatory term. To be known as a Christian was to be considered an overbearing, obsessed *fanatic*, consumed with an enthusiastic, zealous love of the gospel.

Those early disciples, however, comprised a fellowship of believers who operated, in the truest sense, as a single body. They freely lent gifts, resources, and talents for the greater good of the brotherhood. They were closer than family—they were *together*—devoting themselves to the apostles' teaching and to the fellowship, to the breaking of bread and to prayer. They ate together with glad and sincere hearts and praised God day and night, enjoying the favor of the people. It was a unique, irresistible dynamic, never before or since manifested in the church with such selfless surrender and humility.

The result? "Everyone was filled with awe, and many wonders and miraculous signs were done by the apostles. . . . And the Lord added to their number daily those who were being saved" (Acts 2:43, 47). These Christians were *fanatical* about Jesus. They were filled with the Spirit. They talked about Him day and night. They were neither self-conscious nor aloof; they were gladly fools for Christ, stripped of any desire for self-promotion and fearless in the face of rejection. They were of one heart and mind. None so much as claimed "that any of his possessions was his own" (Acts 4:32). They were sold out to Christ and to one another. There were no unmet needs among them. Can you imagine such a state of affairs in the church today?

The church of Acts turned the world upside down. Believers in the early church looked forward to *eternal* rather than earthly rewards. They happily took enormous steps of faith, relinquished control, and humbled themselves to serve God's kingdom. Their total trust in God sparked the revival all others are measured by. It's the kind of church our world is waiting for. God designed us for this upward call. He designed us to be red hot and worked up for Jesus. He calls us to "proclaim from the roofs" what Jesus has whispered in our ears (Matthew 10:27).

What If?

Not long ago, I returned to CU's Dal Ward Center, where the Buffs' athletic offices are located. Walking in the door, I immediately bumped into a senior-to-be wide receiver on the team. This young man, who went on to become a number-one draft pick, came up and promptly started telling me about his forty-yard dash times and what kind of season he hoped to have to increase his stock in the draft. I listened and encouraged him. It was a friendly chat, but as I walked away, I was struck again by an enveloping sense of futility. How easy it is to avoid the things that matter most. I hadn't asked this young man about his spiritual walk. I hadn't encouraged him in his faith or prayed with him. The Lord's name never came up.

I have a recurring dream. It's a picture of how things are *supposed* to be. It's a picture of the world if Jesus had free rein in our lives. It's a picture of how God *intended* our planet to look, with humanity so red hot, so electrified by Jesus that the landscape is visibly transformed. What *would* society look like? For one, the word "lukewarm" wouldn't exist. Everyone would *always* be talking about God, praising Him for His miraculous blessings. Billboards would be plastered with devotional Scriptures; radio talk shows would answer caller's questions about Christ all night; the Top 40 countdowns would be filled with praise and worship. Network television shows and primetime programming would be dominated by stories about Jesus, about Christians living for the gospel and spreading the Word to the lost. Everywhere people would be talking about the miracle of their salvation; people would be wanting to know more about the Savior.

Magazine racks would feature cover stories about people who'd been restored, healed, and transformed by the power of God. Bestseller lists would be jammed with books about discipleship, about becoming more like Christ. Even the weather channel would have a Christian look and feel. If there were a drought in Kansas, or a flood in California, or a fire in New Mexico, the announcer would give his report; then he would call on the Lord. He would make a plea for everyone to fast and pray for relief. Without further prompting, masses around the world would fall to their knees, praying for a rescue and praising God in advance for replenishing the land.

The most brilliant, creative minds would be focused solely on reaching the unchurched in remote lands. Advanced technologies would be developed with the singular motive of communicating the word of Jesus Christ to the most people possible. The lonely, sick, and crippled of the world would be gathered into the church to be loved and provided for, as Christ intended. God's people would all be together, sharing their gifts, resources, and talents. No one would want for anything. When economies and governments began to topple, the church would be the rock-solid bastion of hope, healing, and provision.

In the Old Testament, pagan nations feared the Israelites. But it wasn't because of how great or powerful the Israelites were. They feared the *God* of the Israelites. Today, be honest, how many unbelievers fear the God of the Christians? Who stands up and takes notice when a Christian speaks of the power of God? If you wonder why so few do, or why God has become increasingly irrelevant in our culture, it's because Christians look *exactly* like the culture. The church has become like the world—lukewarm. Many Christians are asleep. Our prevailing view of God is far too small, and we know that Jesus Himself could perform few miracles wherever there was a lack of faith (see Matthew 13:58).

If a searcher wants to know the *truth* of Christ, all he has to do is look in the Bible. But if he longs to see *proof* of Christ, he must look to the Christian—to the church. We live in a world literally dying for Christians to *be* who the Bible says they are. Isn't it time we separated ourselves for God's purposes; isn't it time we *become* the people of God? We have been given the legacy of inexhaustible life from the only One who conquered death. Isn't it time to wake from our slumber and lay hold of this treasured birthright?

Lyndi: Following Bill or Following Jesus

Remember when I said, "Bill was chasing God and I was chasing Bill, choking on the dust"? That's how I spent much of my married life, even after I entered into my own personal relationship with Jesus. Bill wrote about seeking intimacy with God in this last section. I too longed for intimacy with God, but I lived as though the way to find that intimacy with God was to follow Bill.

King David wrote, "O God, you are my God, earnestly I seek you; my soul thirsts for you, my body longs for you, in a dry and weary land where there is no water" (Psalm 63:1). I had it all wrong! I was singing the same song, but I'd been singing it for Bill. I had made him my god, thinking he would save me from all my hurt and pain. Of course, there was no way he could live up to my impossible expectations because God never intended for him to do so.

My idolatry created severe problems in our marriage. I had grown accustomed to blaming Bill for every deficit I felt in my life. I was so focused on blaming him that I couldn't see where I had gone wrong. I lost clarity in my own life along with the ability to fully forgive and fully love, until God started dealing with me on this issue.

I had always thought of Ruth's words to Naomi in Ruth 1:16 as the motto for our marriage: "Don't urge me to leave you or to turn back from you. Where you go I will go, and where you stay I will stay." That's how I operated, by dutifully following Bill. However, I must admit that my biting comments and well-aimed sarcasm probably made him wish I didn't follow quite so close at times. For decades, I followed after Bill, trying to make him give me what only Jesus could give. I thought I was doing my Christian duty. I didn't realize that following Bill, emotionally and spiritually, sometimes meant I ignored Jesus when He called, "Lyndi! Come, *follow* Me."

We have a small brass-plated bicycle on a shelf in our home. It bears an inscription adapted from the verse I quoted as my marriage motto. I always thought the inscription read, "Wherever thou goest, I will go," symbolizing my commitment to Bill. Not that a bicycle has anything to do with the Bible story of Ruth, but it was an apt symbol for what I was doing in chasing after Bill. I was pedaling as fast as I could to catch up with him spiritually. I never came close. The faster I pedaled and the harder I pushed, the further I seemed to get from Bill and from God. My efforts left me self-defeated and exhausted.

Recently, I was sharing this with a friend as I showed her the brass bicycle. She looked at the inscription and said, "Lyndi, this doesn't say what you think it says. It says, 'Wherever *God* leads I will follow.'" Oh! That's a significant difference. She then shared with me something she and her husband learned when they were going through pre-marital counseling. Their pastor had told them that a marriage relationship could be envisioned as a triangle, with three equal sides, the bottom side flat on the ground, with two sides pointing toward the pinnacle. She drew the triangle and a dot at the top representing God, who could be conceived as being at the pinnacle. She then drew two dots—one on each side, explaining that these represented each marriage partner's life. Then she drew the dots closer to the pinnacle, explaining that if each person focused on moving closer to God—individually—they would simultaneously draw closer to each other as they grew closer to God. Well, where was her pastor when I got married? Or even when we both became Christians? What a difference that little diagram could have made in our marriage!

For more than thirty years, I hadn't aimed my life to grow closer to God—not directly. I wanted to be close to God, but instead of moving toward God Himself, I turned to follow after my husband. I figured that since Bill was so passionate about God, following him would get me closer to God faster than going to God myself. If you used my friend's diagram to represent how I'd lived, my dot would have turned toward the bottom of the triangle, gone all the way across the bottom, then turned to try to go up Bill's side. No wonder I ended up further from God and exhausted!

The Lord graciously revealed this to me, even though He did it in a way that was painful. It happened just a few years back, at a moment when I was grasping for Bill's love and affirmation and he pulled away from me. That devastated me, but God used the incident to discipline me. Hebrews 12:11 says, "No discipline seems pleasant at the time, but painful. Later on, however, it produces a harvest of righteousness and peace for those who have been trained by it." I didn't want to waste this pain! I wanted to be trained by it. Somehow, God revealed to me that I had been guilty of idolatry. He showed me that I needed to stop worrying about trying to change Bill and let God change me. I had to stop grasping, to let go of Bill and let God deal with him. I had to turn to follow Jesus. I had to look for my fulfillment in Christ Jesus *my* Lord. This was a realization that came to me quietly, by an inner work of the Holy Spirit who was keeping His promise to lead me into all truth.

This quiet realization caused me to repent of putting my relationship with Bill before my relationship with Jesus. It came as a change of mind and a change of direction. If I were a dot on my friend's diagram, I would have turned around and gone back down Bill's side of the triangle, across the bottom, and back up my side. In real life, it meant turning my thinking around to realize that I don't have to follow the same patterns Bill follows to love God with just as much fervor. I can love God in my own quiet, introverted, reserved way, and that's precious to God when it is sincere and aimed at pleasing Him.

I realize now I made a mistake when I tried to love God like Bill loves God, in terms of how his personality works. I'm not a dynamic kind of person with a gift for evangelism, like Bill. But that does not mean that I cannot love God just as fully, in keeping with the person God made me to be. Bill's personality is unique, and so is mine. And God does not require any of us to act like someone else. God does require us all to seek *first* His kingdom and His righteousness. He does require us not to love anyone more than we love Him and to love God with all our heart, soul, mind, and strength. I found I could love God "Lyndi's way" and still not be lukewarm, even though my way of expressing love for God is quite different than Bill's way.

What a wonderful discovery! My friend's pastor's diagram represented the truth and worked in reality! The closer I grew to God by seeking Him first, the closer I came to Bill. As I turned my attention toward developing my love relationship with Jesus, I found my worth and my foundation for living. I found the true release to love and be loved. The love I received from the Lord filled me up in such a way that I could demand less of Bill. My expectations of what Bill was supposed to give me emotionally began to come into the realm of what was possible. I stopped blaming Bill for every deficit I felt. I guess that took some of the pressure off because now it seems easier for us to come together and really minister to each other's needs. By loving God truly and directly, I became better able to love my husband as myself. And it seems I made it easier for him to love me too. When I stopped grasping, he reached out for my hand.

One of the lessons I see here is that Bill suffered because of things I misunderstood about my relationship with God. In talking with other Christian women and reading Christian books, I see that my tendency to idolize my husband and expect him to do for me what only God can do is not uncommon. Men, you should be aware of this and pray for your wives in this regard. I don't think this is something you can point out to her, but pray that God will open her eyes and He will honor your prayers. I know that Bill's prayers that the Holy Spirit would lead and guide me contributed to my being able to finally see the truth and repent.

Women, if you feel further from God and your husband than you want to be, I believe the answer will be found in God's direction. You can chase after your husband all you want—whether he's a Christian or not—but you will only exhaust yourself. This may require you to stop blaming him for your emotional deficits, and turn those deficits over to God so He can fill them in ways your husband never could. And there is an amazing bonus! When I stopped trying to force Bill to change the way I wanted him to, he changed. The Lord started talking to him about the things I'd been harping on for years, and gave him ears to hear.

Chapter 35
Stand in the Gap

Therefore come out from them and be separate, says the Lord.
Touch no unclean thing, and I will receive you.
I will be a Father to you and you will be
my sons and daughters.
—2 CORINTHIANS 6:17–18

Is This Your Jesus?

At a recent Promise Keepers conference in the Pontiac Silverdome, speaker Bruce Wilkinson, founder of Walk Thru the Bible, recounted the story about a large Christian gathering being held in a particular city. It seems every room in a nearby hotel was booked by its participants. Following the conference, one of the keynote speakers for the conference sat in the hotel lobby with the hotel's owner. He was witnessing to him about Jesus. It was a rich discussion, with lots of questions and a lively give and take. The hotel owner expressed a sincere interest in knowing more. The two agreed to meet for breakfast the next morning to continue the discussion.

When the speaker arrived in the coffee shop the next morning, however, he detected a hardness in the hotel owner's face. As they began to talk, the speaker asked, "Is something wrong? You don't seem to be as receptive as last night." The hotel proprietor looked the speaker squarely in the face and said, "You know that every single room in this hotel is occupied by a Christian attending your conference. This morning I checked our video log from last night, and over half of your people went back to their rooms and watched pornographic movies." The speaker was speechless. The hotel owner paused, then said, "If that's what your Jesus does for you, I don't want Him."

Taking Spiritual Inventory

On October 4, 1997, a multitude of men from across the United States gathered in Washington, D.C., the symbolic heart of the nation, to kneel before a holy God, confess their sins, and declare their commitment to walk in obedience with God. The event was called *Stand in the Gap: A Sacred Assembly of Men*. It was held in the nation's capital, not for political impact or partisan agenda, but because it was the most fitting setting from which to address the spiritual ills besetting its people. Washington is where national tragedies are mourned, where protests are most keenly felt, and where the nation's attention turns to in time of crisis. And we are a church and a nation in crisis.

In Ezekiel 22:30, God said, "I looked for a man among them who would build up the wall and stand before me in the gap on behalf of the land so I would not have to destroy it, but I found none." On October 4, the nation watched as Christian men from every ethnic, socioeconomic, and denominational background accepted full responsibility for failing to stand in the gap for the body of Christ and for this nation. Like Israel of old, they cried out with one thundering voice, repenting for their shortcomings and pleading for His mercy on the land.

They offered no excuses, made no defense. Rather, they simply shouldered the blame for the leadership vacuum, for the breach in the wall of protection God bestows upon His people. As one voice they confessed to abdicating their responsibilities to their wives, children, communities. There were no more games, no more denial on the National Mall that day. Men accepted their role for the blight of fatherlessness across the land, for the plague of illegitimate births touching one of every two households. They grieved and repented for the cancer of racism that has split our communities, divided our churches, and profaned our brethren. With private tears they mourned all the small, countless, private ways we—*all* of us—have shirked our duties before God.

Sandwiched between the nation's Capitol and the Lincoln Memorial, men of faith grappled with their consciences; they came to terms with the plain truth—that in 1997 evil struts arrogantly in the streets of America. As a people, as a Church, men have blinked as our country has descended into depravity; godly men have turned a blind eye as a culture has turned mean and violent; men have watched and waffled as a culture has become the chief supplier of vice to a planet. But on October 4, 1997, the men of Christ cast their vote. They chose righteousness. They stood to be counted—not one, but *legions*—saying, "Here I am, Lord, send me to stand in the gap and rebuild the wall."

Facing Facts

The men in Washington prayed for strength and courage to reclaim the moral vision for the church and for the nation. It was a painful admission that the *lack* of such a vision has taken us into a steep moral decline. In Washington, D.C., Christian men from all walks of life humbled themselves—before God, before their families, before the nation—accepting responsibility for taking a back seat while women, by default, accepted the mantle of spiritual leadership in the home. For generations women have taken their children to church; women have upheld the standard of Christ. *Stand in the Gap* was for men because the men of this generation have abdicated leadership.

Christian men have been making strides. But, frankly, the evidence says men are still far more likely than women to break their marriage vows through adultery, violence, or abandonment. Men continue to impregnate young women in unprecedented numbers, leaving them to deal with the consequences. Men are still abandoning their families; more children grow up without fathers today than at any time in our nation's history. And largely because the absence of morally sound men in the home, teenage boys are the fastest growing group of violent criminals in America. Men, far more than women, are suffering epidemic levels of drug and alcohol abuse; they commit nearly all of the nation's violent crimes; they fill 94 percent of the nation's prisons.

In 1994, Promise Keepers President Randy Phillips, praying on the National Mall, had a vision of a multitude of men gathered in Washington for a day of confession and repentance. *Stand in the Gap* was initiated by God to draw a line in the sand. He brought His sons to Washington to bring them back into accountability; to woo them back into a lifestyle of repentance and help them to turn from the alarming moral meltdown that is taking their families—the Church, a *nation*—down with them. Do we need to take men's spiritual temperature? The most graphic illustration of a moral breakdown among men is the explosive growth we're witnessing in the online porn and video sex industries.

America has long led the world as a peddler of pornography, but now, with the proliferation of video and the advent of the Internet, both the appetite and availability for pornographic materials has soared. According to *U.S. News & World Report*, hard-core pornographic video rentals rose from 75 million in 1985 to 665 million in 1996. Last year the cash Americans (mostly men) spent on this industry exceeded all of Hollywood's domestic box-office receipts—exceeding $8 billion. This doesn't even mention the explicit sexual content now pervading mainstream media.

Now we are seeing something truly frightening for its potential consequences. Advanced technology now being developed for online websites is being driven by an insatiable demand for interactive sex called "cyberporn." What is becoming of us? "Sex" is the most searched-for word on the Internet;[1] a survey by *Interactive Week* magazine estimates that 10,000 "adult" sites are already bringing in more than $1 billion annually, and it's just the beginning. A national news magazine recently reported that in one month a single pornographic site received more than 6 *million* hits.

Men in record numbers are exposing themselves to this trash. Its catastrophic impact on traditional marriage and family can scarcely be imagined. The adulterous symptoms of a cultural pestilence are on the scene: In 1997, 31 percent of all Americans claim to have had or are now having an affair; more than 62 percent of these think there is nothing *wrong* with the affairs they're having; and only 28 percent have any plans to end their affair. An entire culture is being seduced and brainwashed. In 1997, one married woman in four cheats on her husband; one married man in three cheats on his wife.[2]

And What of the Christian?

These trends have manifested deep within the walls of the Church. A Promise Keepers survey tells us that the number one sin Christian men deal with, far more than anything else, is sexual immorality—the spectrum of lust, pornography, adultery, fornication, and homosexuality. Of those who completed the survey, 62 percent struggle in one or more of these areas. Our shepherds are also struggling. A 1991 study by the Fuller Institute of Church Growth reported that 37 percent of pastors have confessed to being inappropriately involved in sexual behavior with someone in the church. And nearly 50 percent of all pastors have admitted to experiencing sexual problems in their marriages.[3]

God's Word about these practices couldn't be more clear: "Do not be deceived: Neither the sexually immoral nor idolaters nor adulterers nor male prostitutes nor homosexual offenders . . . will inherit the kingdom of God. And that is what some of you were. But you were washed, you were sanctified, you were justified in the name of the Lord Jesus Christ and by the Spirit of our God. . . . The body is not meant for sexual immorality, but for the Lord, and the Lord for the body. . . . Flee from sexual immorality" (1 Corinthians 6:9–11, 13, 18).

And, "It is God's will that you should be sanctified: that you should avoid sexual immorality; that each of you should learn to control his own body in a way that is holy and honorable, not in passionate lust like the heathen, who do not know God; and that in this matter no one should wrong his brother or take advantage of him. The Lord will punish men for all such sins, as we have already told you and warned you. For God did not call us to be impure, but to live a holy life. Therefore, he who rejects this instruction does not reject man but God, who gives you his Holy Spirit" (1 Thessalonians 4:3–8).

Men, God has not only called us out of these behaviors, He *demands* that we avoid them at all costs. He has given us His Holy Spirit to empower us, to help us resist, and to purify ourselves. Yet we refuse to cooperate. We continue to dabble in, flirt with, gaze upon and indulge in our carnal pastimes. We've become morally numb to the shame this activity brings to Christ's name, and the havoc it wreaks in our relationships.

It is certainly not the only area of compromise. Others have been as crippling. Who can calculate the damage inflicted by a generation of Christian men who have forsaken their first love—almighty God? How does one measure the damage inflicted by centuries of institutional racism and racial insensitivity within the church? What incalculable devastation has been inflicted on the Christian family by generations of men abdicating spiritual leadership in the home? How terminally have we injured our pastors by our vast indifference to their struggles, and our refusal to pray? How have our petty denominational divisions and competitiveness isolated God's shepherds and sent them fleeing prematurely from their calling? Finally, what of our hearts? Who is able to grasp the breadth of damage to our souls by self-inflicted wounds of pride, fear, jealousy, and mistrust?

Other Sacred Assemblies

> Blessed is the nation whose God is the LORD, the people he chose for his inheritance.
>
> —Psalm 33:12

In 2 Chronicles 7:14, God says, "If my people, who are called by my name, will humble themselves and pray and seek my face and turn from their wicked ways, then will I hear from heaven and will forgive their sin and will heal their land." *Stand in the Gap* was a contemporary Christian response to the mocking irreverence of our culture toward all things sacred. I fully believe it was ordained by God for this precise moment in history. By our obedient response, it may be that God's hand of judgment upon His church and upon a nation has been stayed—at least temporarily. If God's people continue in obedience, humbling themselves, seeking God's face, praying, and turning from sin, there is biblical precedent to believe God will hear and answer our prayers.

Sacred assemblies of the sort held October 4 are an archetype of periodic Old Testament solemn assemblies. In 624 B.C., for instance, young King Josiah, reading from a book of the law given by Moses, tore his clothes and wept because "our fathers have not kept the word of the LORD" (2 Chronicles 34:19–21). Josiah called together the people of Judah and Jerusalem. Together they made a covenant to follow God, to keep His commandments with all of their hearts, and to thereafter obey what was written in the book (see 2 Chronicles 34:31–33). In 951 B.C., Israel was experiencing a time of constant war and bloodshed. The prophet Obed warned, "If you seek him, he will be found by you, but if you forsake him, he will forsake you" (2 Chronicles 15:2). King Asa removed the idols from the lands of Judah and Benjamin, gathered the people in Jerusalem and made a covenant, with a loud voice, to seek the Lord with all their heart and soul. The wars ceased (see 2 Chronicles 15:9–15).

These are but two of dozens of recorded incidents when the people of God made covenants to follow His decrees. Faced with impending doom and convicted of their sin before God, the people rallied together to seek Him for mercy and deliverance. In each case, it was a catalyst for change—a starting point whereby God's people stopped their willful disobedience and rebellious ways. They set themselves apart from pagan peoples and unclean practices to purify themselves before God. We, too, are in a season of crisis; God is calling us out as well. He is calling His church, His people, to separate themselves from a culture of sacrilege and debauchery. On a practical level, He is calling us to turn off the TV; to stop being seduced by Hollywood and an increasingly vulgar, hedonistic media; to quit renting those movies and chasing after all of the worldly pleasures that entice our bodies and enslave our minds. He is calling us, above all, to invest in the things of eternity—in our relationship with Him, in our marriages, in our homes, and in our churches.

The Call to Radical Repentance

Every genuine revival throughout history began with a massive movement of prayer, followed by church-wide outbursts of confession and repentance and a restoration of deep reverence for God's Word. While other particulars may vary, prayer, confession, godly repentance, and high regard for God's Word are the four pillars of genuine spiritual awakening. Today the first pillar is in place. Powerful prayer movements encircle the globe. Untold millions across the planet are meeting and networking, praying and petitioning God with broken hearts to send worldwide revival into the present moral darkness. In some quarters—in some churches—we know of legitimate pockets of confession and repentance, where God's Spirit seems to be moving with hopeful signs of spiritual awakening. To date, however, we have yet to see the requisite widespread, anguished torrents of repentance that always precede true spiritual renewal within the church. God, we believe (and it has been confirmed in countless ways), called His sons to Washington, D.C., for this precise purpose. Men allowed the breach; men needed to take the lead. We pray that all those who poured out their hearts so forcefully on the mall will return home to become conduits of prayer and repentance in the local church.

It's important to understand the biblical meaning of repentance. Godly repentance is not, as many mistakenly assume, a one-time, verbal confession of sins—or simply admitting one's wrong behavior. That is *confession*, not biblical repentance. What God is calling His church to is *radical* repentance—what occurs when a person comes face-to-face with the woeful condition of his heart and flees from sin toward God. It is seeing one's heart from God's perspective—filled with self, sin, and worldliness. Radical repentance is being ready to acknowledge *guilt!* It is a willingness to accept blame for wrongdoing—to say, "I am the one, Lord. I have sinned!" Repentance is not merely about making things right with a person or persons you have personally wronged; it's making things right with God. In every case, *God* is the one who has been sinned against.

David said, "For I know my transgressions, and my sin is always before me. Against you, you only, have I sinned and done what is evil in your sight" (Psalm 51:3–4). A repentant man is one who is so shattered, so distraught, so despairing of his alienation from God that he turns immediately, irreversibly from his sin and begins to obey God and follow Christ, no matter the cost. Radical repentance is daily inviting God to "Search me, O God, and know my heart; test me and know my anxious thoughts. See if there is any offensive way in me, and lead me in the way everlasting" (Psalm 139:23–24). We must lower our defenses and let the Holy Spirit *convict* us to our core. We must willingly *mourn* over the myriad ways we let God down.

The impact of October 4 upon the church will be years in assessing. If it breathes life into the church, it will only be because the men *and* women of God aggressively embraced a lifestyle of radical repentance. We will know if we have by the lasting change, not the momentary conviction, it produces in our lives. Repentance must become the mortar of our faith and the lifeblood of our walk with God. Then we have a chance to be the people God is calling us to be and to accomplish the things He has called us to do. We are sinners saved by grace; we must take God at His Word and *repent* and we must keep on repenting and humbling ourselves and crying out until He answers our prayers. As this supernatural dynamic begins to operate at a deeper level throughout the body of Christ, God is faithful to revive His people.

Forceful Men Lay Hold of the Kingdom

> From the days of John the Baptist until now, the kingdom of heaven has been forcefully advancing, and forceful men lay hold of it.
>
> —Matthew 11:12

For now, however, we must face a chilling truth. Today there is little difference between so-called believers and non-believers; aside from their stated spiritual convictions, it's almost impossible to tell them apart. Recent polls comparing the behaviors of these seemingly disparate groups show that churchgoers still call in sick when they're not, still pad their resumes, still cheat on tax deductions and still lie when it's to their advantage. How can this be? Practiced as God intended, Christianity is an unrivaled force for purity and righteousness in the world. Our faith in Christ offers matchless power to transform lives, to cleanse us of unclean behaviors. So how do we explain it? How, given this tepid state of affairs, do the people of God re-emerge as a potent force for godliness in our society? Since there seems to be stubborn resistance even among *Christians* to obey God's commands, how do we recover the healthy, irresistible fear of God in our lives? God sees our plight; He shows the way.

Spiritual Two-a-Days

In my experience as an athlete and a coach, I underwent two-a-day practices for forty years: eight as a player, thirty-two as a coach. What they taught me is to put in long, hard, tough days while maintaining full concentration and focus. For a player, two-a-days are a physically intense, character-building crucible of adversity. Athletes prepare *months* in advance just to be ready for two-a-days.

For a coach, two-a-days are exercises in mental discipline, planning, and precision. It takes emotional endurance to preside over morning, afternoon, and evening meetings, with film sessions and two rugged practices thrown in between. The repetitive grind of two-a-days prepares a player to compete at his full potential, to fight through fatigue, and to maintain sharpness and clarity under withering pressure. Two-a-days demand that a coach structure his day to the minute, foresee every conceivable problem, eliminate all distractions, and maintain vigor and enthusiasm when he's ready to wilt at the end of a series of marathon days. The day I stepped away from coaching, I stepped away from forty *years* of two-a-days.

I confess I haven't missed them. Still, I'm grateful for having had the experience. It helped prepare me for full-time ministry. The grueling routine trained and groomed me for another type of two-a-day regimen, one that has yielded far sweeter returns than the gridiron version. In its rigorous commitment and disciplined execution, I propose it's the kind of regimen every Christian should be willing to embrace.

Psalm 1:2–3 says: "But his delight is in the law of the Lord, and on his law he meditates day and night. He is like a tree planted by streams of water, which yields its fruit in season and whose leaf does not wither. Whatever he does prospers." Two-a-days on the gridiron steels an athlete for battle in the trenches. But Psalm 1 gives the Christian the spiritual equivalent of two-a-days—the means by which to prepare ourselves for godliness: *Meditate on the Word of God day and night*. It is God's answer to our predicament; it is the antidote to lethargy, to lukewarm mediocrity. It is God's gift to us—our divine weapon—to demolish strongholds and every argument and pretension that sets itself up against the knowledge of God (2 Corinthians 10:4). It is the demanding regimen which cannot fail us in times of testing; meditating on God's Word day and night will make us strong, courageous, and victorious in His service.

On the eve of leading Israel into a promised land occupied by fierce, hostile opposition, Joshua received a Coach's pep talk from the Captain of Hosts. God's instruction: "Do not let the Book of the Law depart from your mouth; meditate on it day and night, so that you may be careful to do everything written in it. Then you will be prosperous and successful. . . . Be strong and courageous" (Joshua 1:8).

With these words, God galvanized Joshua and gave His people the key to victory in the face of fierce opposition: *Meditate on God's Word day and night.* The Coach told the player how to win the game, how to claim the promised land. This is God's Word to His people—if they embrace His Word, meditate on it, and *do it*, then they will have courage to do the right thing, and to stand strong! Who can doubt that this is the level of commitment God requires of us today? Are we willing to accept it to reclaim our own church and possibly a nation? Are we willing to find our identity and delight in God, to be wholehearted and sold out to His Word? God has given us the key—to give our hearts, minds, and bodies over *totally* to Christ. In so doing, He will grant us favor among the lost; He will transform us; He will cause us, well past old age, to flourish in His service.

Getting Back to Team

One more thing about two-a-days: A coach uses this critical time during the preseason to take his players from an inward to an outward focus. Over the course of two weeks, a coaching staff can begin to shift a player's sights from personal to team goals. Part of the reason for such relentless intensity is to shed an athlete of selfish motives, to strip them off one by one, until the *team* becomes the most important thing. Only the teams that truly come together can approximate their potential.

In this same way, spiritual two-a-days—the act of giving our minds and bodies over totally to Christ—has a similar effect. It shifts our focus from an inward to an outward perspective—*exactly* what God intended. Meditating on God's Word day and night softens our hearts, makes us less self-centered, and readjusts our focus toward serving others. As we fill ourselves with Truth, we begin to see that it is the needs and well-being of the church, of God's *people,* that matter most. By fixing our eyes on Christ—who came to *serve* rather than be served, who shed His personal glory for the sake of the lost—His nature is grafted into our own. Where God desires to take us, our focus must shift from self to community. Two-a-days will do that. The Word will have its irresistible effect. We will find ourselves invested in team glory rather than personal glory.

Athletes seeking bronze-plated trophies eagerly devote themselves to a demanding two-a-day routine. Can we, who have so much more to hope for, so much more to gain, commit ourselves to the disciplined practice of radical repentance, of continually seeking Christ through prayer and the Word? The stakes—for the church, for a nation, for our families and communities—couldn't be higher. Only God knows what blessings He has in store for a people consumed by zeal for His name. We have but to do our part. He will do the rest.

Stand and Be Counted

> Is any man afraid or fainthearted? Let him go home so that his brothers will not become disheartened too.
>
> —Deuteronomy 20:8

If God wills, on January 1 in the year 2000, Promise Keepers will hold a roll call for all the churches of this nation. That day we will call all of the pastors of every Christian church to travel to their state capital, where, connected by satellite, we will ask them to stand up and be counted. It will be a day in which every church's colors will fly for every other church to see. It will be a decisive moment for the church, revealing how it responded to God's sacred call.

At the closing of *Stand in the Gap*, every man was asked to return home and report to his local church. He was asked to submit himself to the authority of his pastor, and to begin praying for and serving his local shepherds. Every pastor was asked to go back to his church and lead his flock into discovering their spiritual gifts. By learning what God has uniquely gifted us for, every man and woman will be asked to pour these God-given talents and abilities back into the local church, enriching the body and strengthening and complementing the pastor.

Every pastor was challenged to work with the men of his church to establish a vital men's ministry; to provide small group settings where men can support and encourage one another to go deeper with the Lord. We are challenging each church to form vital prayer networks with the other churches in its region, to step boldly across ethnic and denominational lines in building these mutually supportive relationships. Each church must begin to work toward breaking down racial barriers within its own congregation, and with churches of different ethnic backgrounds in their community.

By the year 2000, we expect God to *eradicate* racism in the church. On that day, any church that names the name of Jesus Christ should be able to stand and boldly say, "We have abolished racism in our church!" I believe that is God's heart for His people.

What does this look like? It starts with the pastors; we're asking each of the pastors in a given community to begin meeting weekly with one another—*face to face*, in the same room—where they will listen to one another, share prayer requests, and go back to their own churches discussing the needs of their brethren. I plead with you: as a body we need to shift from an inward to an outward focus. The only way our churches will discover the *real* needs in the community is by *talking* with one another.

Too many churches today are insulated, worried about the annual budget, membership quotas, and church growth. The burden invariably falls on the pastors—it's *expected* of them. But this must stop. The men and women of the church, as part of their time and treasure, must take some of the pressure off the pastors in these business-related activities so pastors can begin to attend to the more pressing business of ministering to the lost and addressing needs in the community. There are people in our communities who are fearful and alone, who don't know where their next *meal* is coming from. But because our churches are isolated and disconnected—because we have not stood together—many fall through the cracks.

We're asking the pastors to lead the way. We *are* imploring the pastors to work toward a unified vision. Our shepherds need a united strategy to team up across racial, cultural, and denominational lines. They need to encourage one another, to share resources, to pray for one another—to *get to know each other* in the name of Jesus! Then, I believe, our team will potentially satisfy God's heart. On the first day of the year 2000, we will gather in a spirit of rejoicing in our respective state capitals to give an accounting of where God's people stand in each of these vital areas. Those who decline will be making their own statement.

It doesn't end there. We have asked fathers to return home and teach their children, to instruct them in the way of the Lord, to speak to them about God morning, noon, and night. We have asked fathers to invest in their family's lives, to love, protect, and affirm their wives and children. We have asked husbands to return home and lay down their lives for their wives, to nurture them back to health and splendor and radiance, and to embrace them as their God-given teammates.

We have asked pastors to preach to us the truth in all its power. We have made it clear that we don't want to be entertained, that we don't want to be soothed and reassured in our lethargy. We want to be *convicted*, challenged and shattered by the two-edged sword of God's living Word. We want to be revived in our spirits by a stern, firm word from the Lord.

We realize that for this to take place, fundamental changes must occur. We are asking pastors to delegate some of the responsibilities and details of running their churches to elders and volunteers. We are asking the men of the church to help them. It's critical. It will free our shepherds to obey what the apostle instructed in Acts 6:4—to devote themselves "to prayer and the ministry of the word." We need every pastor to be broken before the Lord, anointed by His Spirit, filled with fresh fire, new wisdom, and insight. Pastors, we need you to be spending quality time with Jesus, on your knees, in your prayer closet. To be the people of God, we need our shepherds to become so intimate with Him that you *know* when He is speaking and what He is saying. Then you can speak with authority, accurately dividing the Word, looking through His eyes, and leading the flock in paths of righteousness.

In the final analysis, these requests have one goal: to prompt Christians everywhere to "come out from them," to touch no unclean thing, and to separate themselves from a culture weighted with sin. A culture which shows only hatred for those who love God. We are asking our brothers and sisters in Christ to turn off the TV and invest in the treasures God has deposited in each of your families. The challenges before us are daunting. But they are plain.

Until the children of God say NO! to their preoccupation with the world, until they break its seductive grip on their hearts, heaven will continue to stop its ears; and we will not see revival. We mustn't go another day blaspheming God by our immorality. Jesus Christ hung on a cross to save us from an eternity in hell. Do we dare stubbornly resist His call to repentance? It's too late for games—it's time to put away childish things. I pray, Holy Spirit, convict us. Do not permit us to harden our hearts. God's Word promises us that chains of bondage now enslaving the church, and holding a nation captive, will be broken if only the people of God will stand as one in prayer and *repent*. God's own kingdom will appear in our midst if only forceful men will lay hold of it, and with one voice say, "I have made a decision. I will stand in the gap for my country and church. I will set myself apart for my family and my faith. At this critical time in our history, I want to make my life count for Jesus Christ!"

Lyndi: Looking Back, Looking Forward

As I look back at our life together and what God has done, I am struck by one primary thought: God has continuously been at work in us, while moving us to fulfill His vision for us. What a challenge it is to go through life with another human being—especially one of the opposite sex! And yet I see how God has used our differences and our misunderstandings to drive each of us back to Him, to show us how desperately we need God's love and patience to stay together and fulfill His call on our lives.

I am fully aware that I am not some glorious finished product with all the answers. But God has given me victories and clothed me with His dignity. I'm bolder, stronger, and not nearly so intimidated as I once was by what others say and do. Whereas I used to keep quiet, now I'm speaking up. If I'm not heard the first time, I don't hide within myself anymore. I say it again. If I'm not heard the third time—well, unfortunately I'm still a product of thirty-four years of the sports mentality that says, "Three strikes, and you're out." But now when something needs to be said, God has even given me courage to say it a fourth time. And now Bill is around to hear and is inclined to listen to me.

Just the other day he came home from a meeting where the staff at Promise Keepers had been praying about an important matter. He asked me my opinion. When I offered it, he listened and appreciated what I had to say. He said it gave him a clear view of what he needed to do. It's as if Bill's view is one lens of a set of binoculars, and my view is the other lens. Now we are working together to adjust our combined views so that we can see further and clearer than ever before. In each situation we will have to practice making adjustments, but we are intent on looking to the future together.

Remember that booklet I mentioned that told how our hearts are meant to be Christ's home? I can see how God has been knocking on door after door in Bill's heart, and in mine. There is one room in my heart that God seems to be knocking on now. That's the attic. Over the years, while Bill was focused on outside interests, I stopped sharing the important issues of my heart with him. I figured he didn't care, so I put away many important events and aspects of my life, and our children's lives, without even discussing them with him. Along with these issues, I packed away some hurt, fear, anger, and resentment that can rot those precious memories if I don't go back and clean out that attic.

At one point, after we had gone through that summer of counseling and I started to go down again, Bill thought, "Hadn't we taken care of things?" Well, it was a start, but I think there is more we need to take care of together. So I think part of our future will be spent sorting through what's been stored away in my heart, throwing out the garbage and preserving what is good. Bill missed out on so much, and I believe I will be able to help him appreciate some of what he missed. And he will help me clear out some old junk that is really cluttering up my inner life.

Someone asked me recently if Bill is a man of integrity. I say yes! I don't mean he is perfect by a long shot. But he is a man who is doing as much of God's will as he sees to do. When God shows him something in his life that is out of line with God's Word, he is willing to bring his life into agreement with God's will. He is willing to take a step in that direction, and keep taking steps until his life is on track with what God intends. More and more I see an agreement between his public life and his private life. More and more, I see an integration of what he professes and what he possesses of God's will. I believe that is a man of integrity.

Bill has dared to call himself a Promise Keeper and called a nation of men to join him in calling themselves Promise Keepers. This does not mean he never breaks a promise. The name is really God's promise to him as to what he will become. Bill is on his way to walking in that every day; he is determined not to lower his standard even though he may sometimes fall short. God has given him this vision. God has promised to make him a Promise Keeper. God will lead him toward the fulfillment of that vision and change him into the man of the vision along the way. But I think the road he will take may surprise even Bill.

Bill has always been the one to forge ahead, "forgetting those things that are behind and pressing on" to what lies ahead, that he may lay hold of that for which Christ Jesus laid hold of him. But sometimes God must take a man back so that he can go forward to the fulfillment of the vision God has given him.

I look at what God did with Jacob and see a parallel to what He may be doing with Bill and Promise Keepers. God had a plan for Jacob that He revealed before he was even born. This was God's good plan through which He would lead a nation in the future. He chose Jacob, but not because he was a sinless, upright person his whole life. Jacob was a deceiver; his name even meant supplanter, someone who would just grab what he wanted. By his nature Jacob hurt the people closest to him. He deceived his father and stole his brother's birthright. But he developed a sincere relationship with God. He vowed that the Lord would be his God and that he would follow Him. As Jacob left home, running away from his brother who was intent on killing him, God told him, "I am with you and will watch over you wherever you go, and I will bring you back to this land. I will not leave you until I have done what I have promised you" (Genesis 28:15). Jacob spent the next twenty years working hard and raising a family. Then the Lord said to Jacob, "Go back to the land of your fathers and to your relatives, and I will be with you" (Genesis 31:3).

To become the man God intended him to be, to arrive at the destination God had appointed for him, God told Jacob to go back to get ahead. It was only when Jacob became willing and took steps to go back to reconcile with his brother, whom he had wronged twenty years prior, that God could fulfill the promise and vision He had given him for his life.

God knew that He would one day change Jacob's name to Israel, a name that became synonymous with the people of God. But that change of identity didn't happen fully until Jacob was on his way back home. That's when he wrestled with God, and would not give up until God blessed him. That is when he became who God always intended him to be.

I believe God has a plan for each of us, and a particular plan for Bill. I do believe that it is God's plan that Bill help lead the men of our nation to become promise keepers. Obviously—if you've read this book you know—God didn't choose Bill because he was a sinless, upright person his whole life. He was a man who set out to grasp his dreams. He was sold out to his ideals and to the pursuit of his career, but sometimes that hurt the people closest to him. Bill developed a sincere relationship with God and vowed that the Lord would be his God. Just as God would not let go of Jacob until he had done what he had promised, I believe God will not let go of Bill until he has fulfilled his promise in Him and through Him.

Bill has spent decades working hard, and God has blessed him abundantly. When God called Bill to be a "Promise Keeper" in 1991, when He called him to resign his coaching position in 1994, I believe God was telling Bill to go home just as surely as God called Jacob to go home. And just as Jacob had to face the hurt and anger that he feared would be waiting for him from his brother, Bill has had to face some family problems he had run from as well. That was part of God's ordained journey on the road to becoming a Promise Keeper. Bill also wrestled with God, and would not give up. He still wrestles with God, and—I know the man—he will not give up. Just as I have seen this man wrestle with God, I have seen God bless him. I have seen that God changed his name so that he can be called a Promise Keeper and so that he can be used to lead a nation of men—sinful, misdirected, and self-centered though they may be—to become Promise Keepers to their wives and children.

Men, I believe God has a plan to make you into the Promise Keeper he has always intended you to be. It does not matter how many promises you have broken in the past. It does not matter how deeply you have hurt those you love or were supposed to love but did not. God can still fulfill His vision of making you into a true Promise Keeper. But in order to go forward you too may need to go back home first; to become a Promise Keeper you may need to revisit where you have broken your promises, you may need to face the people you have hurt and seek to make things right. There will be times when it feels like you are wrestling with God. I urge you, don't give up no matter how weak you may feel at times. When the night has passed, when the wrestling is finished, God will bless you if you don't let go. God will change your name. He will make you into the Promise Keeper He always intended you to be. I know it can happen. I'm living with living proof.

Women, I encourage you to be patient with your husbands, and I leave you with these words of encouragement from the prophet Habakkuk:

> But these things I plan won't happen right away. Slowly, steadily, surely, the time approaches when the vision will be fulfilled. If it seems slow, do not despair, for these things will surely come to pass. Just be patient! They will not be overdue a single day!
>
> —Habakkuk 2:3 (LB)

Epilogue
Christ in Me, the Hope of Glory

To them God has chosen to make known among the Gentiles the glorious riches of this mystery, which is Christ in you, the hope of glory.
—COLOSSIANS 1:27

10/3/93

Dear Jesus Christ:

Thank You for dying for me. Now I want to die for You—I confess a proud and haughty heart. I confess arrogance in my spirit. I admit a desire for human glory. I exchange these for Your blood. I agree to yield to Your Spirit. You are my hope for a changed heart and a renewed life. Jesus Christ, please cleanse me and wash me clean, without sin. Please don't take Your Holy Spirit from me. Lord I need You to lead me into true humility. I need You to help me surrender all, just like You did for me. I am tired of living for myself. I desire to live for You. Oh Spirit of God, please empty the sin out of me. Please put a right spirit in me. Thank You, Jesus.

My hope is in You
—Bill McCartney

Blown Cover

It had been a frantic day around Promise Keepers. I was exhausted. We'd had a long afternoon board meeting sandwiched by what seemed an endless series of strategy meetings and financial review sessions. I left Denver late and drove straight out of town toward church, located thirty-five minutes north in the foothills outside of Boulder. I would have to rush to make our 6:30 P.M. church board meeting.

Arriving in the nick of time, I found the parking lot empty. The doors of the church were locked. I thought, *Yes! The meeting's been canceled.* I almost headed straight for home, but just to be conscientious I double-checked the premises carefully—rattled the doors, peeked in the windows. Satisfied that there was to be no meeting, I cheerfully hopped in my car and drove home, relieved to be free of that two- to three-hour commitment. I thanked the Lord for an unexpected night of relaxation.

Pulling into the driveway, I felt lighthearted and free. *Hmmm. . .,* I thought. *Wonder what's on TV.* Yet walking in the door, I heard a voice echoing from the answering machine. It was my pastor. "Mac . . . it's James. I don't know if you got the message. The board meeting's been moved to my house." I stood silently, debating whether to pick up the phone. "Anyway, Mac, we're all over here, ready to get started. If you get this message, come on over. We'll be waiting." *Click!*

Various scenarios were spinning through my mind. My first thought was, *Oh, well, I guess I should go on over there.* But then I thought, M*y cover isn't blown. No one knows I'm home. . . . The answering machine is filled with messages. . . . If I don't return the call . . . or . . . if I just don't show up . . . they'll think I got home late . . . or forgot to check my messages and went to bed. Yeah . . .* that's it! . . . *I got home late and forgot to check my messages . . . . Perfect alibi. . . . I'm* free. . . . Monday Night Football, *here I come!*

It was a neat rationalization all wrapped up in a bow. I ignored the nagging twinge of guilt I felt and proceeded to have a restful evening watching the game. I got to bed early and rose early, primed and alert for my devotional time with the Lord. Lately I'd been waking up at 4:30 sharp without an alarm. It was uncanny, as if

God were nudging me awake at the same time each morning in a kind of personalized wake-up call, wanting to spend as much time as possible with *me*. Our fellowship had never been sweeter. Entering the prayer room downstairs, I went to my knees. I opened my Bible where I'd left off, expecting some immediate sense of His presence illuminating the Word. The Bible had been coming to life for me lately, galvanizing me and fortifying me for the demanding days we'd been experiencing at Promise Keepers. I found my place and began to read. I was distracted. I tried again, but I couldn't get focused. The Word didn't make sense—it looked like Greek.

I stopped reading and tried to pray. But my thoughts were out of focus; I had no direction, no peace. By now I was starting to get agitated. "Where *are* you Lord?" I knew the answer. From a lengthy track record, I knew the problem lay with me—not God. Even before I'd fully formed the question, my mind was riveted on the sequence of events from the prior evening. *I had deceived my pastor. I wanted only my own comfort at the expense of my duty to my church.* That was it. It had seemed innocent enough at the time. In near exhaustion, I'd duped myself into thinking a bit of subterfuge was in order. Now, with the Holy Spirit piercing me with His strobe, I knew I'd committed a grievous breach. *Not again.* It was a sinking feeling, like being punched in the stomach. Kneeling reverently in my study, my true colors were flying.

In a matter of hours, I would be in full swing at work at Promise Keepers, encouraging every staff member to press in to the Lord, to *keep their promises*; I would be exhorting them to obey Christ's standard of holiness and integrity. Yet, here I was, the leader and founder, justifying a blatant deception to get out of a church meeting. As I knelt there, the Holy Spirit's rebuke was sharp. It was as if God were saying, "I will not stand for this behavior anymore. The world is rotting before your eyes and you are content to use little white lies to promote your own ease and comfort. If you intend to grow in relationship with Me, I am calling you to *radical* obedience!"

I stopped where I was. I confessed my sin; I repented and asked for God's mercy and forgiveness. "Lord, I know You require a soul who listens to You, yields to Your subtle prompting, and obeys You. Forgive me, Jesus. I have been selfish and disobedient. Please restore Your Spirit to me." In the following moments the heaviness and confusion lifted. God's warming presence returned. I proceeded to have a rich time in prayer and in the Word. My spirit was revived to face the day's rigors.

Later that morning I called my pastor. I confessed my crime and asked his forgiveness. He was stunned. "No one ever calls and confesses something like that to me," he said. "In this day, that *is* radical obedience." His affirmation felt good at the moment. Yet it was just another bitter reminder of all the ways I continue to fail God every day; another lingering memento of how far I have yet to go.

Valentine's Day Shocker

What a Valentine's Day gift. Lyndi gave me a *9 out of 10 ranking in our marriage!* Glory to God! I was speechless. It happened February 14, 1997. Lyndi presented me a Valentine's Day card with the long-awaited score tucked at the bottom of her note. It was one of the best days of my life. It told me that since that day in Dallas when I gave my marriage an embarrassing 7, we'd made steady progress. I'd vowed to become the husband Lyndi needed and had taken deliberate steps to bring it about. Over the course of two years, our marriage had gone from an 8.0 to an 8.5, to a *nine*. I don't pretend we've arrived. Lyndi is probably generous in her scoring system. There is still much room for improvement. But my wife was telling me things were improving. It felt like a ray of sunlight after an endless pitch black, stormy night.

Some may think it a silly exercise to rate one's marriage. Perhaps, but it has given me a concrete goal to reach for. I've always believed you achieve what you emphasize. Finally, I was putting proper emphasis where it needed to be.

Why does a sick marriage improve? There are many reasons. But if you were to ask Lyndi what changes took place to make the biggest difference, she'd tell you in very simple terms—"He *listens* to me now." It breaks my heart to think of how many men might soar in their score with their wives if they'd just stop what they were doing and *listen*. In my case, I had to first stop defending myself as if my honor were at stake against Lyndi's every subtle critique or suggestion. I've learned that women instinctively know what makes a good relationship—it was time for me to shut up and listen. It wasn't as if I'd been blatantly ignoring her for years and years, but during that pressure-cooker ten months of the year when my mind was given over to football season, even though I *heard* her, I didn't make an earnest effort to retain what was being said. It created enormous tension and resentment in her heart toward me. Two months out of the year listening to your wife doesn't cut it.

The real catalyst for the breakthrough was my retirement from football. It doesn't take a genius to see that it freed me to be far less consumed by the demands of a job. Working full-time for Promise Keepers still keeps me very busy. I travel often. But the environment is altogether different. Every day I'm around men and women who love Jesus with all their hearts and who are committed to honoring Him in their marriages and families. It helps me to continually reevaluate how my convictions are lining up with my actions; it forces me daily to examine my relationship with Lyndi. Am I bringing her to radiance? Am I hearing her? Am I loving her and affirming her?

I was locked in a system called professional coaching. Yet I contend the *system* is anything that prevents us from living out the gospel mandate. It is letting society determine how we're going to live life. It puts success, career, money, and prestige ahead of God and family. It's a recipe for a lukewarm heart. Allowing our hearts to become captivated to the system—whatever that may be for an individual—dulls us to that which is most important. And the most important person in *my* life—my *wife* —was failing to thrive.

Today, I know I still disappoint Lyndi, still frustrate her. It seems some days we take one step forward and two steps back. I think some days I'm becoming the husband she needs; others I don't think it's happening at all. In the final analysis, whatever progress we've made—whatever *growth* we've experienced—is due to Lyndi's faithfulness and perseverance. She has carried the burden to bring us to this second chance. My part has been to establish her as my teammate, my prized priority; my part has been to pray every day that God would improve our marriage and to continue to ask God daily that He would help me become a person Lyndi can share her heart with, feel treasured by, have fun with; to be someone who makes her feel valued and affirmed. He responds by convicting me every day of something I should be doing to build our relationship.

It sounds so simple, realizing the one thing I do that blesses Lyndi more than *anything* else: When she's talking to me, I'll quietly put down whatever I'm reading, take off my glasses, sit back, and just focus in on her. It validates her and makes her just glow to know we're emotionally connected, that she *matters* to me. Such simple, easy steps. It has not come naturally. I have far to go. But I've seen the fruit. And it's delicious, delectable—I'll never turn back.

God Walked Down the Aisle

Fifteen months after I coached my last football game, a friend of ours, a woman, approached me with a reassuring smile. She said she was finally beginning to see true contentment in Lyndi's face. And she wasn't just saying it—I could tell she *meant* it. Nothing on earth could have given me more joy—for someone who knows us both to tell me my wife looks happy and fulfilled was the highlight of my year. Only the Lord can do something like that. Through me, He is weaving a miracle in Lyndi. She is slowly recovering her splendor. God chooses the man as His representative to complete the woman—and the woman to complete the man. Together in Christ we are whole.

It's perhaps too easy to forget: At the beginning of creation, God didn't create a church committee first, or even a church. God personally breathed life into two human beings, one handcrafted specially for the other. Then He walked down the aisle with Eve and tenderly presented her to Adam as his wife, as his helper. God knew man needed help. God did that *first*, to demonstrate the paramount importance He places on the marriage covenant. For a husband and wife, *this* is the relationship, more than any other human association, that certifies the depth of our relationship with God. Only as I continue to die to myself and willingly give away my rights does Lyndi flourish. And as the cycle deepens and matures, she happily pushes me toward the things I enjoy as a man. It is the same with Jesus: As I die to myself and surrender my rights, I tap into the full breadth of His love. As the relationship deepens and matures, He causes my cup of joy to overflow.

I have determined that, God willing, Lyndi and I will live our remaining years as full-fledged teammates. I've learned so much from her; God has gifted her in so many ways, none so much as the instinctive wisdom she brings to almost every situation. More than anyone else (and this includes some incredibly wise, godly mentors), I seek Lyndi first for the counsel I need on a daily basis. She amazes me with her deep understanding of how God works in our lives. I still marvel at how it took me so long to wake up to it.

If for no other reason than to honor Lyndi's perseverance throughout, it may be that God has a blessing for us in years to come. Either way, I have resolved that, if God grants it, I will care for Lyndi in her old age. So often it is the woman who outlives the man, who cares for him in his infirmity. I pray that God will allow me to be the one to care for Lyndi. Nothing can ever compensate for the sorrow and futility I put her through, but perhaps, in the end, it will show my gratitude for all the years she cared for me when *I* was sick, lost, and floundering.

Battling Strongholds

This is where I am today, still fighting the fight, still forging ahead—sometimes with blinders on, sometimes with my eyes wide open and alert. I gain ground, then I lose it. But I never stop looking to my Savior for mercy and deliverance. Then I am free to move on. It has been three years since I left coaching. But coaching has not altogether left me. It is with some frustration that I recognize how I have retained many residual thoughts and behavior patterns drilled into me over a career. To this day, for instance, if anyone even mentions college football in a passing conversation, my insides start to churn, my pulse quickens, and the competitive juices start to burn all over again. All the emotions and memories—the insecurity, fears, and pressure to succeed, and to perform—well up in me. I unconsciously start to compare myself; I'll flash back to all the battles, the excitement, the criticism. I begin to feel out of place, unneeded, worthless. It can absolutely steal my joy. I can become miserable.

Moments earlier I might have been basking in the Lord's serenity. But then I hear the word *football* and my spirit turns sour—bitter. It is vile, faulty thinking; it is horrible ugliness to Jesus. Such pride raring up dishonors His name, insults Him by my warped sense that I had anything to do with past achievements. *He* had granted me success. Yet I still play into the enemy's hands—I get caught in the sick web of envy and paranoia. By God's grace I am no longer immersed in an environment that can spark me to rage, as when I stalked the sidelines. But when I choose to go to this dark place, my closeness with Lyndi, family, friends, and Christ is undermined. All I can do when it happens is confess it, repent, and claim God's sovereignty once again over my life. It brings me back to what's real.

Spiritual strongholds, personal fears, still persist. They subtly dull my life in the Spirit and choke off the freeing truth of who I am in Christ. I still battle insecurity, the sullen belief that deep down I'm unlovable. I trace it back to drinking, to internalized taunts I weathered as the undersized freshman linebacker at Missouri. They are deep waters, too deep and choppy for me to navigate solo.

Television sports remain a powerful temptation. It creeps up on me when I'm tired and want to zone out. Lately, as I've found the will to press through and resist its slick allure, when I make a conscious *choice* to meditate on God's Word—to stick with my spiritual "two-a-day" regimen—I end the day strong and victorious. My focus turns to family, to my grandchildren. And next morning, even before I go to my knees, I'm already in God's wondrous presence. My heart is filled with His Spirit from the night before.

I still battle impatience, though I'm getting better about relaxing at meals and enjoying a good conversation. On a recent trip to Mexico, for example, I sat and chatted with Lyndi for almost three hours at dinner—and *enjoyed* myself. It was a record. So I'm learning. But I am still a fumbling novice in my efforts to bless others. I tend, too often, to defend myself, to promote myself. There remains in me an extremely self-centered streak, the propensity to focus on me rather than on the needs in others. Far too often I find myself looking to man, rather than to God alone, to affirm my sense of worth. I have not arrived at a point where I trust God implicitly, automatically, for *everything*, though I know that's precisely where He's calling me. In stressful situations, I fall back on my own strength and ingenuity, and usually make a mess of things. In random encounters, I find myself *questioning* people rather than loving them. *Please forgive me Lord. I have not loved my fellow man like You require. Have mercy on me; Holy Spirit, please fill my heart with Your love for all men.*

This is who I am—the man with the Fortune 500 resumé who is still trying to align his convictions with his actions. There is no doubt—in me, God has a broad canvas to work with. But that's the good news—the *great* news! Because in these great empty spaces and craggy valleys—in this spiritual no man's land—is where Jesus meets me. He seeks me out where I am, standing at each shadowy doorway where I'm the weakest and most flawed. And He knocks, and knocks patiently. When and where I invite Him in is where He engages me—rarely where I want Him to enter, but always where I need Him most.

When Jesus said, "My grace is sufficient for you, for my power is made perfect in weakness" (2 Corinthians 12:9), He was talking about *me*. I receive His grace like a hungry child; in my rampant weakness I gather up His power. It is why, like the apostle Paul, I boast all the more gladly about my weaknesses and flaws, so that Christ's power may rest on me. "For when I am weak, then I am strong" (2 Corinthians 12:10).

So you see, despite my shortcomings, God has smiled down upon me. Glory of glories, He *chose* me to participate with Him in sculpting out a life from this wreckage. Not because I had anything to offer. But because He knew He could be strong in my weakness, that He would get the ultimate glory for being the *only* Promise Keeper worth emulating.

If *anybody* had reason to place confidence in the flesh, it was me. I willed myself to the top of a demanding profession, stepping over anything in my path. I could also work up quite a religious lather. If anyone had potential through his own high-revving resources to be sold out to all the *right* things, it was *me*. It wasn't as if I didn't *know* the right path; it boiled down to the simplest of choices: stop drinking; stop letting your job dictate your walk with God; find balance in your relationship with your wife and kids. And I *tried*.

With every ounce of his tenacity and resolve, Bill McCartney tried. I fell miles short. Promise Keepers has adopted what are known as the Seven Promises—vows of commitment men at conferences are asked to make to Jesus Christ, to their families, and to a few other men. They call men into spiritual and moral purity, into strong marriages based on biblical values, into a deeper commitment to their church and pastor. They call men to reach beyond racial and denominational barriers to spread the good news of Jesus Christ to the world.

They are promises to base one's life on. I have no doubt that if every Christian man practiced them to a fault, our land, our planet, would be healed in Jesus' name. To this day I make an earnest attempt to practice *all* of these promises. Some days I succeed in some respects; other days I fail miserably in all of them. The truth is, on my own, I can *never* be a bona fide promise keeper. And that's OK—it's not about me—it's about what Jesus can do *in* me. I can never keep the seven promises. But Jesus can keep them *through* me. His Spirit operating unhindered in me is the only hope I have of living a consistently righteous life. I will never give up the fight; I will *always* strive to keep my promises. But without Christ I am helpless. He is my strength; He is my power, my joy. It comes from no other source. It comes from no other person. We can't get it from *people*. We can only get it from the Way, the Truth, and the Life. Christ in *you!*—that's your hope of glory.

In Galatians 5:5, Paul says, "But by faith we eagerly await through the Spirit the righteousness for which we hope." There is *no* righteousness apart from the Holy Spirit. There is no goodness. The Spirit of God in us is fundamental to a victorious life. Our *only* hope is to let the Holy Spirit lead. It's our only hope of coming together. Regardless of our background or our denominational affiliation—regardless of how we dot our i's and cross our t's—it is Christ in us, as a *body*, that is our hope.

My life is insurmountable proof: On my own I made every wrong turn, hurt everyone I loved, nearly lost all that meant anything. Renewed in God's Holy Spirit, with His power operating in me, my life has been steadily transformed. And, yet, it's still the *beginning*. But I am on the path of *Life!*

As the psalmist says, I am seeing the goodness of the Lord in the land of the living (Psalm 27:13). Jesus, my wonderful Savior, looked beyond my shortcomings. He made me an heir to His life of power, holiness, and incomparable joy. In Him, I am complete.

As God has worked His hard, unbending truths into my life, He has kept me in the race, still battling, still wrestling. Praise

God, I wasn't disqualified. I still have my beloved family nearby and bound up in my affections. It is to my joy. My own children and I are learning to be of one accord, trying to make the most of our belated opportunity. It stands as perhaps the most eloquent testament of all to God's love. There has been no more tender victory than to now be able to share my pain, my joy, my love, and my shortcomings with my children, all now adults. The ready access I have to my grandchildren is an unmerited treasure. Even late in life, God permits me the honor of serving in that capacity—in the father's role as the grandfather. I know He always intended it for me.

It's never too late with Jesus. Brothers and sisters, it's *never* too late. God is eager to restore what our youthful ignorance stripped from us. He doesn't do it begrudgingly—He does it enthusiastically. He is always redeeming the time. He wants to restore proper order in our homes. If I have been granted a larger stage from which to share, it is only because His lessons have been—are still *being*—forged in the proving ground of my heart. I, more than most, know nothing is guaranteed. The test is to walk these lessons out daily. But in my home, at least *today*, order is being restored. Balance is returning. In the power of the Spirit, a father is working out his salvation in the company of his family. Relationships have been reborn of the miracle of second chance. With restored vision, with restored sanity, I have been allowed to come home where I belong. He granted me the will and the desire; He made my family patient and long-suffering. Together we are learning to live His gospel. If we want it, He is more than able to grant it (see Romans 4:21). Of all the unsearchable gifts in God's storehouse, to me this is the grandest.

There Are No Limits

Journal Entry 12/23/96—*Where is the answer? What is flawed and missing in me? Why is my love always coming up lacking? I have been damaged, and where I have been damaged I damage others. Father, Your love is perfect—You are not damaged; Your Spirit is not impaired. You provide just the right ingredients in this relationship You offer to us. You make up the difference in the ways that we fall short. You alone know where I hurt and whom I've hurt. Repair the breaches, sustain us and draw us to You. We desperately need You. We can be healed if You say the word. You are the Lord God Almighty. I ask Your forgiveness for not asking You sooner, repenting sooner and turning to You completely.*

Journal Entry 12/26/96—*When I think about writing a book, doing a television special, participating in the production of several large conferences—going to Washington, D.C. with a multitude—it is frightening. Then I remember: I have a great big God Who loves me; He will never forsake me—no never. He is looking to and fro for someone He can depend upon to step out in faith and trust Him to do the things which are impossible for man. If this is radical, it indicts the present Christian culture—because it should be routine. Our God is glorious. He is extraordinary; we are ordinary; He is infinitely more than ordinary. We are quite limited; He is unlimited. There are no limits to His power, love, and mercy. Without faith, it is impossible to please Him!*

A Note to the Reader

AS THIS BOOK HAS SOUGHT TO UNVEIL and explain the uneven dips and arcs of my private spiritual journey, it would be shortsighted, even negligent, to close this work without a consolidating word from my four exceptional children. Apart from Lyndi, they have been closest to this elusive, often troubling testimony. As you will see, they each have a different story to tell. But they, more than I, are most qualified to assess who I was, and who I am still becoming, as their father.

I bear much heartache for the ways I've failed or disappointed my children through the years. Yet for every lingering regret, I find endless consolation in knowing they each have an abiding, personal relationship with Jesus Christ and are bound for eternity swathed in the Father's love. Whatever the past has held for us, today I rejoice that each of my children know and *feel* how deeply I treasure and love them. We are reclaiming lost time. Short of my own walk with Christ, nothing has been as sweet as their unconditional love for me in the midst of my shortcomings.

Today, our oldest son Mike, 33, is a devoted Christian man and a scout for the Chicago Bears; he and his wife, Jenni, have a young son, Nickolas Chase, and expecting their second child December 14, 1997.

Our second son Tom, 32, is following in his father's coaching footsteps, presently serving as the head football coach at Fairview High School in Boulder. He and his wife, Pam, have been married for three years. My gentle, beautiful daughter Kristy, 29, who clearly felt the sting of my coaching preoccupation more acutely than my boys, is a devoted mother to two beautiful young boys, Timothy Chase and Derek William. She now works as project facilitator in Promise Keepers' Racial Reconciliation Division. Our youngest son Marc, 25, has perhaps benefited most from the mistakes I made and the lessons I learned with his older siblings. He and his wife Robin live in Mesquite, Texas, where he works as the southwest regional volunteer manager for Promise Keepers.

I have asked each of them to share briefly, yet candidly, the highlights and low points of our family experience—what it was like growing up in the McCartney household. Raised in the eye of the hurricane that marked much of my career, I often worried that the burden might be too heavy for them. I have been consistently amazed, and undeservedly blessed, at how God uniquely gifted each of them to weather the storms of the past three decades with poise and maturity far beyond their years. They are my priceless legacy—proof that Jesus redeems a father's mistakes and sheds His love abroad through even the most flawed vessels. I am above all men most blessed.

Reflections of Three Sons and a Daughter

Mike McCartney

Dad, you are a man of tremendous integrity, principle, and character. I admire the work ethic and discipline in your life. Everything you ever get involved with seems to be great or turn great. You have so many talents and are unquestionably the greatest source for me to turn to for advice. You taught me how to be gracious in defeat and humble in victory. I am grateful that I always knew of your great love and affection for Mom and your children. I love and respect you very much.

I remember growing up in a home with three dads. My first dad was very religious—it was a religion of do's and don'ts and was very strict. He was the kind of dad that was very disciplined and strong. He went to church every day for ten years. Yet, he didn't have a personal relationship with Jesus Christ. And as a young person, a faith centered on do's and don'ts is not attractive.

My second dad accepted Jesus Christ in 1974, and things immediately changed. He quit drinking and led the entire family to Christ. He had a heart for sharing the Gospel with others and initiated a nightly devotional at home. Yet, his priorities were out of whack. He always said it was faith first, family second, and football third. But we knew it was faith one-A, football one-B, and family a distant third.

My third dad shocked the football world and resigned his lucrative and prestigious position in order to heal his marriage. The changes have been dramatic. Despite his motivation being for my mother, he has become much more attentive as a father. He's truly interested in my life, and the effect has been terrific on me. Once my relationship with my earthly dad was restored, it allowed me to receive the love of my heavenly Dad as well!

Growing up, I thought my dad was the greatest. He was always a coach. When I was little, he was a high school football and basketball coach. I can remember many games and bus rides. When I was about ten, he went to Michigan as an assistant football coach. Now, most of the time being a coach's kid was the greatest. We went to four Rose Bowls, as well as other bowl games. I sat on the sidelines for all the home games. I do remember getting booed in sixth grade upon returning from a Rose Bowl loss. There were a lot of good memories. But there were some painful ones too. My dad is an all-out guy. When he sets his heart on something, it generally will happen. He was really devoted to becoming a head football coach. And so, he wasn't around much. Sometimes he would swoop in for a quick dinner before going back to the office. The real issue was when he was home physically, he wasn't there mentally. It was like talking to a blank wall, with a lot of "huh-huhs" and "sures." There wasn't a whole lot of one-on-one time. Plus, he had a strong temper. He could really intimidate people by just being louder and angrier than the other person.

But that was life, so we all adjusted through the years and learned when our dad was approachable and when he wasn't. Obviously, my dad wasn't abusive, and there were some great aspects of him being a father: He certainly loved us, he instilled good values, and he did lead each of us to Christ. And yet, I can't deny there was pain.

I'll fast forward a few years. When I moved away following college, I began to come to grips with the fact that I had some unresolved issues and pain regarding my dad. I had become good at stuffing pain. Thoughts of my dad always triggered defensive thoughts against things that had happened in the past. Did I mention he had a coach's temper? Well, at this point in my life, I could see it was time to take care of some things. I had just arrived in Chicago. I knew I would eventually meet the right girl, and I really didn't want to bring a lot of baggage into my marriage. So, I decided to see a counselor. I wrote a local pastor and asked him to recommend a Christian counselor, and I started going. After a couple of sessions, the counselor encouraged me to confront my dad about some issues and share some examples of painful memories. It so happened that I was going home for a visit, so the timing was right.

My dad and I sat down, and I asked him if he could allow me to get some things off my chest; I explained that I really needed just to say some things face-to-face. He said okay, and I started to explain some pain. After the first example, he defended himself. My reaction to him was, "If you're going to defend every issue, then we can quit right now." Thirty minutes later, tears were running down his face and he was apologizing. The truth is, none of the examples was earth shattering or caused any great pain. But it was the first time he had realized he had hurt me, and that hurt him. He asked for forgiveness, and I forgave him. Things were better, but he was still a coach and still focused on winning.

Following his resignation from CU, we kids decided to honor our parents in a special way. Prompted by my brother Tom, we each decided to eulogize our parents while they were still alive (these tributes have been printed in their entirety in the Appendix). Each of us wrote a tribute based on God's fifth commandment, "Honor your father and your mother" (Exodus 20:12). We gathered as a family on July 4, 1995, and individually read our tributes. I had mine typecast on a plaque and read first. Afterwards, I knew why God had commanded us to honor our parents: to give us a tremendous blessing. Since writing the tribute, I have felt only positive feelings about my dad. I no longer have the defensive thoughts I once had. It was very cleansing to honor him, and reading my tribute to him was an incredible moment in our relationship.

Tom McCartney

> *Dad, you raised our family to seek the Lord. Thank you for all those nights we turned off the television and you read from the Bible. Thank you for all those mornings you prayed over each of us. Thank you for never missing church on Sunday and for always including us in saying the Rosary with you in the car. Dad, I have always wanted to be just like you. Thank you for your footprints.*

Frankly, I always thought that being the son of a coach was pretty cool. I was always intrigued with big-time collegiate athletics, and I liked growing up that way and being part of Michigan and Colorado football. I loved my dad. And now that I'm coaching, I'm finding I have some of the same characteristics as he did: that same competitive nature, that same drive. It's kind of neat in a way.

I don't remember when I was *really* young, but I do remember Dad always being there for me. As a child, our life was church and sports. Those are the things we did as a family. I remember going to Catholic church every Sunday and praying and reading the Bible as a family each night. Dad would lead us in family devotions. Each night before we went to bed, Dad would come in and we'd turn off the TV. We'd read a couple of verses and Dad would ask us to discuss them. Then we'd pray before going to sleep.

Summer vacations, Dad would take us to the Fellowship of Christian Athletes camp. I used to joke that when I was born, the doctor slapped me and I thought I was a Christian. That's the only thing I knew at home. I had a lot of fun growing up—when we weren't with Dad at his practices, we were at our own. I look at it this way—I've had an ideal life. I love the way I grew up. I know Dad's reflecting on things he should have done differently, but I've personally benefited from his experience.

I feel like my dad has hand picked me, because I've chosen to go into coaching, to teach and share different things with—like how to be a loving husband and still be an effective coach. The biggest thing he's emphasized is how much time I need to devote to my marriage and how I need to be a servant to my wife. He's shown me how to pray and have quiet times with my wife. Dad may have done things differently, but he's investing all that in me so I won't have to go down the same tough path. I give my dad most of the credit that I'm on the right track.

Kristy McCartney

> *Dad, I don't think you realize how much I admire and respect you. When I have trouble with something and need help, I think of you. You have so much wisdom. You speak with such passion and conviction, and you live that way too. You are someone I look up to and strive to be like in many ways. You are a man of God, and I am proud to call you my father. You instilled in all of us the need*

for God in our lives. I am thankful for those vital truths you have given me. I thank you, I honor you, and I love you, Dad.

I remember once, in eighth grade, I tried out for cheerleader and didn't make it. I came home really upset and crying. Dad was very gentle and sweet with me. That meant a lot to me, but I also have some very bad, painful memories. There was always a lot of tension in our home. I think it was a reflection of my mom having so much on her shoulders—she was a single mother in a lot of ways. Dad never seemed to be home to do a lot of stuff with the family. In many ways, I don't think Dad understood what a family really is. So whenever he was around, there was a lot of dictating and orders, and him expecting things to be done a certain way. Looking back, I think Dad and I were sort of afraid of each other. Once, in high school, I got caught drinking. Dad confronted me and said, "We need to talk about your drinking." I just sat there and said, "Okay, Okay, Okay." I was scared. I told him what he wanted to hear, but I remember thinking I really didn't know him.

The biggest thing for me was that he just wasn't around. He was never there to really know me. Growing up, his absence spoke rejection to me, that I didn't really matter much to him. That was awful. Now I realize he probably just didn't know how to relate to a girl. He definitely related better to my brothers, because they were boys. I was always trying to excel in athletics, but I never did. When Dad coached at Michigan, I hated football. Family devotions were not fun for me. I couldn't be myself. I've since come to appreciate the value of those times, but as a kid I wasn't interested in hearing about the Bible.

At first, I didn't understand the impact of Promise Keepers. Once I did, I was just in awe of what God was doing with men. But I confess, at times I've felt my dad was a hypocrite. Sometimes I thought, "You've got a lot of nerve saying those things. You don't have your own house in order." We've made great progress, my dad and me. Much of it has coincided with my own growing walk with the Lord. Working at Promise Keepers has been such a blessing; the Lord has really been working in my heart.

I know Dad has always done his best. I know he loves me, even though it's still hard for him. We're still getting to know each other. He knows that I've been hurt, and I can see him trying to really make up for it, to really nurture me. He does so much for me now. At work, he leaves me little notes. He writes, "I love you" or, "I think you're beautiful." He reaches out to my kids. He's trying to fill that role of a man in their lives, and he's proving to be a fantastic grandfather. I love my dad, and I'm really proud of him—I'm proud of the way he loves me.

MARC MCCARTNEY

> *My dad is the greatest Christian man I know. If the Bible were written today, there is no doubt in my mind that there would be a book called "Coach Mac." I can remember going to two-a-days to watch my dad's team practice and walking to lunch with him after practice. People would always want to walk with us, and when they did my dad would never fail to share the Gospel with them. I remember his prayer list and how he would read it even when he was driving. I remember waking up each morning to the sight of my dad in the living room reading the Bible. I also cannot recall a day in my life that Dad didn't tell Mom how beautiful she looked, or kiss her in front of us. His example taught me to bring my wife, Robin, to splendor.*

I was probably the luckiest one. When I was a kid, Dad obviously worked hard. But he was my hero; everything he did just seemed incredible to me. I know my brothers and sister have different memories, but Dad was a Spirit-filled Christian *my* whole life. Sure, it was hard not having him around during the season, but you've got to understand, I wanted CU to win more than anything. I knew he had to do whatever it took.

The thing that impacted me most was his lifestyle. It's funny, but I didn't listen all that carefully to Dad when he tried to counsel me in sports. But I always listened closely any time he talked about God. I remember Halloween morning 1992 when we were about to play Nebraska in Lincoln for the Big 8 Championship and a shot at the national title. Instead of getting ready for one of the most important games of his life, Dad called a family meeting. He told Tom and me that the McCartney men needed to do a better job at showing Mom and Kristy how valuable they were to us. It was an incredible moment. We began to hug on and cry with each other. Dad taught us long ago that it was okay to cry.

When CU lost to Miami in 1993, we were all devastated, and I was particularly upset. However, instead of feeling sorry for ourselves, my parents called some of their friends over and we praised Jesus together for hours. It was a moving time when I was able to tell my mom and dad how much I loved them. Everyone knows that the greatest gift God ever gave us was His Son, but He gave me something different; God gave me Jesus through my mom and dad.

It is no secret to me why God chose my dad to be the one who is casting the vision for Promise Keepers. It's because my dad starts every day with God. I mean, he spends the first two to three hours of every day with the Lord. Not many do that. I'm still struggling with thirty minutes. But Dad prays for an hour or two, then reads the Word for an hour or two. That's his passion. And he's spreading it to me. He taught me that if I get down on my knees for fifteen minutes a day, God will give me the desire and I'll keep coming back until I can't get enough. I'm learning what that is. To this day, I don't know why God decided to bless me so much with the parents He gave me. But I honestly feel like the luckiest, most loved person in the world.

Appendix: The Children's Tributes[1]

Footprints to Follow

Two sets of footprints represent the good times. One set of footprints represents the tough times. The Lord says where there is one set of footprints, those are the times He carried us. Mom and Dad, thank you for the footprints you have left; the Lord has blessed the two of you, and your children follow in your footprints.

Dad, you raised our family to seek the Lord. Thank you for all those nights we turned off the television and you read from the Bible. Thank you for all those mornings you prayed over each of us. Thank you for never missing church on Sunday and for always including us in saying the Rosary with you in the car.

Mom, your treasure on earth is your family. The Lord blessed you with many talents: playing the piano, playing the guitar, teaching, singing, and writing. However, the gift you chose as a career is loving your family. Thank you for the sacrifices you made to be with your family and the footprints you left. Mom and Dad, thank you for modeling to your family the key to living, which is giving. Mom, I remember when I was a teenager and I said no when you asked if I was going to Marc's baseball game. You told me how you had brought Marc to all my games and how much it would mean to him if I came to his game. Mom, thank you for teaching me, by example, how to give to others.

Dad, I recall times when you and a family member were in a disagreement. Before too long, I saw you go to the family member and ask for his or her forgiveness. Dad, forgiving and giving equals living, and you and Mom make a great team.

> I have sent you to reap what you have not worked for. Others have done the hard work, and you have reaped the benefits of their labor.
>
> —John 4:38

Mom and Dad, you are leaving behind a legacy. Thank you for building our home on a strong foundation. I thought about separate tributes for each of you, but the two of you have never been separate. I love you both, and I ask for your forgiveness. Mom, you once told me that I didn't have a clue, and you were right. I have taken my loved ones for granted. Why do we take our loved ones for granted? I believe it is because the two of you have always been there for me and have been servants to me. Forgive me, because I have not been a servant back to you. Mom, I always wanted to marry someone like you, and the Lord has blessed me. Dad, I have always wanted to be just like you. Thank you for your footprints.

I love you both,
Thomas Chase

A Tribute to Mom and Dad

> I, the LORD your God, am a jealous God, punishing the children for the sin of their fathers to the third and fourth generation of those who hate me, but showing love to a thousand generations of those who love me and keep my commandments.
>
> —Exodus 20:5–6

Mom and Dad, my life is richer because you have given so much to me. Together, you have taught me love, honor, respect, responsibility, devotion, discipline, ethics, morals, and commitment. I've learned from your words, and I've learned from your actions. You provided a safe and godly environment to grow up in. I have so many great memories of growing up. I want to share them here with you so that you will always know my appreciation for you.

Mom, you are the most tender, loving person I know. You make everyone feel so comfortable, never judging anyone. Your caring nature is obvious to anyone who knows you, as is your devotion to our family. I love you and hold you in the highest regard.

Mom, the most special times I've shared with you have been our three driving trips, especially the one to North Carolina. Yes, it was the longest, yet it also gave us the most time to talk. It was such a great honor to hear of your past, your dreams, your struggles, and your love for Dad and the family. Saying good-bye at the conclusion of the drive to Kansas was the hardest thing I've ever done in my life.

As I reminisce about growing up, so many moments come to mind. I want to thank you for attending every Little League baseball and basketball game, even when they started in the early hours. Thanks for believing that every injury was legitimate, despite sixteen broken fingers. Your tenderness and affection when I was sick and the way you rubbed my stomach are special memories. You taught me how to drive a stick shift. You demonstrated the importance of tithing by giving me a dollar for church when I was young. Two other memories truly stand out and are of such significance to me: your devotion to Dad and knowing that Jenni was the one from the onset, welcoming and loving her into our family.

Dad, you are a man of tremendous integrity, principle, and character. I admire the work ethic and discipline in your life. Everything you ever got involved in seems to be great or turn great. You have so many talents and are unquestionably the greatest source for me to turn to for advice. You taught me how to be gracious in defeat and humble in victory. (You had much more practice at humbleness.) I am grateful that I always knew of your great love and affection for Mom and your children. I love and respect you very much.

Dad, Saturdays when you were a basketball coach were very special days. We would start out at the donut shop before practice. Shooting hoops and being around the players were great times. I still remember you trying to teach me what double dribble meant. Following practice, we would often head to Miller's Bar for the best burgers in town. I also remember state playoff games at the Silverdome, watching Mark "The Bird" Fidrych pitch, chapel services at Tiger Stadium, lunch at the Michigan training table, sideline passes, making sure I got into the locker room after the Rose Bowl win, and all of your stirring pre-game talks (I'll never forget the fifteen rounds at Oklahoma). These are great memories. I loved being a "coach's kid," even if it meant getting booed in the sixth grade upon returning from the Rose Bowl.

Mom and Dad, you have added so much to my life, yet the greatest gift you have given me is showing me the door to eternal life. Dad, thanks for leading the family in daily devotions and teaching us about the love of Christ. Mom, thanks for your example of servanthood. I thank you both for praying over me and illustrating God's love daily. I have learned so much from each of you and strive to be more like you. Dad, you're my example of being a godly man at home and at work. And Mom, if I could be as selfless as you, I would truly be fortunate, as would those around me. I have been blessed beyond measure and owe it to the two of you. Mom and Dad, I love, honor, and thank you.

Mike

The Luckiest Person in the World

It was a rainy and humid Sunday night in Waco as the two Baylor freshmen, Marc and Blair, discussed what the preacher had talked about that morning. The preacher told of the awesome gifts God has for everyone. The two students each had the same thing on their minds that night. Marc told Blair about the greatest gift God had ever given him. . . .

Growing up as a McCartney you learn one thing quick: Jesus Christ is Lord!

As a kid, I can remember going to hear all kinds of different Christian singers and speakers and reading the Bible together as a family every single night. I was taught at a very young age that Jesus is Lord and that there is no compromising on that fact. However, the greatest teaching came in my relationship with my parents.

First of all, my mother is amazing! All of my close friends will tell you that she is the heart and soul of our family, and they are right. She's like an offensive lineman, never getting the credit she deserves. My mom has taught me many things, but the greatest lessons have come by the way she lives her life. Some words that come to mind about my mom are humorous, loyal, and compassionate. My mom's humor has always shined through, whether it's the silly way she can make us all laugh or the kid in her that will let her seven-year-old son go to Taco Bell for his First Communion breakfast (by the way, Mom, Taco Bell is still my favorite).

My mom's loyalty has always been an inspiration to me. I can remember the time she scolded and grounded my brothers because they didn't go to one of my soccer games. She got her point across, because some of my greatest memories growing up are of Mike at my junior high football games, or Tom driving all the way to Pueblo to watch me in the State Championship. My mom also displayed her loyalty in the way she stuck by my dad no matter what was going on. I'll never forget waiting for Dad after his football games. I think my favorite part of the games was to see Mom and Dad afterwards.

My mom is definitely compassionate. I'll always remember the cake she made me when I didn't make the Little League all-star team and how the whole family came out to my last game and told me I was their little all star.

My dad is the greatest Christian man I know. If the Bible were written today there is no doubt in my mind that there would be a book called "Coach Mac." I can remember going to two-a-days to watch my dad's team practice and walking to lunch with him after practice. People would always want to walk with us, and when they did, my dad would never fail to share the Gospel with them. There are certain images that I have of my dad that will always be with me.

I remember his prayer list and how he would read it even when he was driving. I remember waking up each morning to the sight of my dad in the living room reading the Bible. I also cannot recall a day in my life that Dad didn't tell Mom how beautiful she looked. His example has taught me to bring my wife, Robin, to splendor.

I remember Halloween morning 1992 when we were about to play Nebraska in Lincoln for the Big 8 Championship and a shot at the national title. Tom, Kristy, and I were there for the game, and instead of getting ready for one of the most important games in his life, he called a family meeting. He told Tom and me that the McCartney men needed to do a better job at showing Mom and Kristy how valuable they were to us. It was an incredible moment as we began to hug on and cry with each other. You see, our dad taught us long ago that it was okay to cry.

One thing about my mom and dad is that they are a great team.

When we lost to Miami in 1993, we were all devastated, and I was particularly upset. However, instead of feeling sorry for ourselves, my parents called some of our friends over and we praised Jesus together for hours. It was a moving time, and I was able to tell my mom and dad how much I loved them.

"Hey Blair, everyone knows that the greatest gift God ever gave us was His Son. He gave me something different, though. He gave me Jesus through my mom and dad. I don't know why God decided to bless me so much with the parents He gave me, but I honestly feel like the luckiest, most loved person in the world." After Blair told Marc about his parents, the two knelt down together to praise God. Marc prayed and thanked His Savior for the greatest gift of all, his mom and dad.

Marc

I Thank You, I Honor You, and I Love You

Parents are the pride of their children.
—Proverbs 17:6

Mom and Dad, you are worthy of honor and praise for the love, commitment, and selflessness you have shown me. I am thankful you were married, had me, and stayed together through all the hard times. Your love and commitment to each other has enriched my life and the lives of my children. I thank you for giving your lives to Christ and sharing His love with me. For this I am eternally grateful.

As a family, we have had many good times. These are some of the memories I cherish: F.C.A. camps, bowl games, vacations in Florida at the McCartney's trailer, help with science projects, extra gifts at Christmas time, visiting Grandma and Grandpa Mac, Mom sponge-painting the walls, Dad making us clean the garage and do yard work, hugging and loving me when I didn't make cheerleader, playing telephone, Mom making our Halloween costumes (and dressing up too), how special you made our birthdays, visiting Dad at practice, playing pinball at Dad's office, all those Girl Scout meetings, getting lost at camp, our trip to the mountains with Mom's family, fighting in the car on road trips, Dad threatening to pull the car over, the millions of football, basketball, and baseball games, beating Notre Dame (twice), reading the Bible before bed. There are so many memories we have made. Thank you for all of them.

Mom, as you look back on your life, it might not have gone the way you planned. But I want you to know you have raised a daughter who thinks the world of you. You are so beautiful to me. You are elegant, graceful, and classy. It shows in everything you do. You are supportive, loving, kind, generous, forgiving, patient, funny, and incredibly talented. I am in awe of your writing abilities. You have been through so much pain in your life, yet you find a way to be positive and forgiving. I admire that and long to be like you. You are a role model for me as a Christian woman and mother. You have sacrificed so many things for me. I appreciate each and every one of those sacrifices with all of my heart. You have been my best friend through many tough times, never judging me, only loving and accepting me. I trust you with my deepest thoughts, fears, and joys. I am so proud that you are my mother. I thank you. I honor you and I love you, Mom.

Dad, I don't think you realize how much I admire and respect you. When I have trouble with something and need help, I think of you. You have so much wisdom. You speak with such passion and conviction, and you live that way too. Your discipline has not gone unnoticed. You had an impact on me. You are someone I look up to and strive to be like in many ways. You are a man of God, and I am proud to call you my father. You have no idea what joy and excitement it brings me to hear you speak. At Promise Keepers '94, I was so excited to hear you speak I could hardly contain myself. I search the radio for your speeches. For all the speeches I have been to, from Buff Belles to Phoenix '90, I am so proud of you. You instilled in all of us the need for God in our lives, the importance of church every Sunday, and the value of reading the Word daily. I am thankful for those vital truths you have given me. Dad, I thank you, I honor you, and I love you.

I love you, Mom and Dad,
Kristy

Attention Married Couples!

You've read the book . . . now, take the next step.

Coming in the Spring of 1998 are an *Interactive Workbook* and *Marriage Journal* by Bill and Lyndi McCartney and Connie Neal, both designed to strengthen your marriage relationship. They will help you and your spouse to rekindle the passionate love of your early years and fully experience unity in an atmosphere of mutual respect and love. Look for these great resources at your local Christian bookstore.

Endnotes

Chapter 1: Legacy of Pain

1. A.W. Tozer, *Of God and Men* (Camp Hill, PA: Christian Publications, 1995), p. 15.

Chapter 2: The Privilege of Prayer

1. Charles Spurgeon, *The Power of Prayer in a Believer's Life* (Lynnwood, WA: Emerald Books, 1993), p. 172.

Chapter 10: Disciplines of a New Believer

1. Tozer, *Of God and Men*, p. 72.
2. Tozer, *Of God and Men*, p. 84.

Chapter 12: Power in Discipline

1. Robert Boyd Munger, My *Heart—Christ's Home*, rev. ed. (Downers Grove, IL: InterVarsity Press, 1986).

Chapter 15: CU: A New Season

1. Oswald Chambers, *My Utmost for His Highest*, updated edition (Grand Rapids, MI: Discovery House, 1993), August 3.

Chapter 19: The Truth About Team

1. *Webster's New World College Dictionary*, 3rd. ed., s.v. "team."
2. Rick Reilly, "Wrong Man, Wrong Time," *Sports Illustrated*, October 2, 1995, p. 38.
3. Pat Riley, *The Winner Within: A Life Plan for Team Players* (New York: Putnam's Sons, 1993), p. 15.
4. Tom Osborne, *On Solid Ground* (Lincoln, NE: Nebraska Book Publishing, 1996), p. 187.
5. J.T. Jeyachandran, "Was Jesus Typical or Exceptional?" *Just Thinking Newsletter*, Ravi Zacharias Int'l Ministries, Spring/Summer Edition, 1997.

Chapter 22: Promise Keepers: Memories to Last a Lifetime

1. Chambers, *My Utmost for His Highest*, July 30.

Chapter 25: Idolatry: The System

1. Dallas Willard, *Spirit of the Disciplines* (New York: HarperCollins, 1988), p. 201. All material in this book taken from *Spirit of the Disciplines*, copyright © Dallas Willard, is used by permission of the publisher.

Chapter 27: A Question of Integrity

1. *Webster's New World College Dictionary*, 3rd ed., s.v. "integrity."

Chapter 31: Saying Goodbye to CU

1. Richard Hoffer and Shelley Smith, "Putting His House in Order," *Sports Illustrated*, January 16, 1995, pp. 27–32.

2. Ibid.

Chapter 32: Training for Holiness

1. Willard, *Spirit of the Disciplines*, p. 2.
2. Ibid., p. 18.
3. Ibid., p. 6.
4. Ibid., p. 2.
5. Ibid.
6. A. W. Tozer, *Rut, Rot or Revival* (Camp Hill, PA: Christian Publications, 1993), p. 20.
7. Oswald Chambers, *The Psychology of Redemption* (London: Simpkin Marshall, 1947), p. 51.
8. Willard, *Spirit of the Disciplines*, p. 5.
9. Arthur Wallis, *God's Chosen Fast* (Ft. Washington, PA: Christian Literature Crusade, 1968).
10. Chambers, My *Utmost for His Highest*, February 13.

Chapter 33: Prayer: Realizing His Presence

1. Spurgeon, *The Power of Prayer in a Believer's Life*, p. 20.

Chapter 34: The Lukewarm Generation

1. Tozer, *Rut, Rot or Revival*, p. 29.

Chapter 35: Stand in the Gap

1. *Rocky Mountain News*, June 22, 1997.
2. James Patterson and Peter Kim, *The Day America Told the Truth* (New York: Prentice Hall, 1991), pp. 94–96.
3. *Leadership*, Fall 1992.

Appendix

1. Our children were inspired to write these tributes after reading *The Tribute* by Dennis Rainey (Nashville: Thomas Nelson, 1994).